WITHDRAWN

STRUGGLES IN SOUTHERN AFRICA FOR SURVIVAL AND EQUALITY

Also by H. J. Simons

AFRICAN WOMEN: Their Legal Status in South Africa
CLASS AND COLOUR IN SOUTH AFRICA, 1850–1950 (*with R. E.*)
JOB RESERVATION AND THE TRADE UNIONS (*with R. E.*)
MEMORANDUM ON THE NEED FOR PENAL REFORM IN SOUTH
   AFRICA (*with M. L. Ballinger*)
SLUMS OR SELF-RELIANCE? Urban Growth in Zambia

Struggles in Southern Africa for Survival and Equality

H. J. Simons

First published in Great Britain 1997 by
MACMILLAN PRESS LTD
Houndmills, Basingstoke, Hampshire RG21 6XS
and London
Companies and representatives
throughout the world

A catalogue record for this book is available
from the British Library.

ISBN 0–333–65664–4

 First published in the United States of America 1997 by
ST. MARTIN'S PRESS, INC.,
Scholarly and Reference Division,
175 Fifth Avenue,
New York, N.Y. 10010

ISBN 0–312–16260–X

Library of Congress Cataloging-in-Publication Data
Simons, H. J. (Harold Jack)
Struggles in Southern Africa for survival and equality / H. J. Simons.
p.   cm.
Includes bibliographical references and index.
ISBN 0–312–16260–X (cloth)
1. South Africa—Race relations.   2. Ethnology—South Africa.
3. Women—South Africa—Social conditions.   4. South Africa—Social
conditions.   5. Zambia—Race relations   I. Title.
DT1756.S53   1996
305.8'00968—dc20   96–2812
                                                                 CIP

10   9   8   7   6   5   4   3   2   1
06   05   04   03   02   01   00   99   98   97

Printed in Great Britain by
The Ipswich Book Company Ltd
Ipswich, Suffolk

Contents

Foreword

On Monday, 17 July 1995 my father signed the contract with the publishers for this book. I discussed the Foreword with him on the Wednesday, and he arranged to start writing on the Saturday. Saturday, 22 July he died.

He was very happy that this book was to be published. Arrangements to collect together some of his other pieces which had been published in various journals had also been made. All that remained was this Foreword.

There are two common threads which unite the chapters. The one is the interaction between indigenous peoples, anthropologists/sociologists and colonial or imperial governments. The second is the struggle for liberation; the struggle that takes place either against the colonialist government or within indigenous society against the patriarchy.

'Early Cape Societies' deals with the indigenous peoples at the Cape (and further afield) at the time of the Dutch colonisers' arrival. It goes on to discuss the different involvements and perspectives of anthropologists and sociologists as they took sides in the conflict between the colonial powers and the indigenous peoples, and the way in which knowledge was often subverted to the cause of the colonisers.

'The Colonial Conquest of Zambia' explores this latter theme further and in more detail, and expands too upon the role played by venture capital and the demands of manufacturing capitalism in the colonisation of large parts of Africa. As suggested by the title, it concentrates on the situation in Zambia, leading the reader from the pre-colonial era through to the present, and examining how the colonial mechanisms for dealing with revolt have persisted in the post-colonial present. It thus introduces the theme of the struggle for liberation, primarily against the colonial rulers, but also within indigenous society against patriarchal rule.

The next essay, 'Patriarchal Rule', extends the arguments begun in the previous essay. It deals with the colonial powers and their relations with the colonised indigenes, which were patriarchal in nature, as well as the place of women in both colonial settler society and indigenous society. The place of women was a subject of abiding interest to my father, and one about which he had written for a great deal of his career.

'The Struggle for Equality' details the rise of African national-ism and the liberation movements against the backdrop of the demands of capitalism for workers, the development of white domination and the evolution of apartheid policies. It picks up again the theme of the role of sociologists and anthropologists in the determination of apartheid policies. This theme is one which my father had first become interested in when doing postgraduate work under Edgar Brookes, one of the intellectual founders of apartheid, in the 1930s.

'The Apartheid Years' explores the gritty details of jackboot heels, detentions and trials, torture and exile. It is a compendium of nastiness detailed fairly drily, but one cannot remain unmoved. Many (but not all) of the individual stories have been told elsewhere, but it is important to have these stories told again. The reader must remain aware that the consequences of social engin-eering are real, and felt by flesh and bones. Social engineers cannot simply claim (as has been done) that apartheid was 'simply' an 'unfortunate (and failed) experiment'.

Through all the essays runs the thread of the lives of common people, and how their interactions are circumscribed by social conditions. This awareness starts in the first essay, and continues throughout; it serves to underline my father's humanity and common touch, which are two of the attributes that made him a great teacher and a wonderful person.

Johan Simons

Acknowledgements

I am indebted to my daughters Mary Simons and Tanya Barben for information about statutes, and to my niece Mrs Twinkle T.E. Brugge for her highly skilled secretarial work, which she carried out with unflagging energy. My wife Ray Alexander Simons has as always been a great standby and, because of my inability to type, wrote and prepared many references. I thank the University of Cape Town African Studies librarians for their assistance. I thank my son Johan who edited and prepared the book for publication to my satisfaction.

H.J. Simons
18 July 1995

Harold Jack Simons:
A Biographical Note

Professor Harold Jack Simons was born on 1 February 1907 and educated in Riversdale, Cape Province. His mother, Gertrude Morkel, was a teacher; his father, Hyman Simons, born in Birmingham, came to South Africa with Cecil Rhodes. He disapproved of the treatment by the De Beers Company of the African workers in Kimberley, and of the lifestyle of the colonials, and so left Kimberley for Johannesburg. But there he found the lifestyle equally unappealing, and departed for Riversdale. There he joined Gertrude's father's legal office. Over his lifetime he was Town Clerk, Librarian, and Editor of the *Western Echo* and of the *Mossel Bay Advertiser*.

After matriculation in 1924, Jack joined a local firm of attorneys as an articled clerk. After completing Part 1 of the Law Certificate, he resigned to join the public service in Pretoria in 1926, where he worked for the next six years in the Auditor General's Department. During this period he obtained a BA (Law) degree as an external student of the University of South Africa (now UNISA), and was awarded a scholarship for postgraduate study. He used it to complete an MA in political science at the Transvaal University College (TUC) in Pretoria, which he obtained in 1931. He was awarded the Porter Scholarship and enrolled at the London School of Economics (LSE) in 1932 in the Department of Social Anthropology and obtained his PhD in 1935. His experience as a civil servant in the Auditor General and Justice Departments formed the basis of his PhD thesis: 'Crime and Punishment in South Africa with Comparative Studies'. He spent the next two years on the editorial staff of Lord Hailey's *An African Survey*, for which he wrote several chapters. He also signed a contract with Gollancz to publish his thesis as a book, but he wanted to revise parts on his return to South Africa, and this he did not do. Instead, he used it to write a chapter on 'The Law and its Administration', in the *Handbook on Race Relations in South Africa*, published by Oxford University Press for the South African Institute of Race Relations in 1949.

In 1933 he joined the British Communist Party and so fell foul of the university authorities. It was only his prowess as a rugby player which saved him from rustication.

In November 1937, equipped with a PhD and a Communist Party card, Jack moved to Cape Town to take up a lectureship in Native Law and Administration at the University of Cape Town (UCT). He did not approve of the term 'Native' and soon changed the Department's name to Department of Comparative African Government and Law.

His political activities paralleled and complicated his academic pursuits. The starting-point of his shift to political radicalism was the period he spent at UCT studying political science under Professor Edgar Brookes, author of *South Africa's Native Policy*. Brookes was a firm Christian and liberal of the J.S. Mill school, who managed to reconcile these values with whole-hearted approval of General Herzog's segregation programme for Africans. Jack rejected racism, segregation and eventually liberalism of the classical type and gravitated towards Marxism as being more consistent with social realities and his concepts of social justice and equality between race and national groups.

This process of change towards radicalism was accelerated by his experience at the LSE, then the centre of Marxist studies and revolutionary thought among British students. He became chairman of the Cosmopolitan Club, specialising in bringing foreign students together, organising hikes and debates at the weekends, and promoting a radical outlook. At the same time, he organised Marxist study classes. This was during the Great Depression – the Hungry Thirties – when the rise of Italian Fascism, German Nazism and the Spanish Civil War appeared to provide convincing evidence of the Marxist-Leninist thesis that the world was moving into a 'new round of wars and revolution'.

On his return to South Africa he took an active part in reviving the South African Communist Party (SACP) which had fallen into the doldrums and was barely limping along. He wrote editorials for the leftwing newspaper *The Guardian*, where he used the term 'African' consistently.

In 1941 he married Ray Alexander, a leading communist trade union organiser. Ray introduced him to the practical problems of trade unionism, which left him even less time for serious writing other than for the radical press, and he wrote pseudonymously for *Freedom*, *Fighting Talk* and *Africa South*.

In 1946, together with other members of the SACP Central Committee, he was put on trial on the charge of sedition for assisting the 1946 African miners strike. He defended himself and the Party successfully.

In 1950 the Nationalist Party government introduced the Suppression of Communism Act.

In 1960 after the Sharpeville massacre he was detained with over 2000 South Africans of all colours. The UCT staff and students demanded his release, and he was the first detainee to regain his liberty. As a result of his continual opposition to the government's racist policies, he was banned in 1961, and only allowed to lecture to his students, but not to publish.

In December 1964 his banning order was expanded, preventing him from entering any educational establishment. It was thus impossible for him to continue his academic career. After family discussions, he left South Africa in May 1965, having lectured at UCT for 27 years. He took up a Lord Simon Fellowship at the University of Manchester, and together with his wife, completed *Class and Colour in South Africa 1850–1950*, which was published in 1969.

In December 1967 Jack and Ray settled in Lusaka, Zambia, the closest independent state to South Africa. In 1968, he took up the post of Reader (later Professor) in Political Science and Sociology at the University of Zambia. He gave series of lectures to selected cadres of the United National Independence Party (UNIP): governors, military and intelligence officials and Kenneth Kaunda's cabinet, among others.

He retired in April 1975, but remained on the editorial board of *African Social Research*, the journal of the Institute for African Studies. At the request of the African National Congress (ANC) he spent two stints in the Umkhonto We Sizwe camps at Nova Catengue in Angola: six months in 1977–8 and three months in 1978–9, teaching political sociology. He also lectured at the Solomon Mahlangu College in Tanzania.

In the ANC he worked with its president, Oliver Tambo, on the constitutional committee, and drafted the guideline constitution for a free South Africa. He also worked in the ANC Education Department.

His interest in the position of African women produced *African Women: Their Legal Status in South Africa*, published in 1968.

Jack and Ray returned to South Africa in March 1990, after

the unbanning of the ANC, PAC and other organisations. He was awarded an Honorary Doctorate in Law by the University of Cape Town in 1994. He continued writing and attending Communist Party meetings right up to his peaceful death in July 1995.

1 Early Cape Societies

BEFORE RECORDED HISTORY

Reading, writing and arithmetic were unknown in Africa south of Islam and the Sahara before the coming of empire-builders and their offshoots, the colonial settlers. To find out what kind of people lived at an earlier period in the subcontinent we must look at the discoveries of archaeologists and antiquarians.

A good starting point is Zambia. It lies within the crossroads between Eastern and Southern Africa where the earliest human beings are thought to have evolved. Brian Fagan and David Phillipson (in Fagan, 1966: 1–2) wrote that 'For all but two thousand years of their history, Zambians have not had the benefit of agriculture, herds of cattle, or metal tools.' Called 'Bushmen' by the colonists, the indigenous inhabitants kindled fires, hunted, fished and collected vegetable food from trees, bushes, roots and wild plants, using stone, wood and bone for their tools, utensils and weapons.

These are the hallmarks of a Stone Age, the first technological stage in human development. It passed through various phases – Early, Middle and Late – distinguished by the quality and range of their manufactured products. Late Stone Age peoples, who appeared 25 000 years ago or earlier, were humans, *Homo sapiens*, modern men and women. 'In interpreting [their] remains, the archaeologist can legitimately and fruitfully compare them with Stone Age techniques which survive today, and among the few remaining bands of 'Bushmen' in the Kalahari desert south-west of Zambia' (Roberts, 1976: 19).

Most authorities agree that the 'Bushmen' – more properly called the San – were Southern Africa's original inhabitants. G.W. Stow (1905: chs 1–3) wrote that they were the 'aborigines'. G.M. Theal (1919: 8) claimed that their widespread distribution throughout Africa, parts of southern Europe and southern-eastern Asia was certain, the only unsolved question being, 'where do they have their birth and early childhood?' Isaac Schapera (1930: 26–7) considered that earlier and middle Stone Age cultures were prior to the Bushmen, who were 'not indigenous to the country, but constitute an invading element which penetrated into it from the north-east and superseded the two pre-existing Stone cultures'.

Perhaps we could do with a definition of 'indigenous'. The one provided by the International Labour Office (1953: 3–4) seems appropriate:

> Four centuries ago in what is now Latin America, and up to about a century ago in other parts of the world, the term 'indigenous' was easily defined. The 'Indian' or 'Native' was the original inhabitant of the land at the time of its conquest or settlement by Europeans. He was different from the invader in physical appearance, culture and customs. The impact of a foreign culture, with superior techniques and fighting equipment, brought swift defeat for the aborigines. The long struggle between the two groups resulted in the extermination of aboriginal nuclei in various parts of the world; others were forced into distant and barren areas of their former territories; and yet others were segregated in reservations or settlements. For most of them, however, the results of such contact were the establishment and development of a master–serf relationship between conqueror and conquered. In various countries life in common gradually broke down the physical and ethnic distinctions between the two groups. Today the result of this common life is often a kaleidoscopic process of biological and cultural hybridism.

It will be seen in due course that such a lot fell upon all the indigenous peoples in South Africa: the San, their first cousins the Khoikhoi whom the colonists nicknamed 'Hottentot', and the African chiefdoms. The San and Khoikhoi were distinct entities, but formed an ethnic unit, known as Khoisan, a word coined by I. Schultze, a German ethnologist, in 1928.

The Khoikhoi ('men among men') were nomads who raised cattle and sheep. They are thought to have entered South Africa from Botswana about 20 000 years ago in search of grazing and water. Having a regular supply of meat and milk from their herds, they tended to be taller than the San. The Khoi were also more stable, requiring far less space that the San hunter-gatherers, with whom they competed for game, water and plants. Their southward migration brought them to the confluence of the Orange and Vaal Rivers where, according to oral tradition, the settlement split into three groups. One group, the Korana, remained; another, the Namaqua, moved towards the Cape peninsula; and the third group, the Einiqua, followed the course of the Orange River westwards. As a result of more splits, one group went into what is now Namibia, and another through little Namaqualand into the south-western Cape (Oakes, 1988: 21–2).

South Africa's Early Iron Age communities, who followed the Stone Age peoples, began as long ago as 200 AD and lasted until the year 900. The communities are said to have been Bantu-speaking, though there is no way of knowing what languages they spoke. They herded cattle, sheep and goats, hunted, fished and gathered wild plants, cultivated sorghum and millet, mined and smelted iron ore. Later Iron Age people settled in the Messina district of Northern Transvaal in about 1050 and lived there continuously for some 200 years. In the absence of hard evidence to the contrary, archaeologists surmise a period of relative stability among Later Iron Age people, which lasted for almost 800 years. Oakes (1988: 26–30) reported that:

> People learnt to spin and weave fibres into cloth, to twist and plait robes and there was a greater reliance than before on domestic livestock as a source of meat. It is estimated that about 50 percent of the meat intake was supplied by cattle, sheep or goats, and the remainder obtained by hunting. Millet and sorghum were the staple crops, supplemented by maize after contact had been made with Portuguese traders. Trade with the Mozambique coast increased dramatically during the Later Stone Age, and the demand for ivory reflected confidence in weapons with iron tips – although Stone Age man, too, had occasionally tackled elephant.

ANTHROPOLOGIST HISTORIANS

The first modern batch of South African social scientists took the stage in the early 1930s to study what they called 'primitive societies'. Long before they emerged, the Stone Age and Iron Age peoples, who once had freely roamed, mixed and fought among themselves on mountain tops, along plains and on the beaches, had been broken, plundered and subdued by white colonisers and agents of imperial expansion.

Isaac Schapera, a youthful leading light among like-minded colleagues, often deplored the virtual disappearance of South Africa's indigenous peoples. His observations on this score are set out below in short extracts from some of his early publications, following this biographical note.

Schapera was born on 23 June 1905 in South Africa, being the third and penultimate son of immigrant East European Jewish parents. During his boyhood his parents lived in the small town of Garies, close to the border of Namaqualand. Whilst at the University of Cape Town in the 1920s he was fascinated by and displayed an interest in the study of the indigenous people of South Africa, which led him to social anthropology.

An outstanding undergraduate career at Cape Town led to a postgraduate scholarship which brought Schapera to the London School of Economics in 1926, where he worked with Brenda Seligman and Bronislaw Malinowski, whose students included Raymond Firth, Audrey Richards, Evans Evans-Pritchard, Gordon Brown and Lucy Mair. Schapera had a short spell as Malinowski's research assistant.

After gaining his doctorate Schapera returned to South Africa to begin his fieldwork and a post at the University of Witwatersrand (1930), where Mrs Hoernle was in charge of the department. There Hilda Kuper, Max Gluckman, Ellen Hellman and Eileen Krige were his students.

From Witwatersrand he went to a post at the University of Cape Town, and in 1935 he was promoted to the Chair of Social Anthropology, which Radcliffe-Brown had inaugurated.

In 1928 he began research in what was then the Bechuanaland Protectorate, which resulted in his most complete and comprehensive body of knowledge relating to the history, social and political life and contemporary situation of any single group of African peoples sociology and anthropology. A meticulous documentary research covered every aspect of Tswana social life. His writing is notable also in another respect. It is presented in a style and language that have made it accessible to the Tswana peoples themselves. His works are accepted as authoritative records of their customary laws and social history by Tswana leaders.

Later, Schapera did a spell as Visiting Professor at the University of Chicago. He returned to the LSE in 1950 to a Chair in the Department of Anthropology. He served on the Colonial

Social Science Research Council, was chairman of the Association of Social Anthropology from 1954 to 1958, and president
of the Royal Anthropological Institute from 1960 to 1963. He
retired from his Chair in 1969.

Retirement, however, has not meant an end to Schapera's
scholarly work. In 1971 *Rainmaking Rites of the Tswana Tribes*
appeared. His enormous, wide-ranging scholarly output extends
over eight substantial books and many other publications. His
famous *Handbook of Tswana Law and Custom* (1955), *Native Land
Tenure in the Bechuanaland Protectorate* and his book *Praise Poems of
Tswana Chiefs* all demonstrate his mastery of the Tswana language, literary sensitivity and a gift for translation.

I joined the School of African Studies at the University of Cape
Town in 1937. Schapera was then head of the department in
which I taught Native Law and Administration, and later Comparative African Government and Law.

The School was founded to equip students for positions of
colonial administration similar to those established in Britain and
France. I personally did not agree with colonial administrators
who were part of the pattern of white domination and discouraged students from becoming officials in government departments. I was not an anthropologist; I preferred to call myself a
specialist in political sociology.

The appointment to the post of assistant in the Department of
Anthropology at the London School of Economics in 1928–9
provided Schapera with an opportunity to write *The Khoisan
Peoples of South Africa. Bushmen and Hottentots* (1930). Parts of the
book, describing the culture of the two indigenous peoples, were
incorporated in a thesis on 'The Tribal System in South Africa',
which the University of London accepted for the PhD degree.

He pointed out in *The Khoisan People* (p. 233) that the only
Hottentots whose social organisation was at all well known were
the Nama of South-West Africa, of whom a special study was
made by Mrs Winifred Hoernle, Senior Lecturer in Social
Anthropology at the University of Witwatersrand. The original
organisation of other Hottentots had long since been totally
obliterated, and the information bearing on it was far too
fragmentary to provide much material for discussion. As far as
could be gathered, they appeared to have essentially the same
system of social grouping as the Nama, whose traditional system
had been almost completely destroyed.

In 1933 the Van Riebeeck Society published *The Early Cape Hottentots* as described in the writings of Dr O. Dapper (1668), Willem Ten Rhyne (1686) and Johannes Gulielmus de Grevenbroek (1695). The book contained the original texts which were translated from the Dutch into English by Schapera and Benjamin Farrington, Professor of Latin, both men being at the University of Cape Town. Schapera, who also edited the book, wrote in an introduction (i–iv) that these three accounts were among the most celebrated of the early descriptions of Hottentots, and added that a 'small tract' published in Amsterdam in 1652 described parts of the sea coast from St Helena to Mossel Bay and contained fairly lengthy accounts of Hottentots or Hottentoots, based mainly on published accounts but partly on oral statements by men who made the Indian voyage.

Before Jan van Riebeeck sailed with his wife and daughters to Batavia on 7 May 1662, he wrote a memorandum for the benefit of his successors, setting out all that was known to him of the Hottentot tribes, their political divisions and distribution. He received little thanks for his work in raising the status of the Cape from a refreshment station to a colony. The Dutch East India Company directors blamed him for the failure to stop the import of rice and put the settlement on a profitable basis. Furthermore, an accusation by Governor-General van der Lijn, that he had filled his pocket at the Company's expense, stuck and apparently blocked his promotion (Böeseken, in Muller, 1980: 33; and 'Aventuur in die Vreemde', 1971: 97; Gie, 1924, vol. 1: 86).

Schapera next undertook the formidable task of organising and editing a collection of essays, which appeared in 1934 under the title *Western Civilization and the Natives of South Africa: Studies in Culture Contact*. His introduction contained a sad account of the tragic fate that had overtaken the country's original inhabitants:

> Under the impact of European civilization the Bushmen and the Hottentots have declined so considerably in strength and in numbers that they are relatively negligible as far as the problems of interracial adjustment are concerned. Their modes of life and forms of social organization have become almost completely broken down, while the peoples themselves have virtually disappeared as racial entities. (p. 3)

A few other specialists in African studies produced first-hand descriptions of African customary society. Professor J.A. Engelbrecht, head of the Bantu Languages Department at Pretoria University, wrote a book (1936) about the Korana, a widely scattered people from whom he collected oral evidence during nine years of fieldwork in the Orange Free State, Kimberley, Barkly West and the Vaal River diggings. He used information from books and manuscripts to supplement his observations, and wrote comprehensive accounts of Korana history, language and culture. C.M. Doke (1937: 31–41), a leading authority on African languages, noted that Korana and Nama were the only surviving Hottentot languages. 'Hottentot had very early contact with Bushman resulting in the acquisition of the clicks and a certain amount of intonation, as well as additions to the vocabulary. Hottentot too must have contributed vocabulary to Bushman.'

THE MISSIONARIES' INPUT

The missionaries, who compiled the dictionaries and grammars needed to give African languages a written form, arrived at about the same time as the colonial invasion. They were an important part of the conquest, ranking equally with traders, money-lenders, officials, soldiers and other agents of European imperialism.

Dr W. Eiselen (1899–1977), Professor of Bantu Studies at Stellenbosch University in 1933, was a close associate of Schapera. The two men at this stage in their careers agreed that Africans were bound to be absorbed in the Western social and economic structures. Schapera made the point in the preface to *The Bantu-speaking Tribes of South Africa: An Ethnographical Survey* (1937: xiv):

It has rightly become the fashion in modern ethnography to study 'the changing Native', and not to concentrate merely upon his traditional culture. But the understanding of present-day Native life must rest largely upon a knowledge of the former culture, and the time is rapidly approaching when such knowledge will no longer be obtainable to the field. It is highly desirable, therefore, that more intensive fieldwork should be done in this country before too much of the old culture has been obliterated; and if this book succeeds in stimulating any of its readers to inquire more fully into some of the topics or peoples dealt with, it will, for that reason alone, have been worth compiling.

Born and bred on the Berlin Mission Station at Botshabelo, of which his father was superintendent, Eiselen had an intimate knowledge of mission life and the language and culture of the Northern Sotho. He wrote (1934: 65–82) that missionaries came to 'uproot heathen beliefs and customs' and replace them by the Christian way of life. In so doing they added more than any other body of men to our knowledge of tribal law and institutions. The Gospel was the most powerful agency in the disintegration of South African tribes. Beliefs in ancestor spirits could not withstand the impact of the Gospel and western civilisation, which helped to undermine heathen ways. Regrettably, some missionaries, notably those of the London Society, agitated for political rights for the Hottentots, thereby alienating the bulk of the 'rural population' who became bitter enemies of the missionaries (pp. 71, 82).

By his own showing, Eiselen regarded missionaries as exercising a highly subversive influence among indigenous people whose institutions they set out to destroy. They might have understood, but had little sympathy with such customary practices as polygyny, *lobolo* and the rules requiring a widow to bear legitimate children in the name of her late husband. Converts were segregated on the mission stations, forbidden to fraternise with the great majority who clung to traditional ways, take part in their dances, beer drinks and initiation rituals, or listen to the exhortations of their priests (called 'witchdoctors', sorcerers, witches and witchfinders by the colonists), who blessed crops, made rain, cured sickness and appeased the ancestral spirits.

Chiefs and priests were pillars of the traditional society and consequently major targets of attack by government officials and missionaries, working hand in glove to promote western civilisation. Its seamy side in Southern Africa was the seizure of indigenous land, migrant labour, rotating migrant workers and millions of low-paid black workers residing or seeking employment in 'white South Africa', which claimed sovereign rights over 87 per cent of its surface area and nearly all its stored-up wealth.

On a more positive side, mission stations throughout Africa were centres of learning, 'the gateway to modernity' during the era of *mission civilisatrice* (Igbozurika, 1976: 23). They were often sanctuaries for people fleeing from oppressive colonial masters, slave-traders, tribal tyrants, drought and famine. The Kat River Settlement, established in 1828 on the Cape Colony's eastern frontier as a bulwark against the Xhosa vanguard, was such a place of refuge. It attracted Khoikhoi, Bastards and Gona, persons of mixed Khoi and Xhosa descent. They came from many parts of the Colony, including overcrowded settlements managed by the London Missionary Society.

THE COLONIAL SETTING

Anthropology took root and grew in the soil of colonialism, a system of rule by aliens over dependencies which, as René Maunier (1949, vol. 2: 431), the distinguished French authority on colonial affairs, remarked, 'always include a greater or less degree of domination' in the form of 'explicit and defined actions and deeds' imposed by the legislator on the native inhabitants, the original owners of the land.

Lord Hailey (1957: 50–72), the equally distinguished British authority on colonial rule, devoted much time to tracing the efforts of governments to promote the study of customary social systems. Early administrations in Africa, he observed, were far less interested in surveys of this kind than the Dutch in Indonesia, who had decided from the outset to enforce local government systems only through indigenous authorities. Sooner or later, however, colonial governments in all countries found it necessary to make up for lost time by identifying and coming to terms with chiefs and priests, who defended the old order against the invaders.

At the outset, Britain's colonial administrations relied on district notebooks compiled by commissioners, the writings of missionaries, observations of travellers, studies of traditional folk music, and ad hoc investigations of crisis situations, such as ritual killings in Lesotho, local disturbances in Ashanti and southern Nigeria, and alleged Mau Mau murders in Kenya. From 1909 onwards they appointed trained anthropologists to carry out ethnographic surveys in the Sudan, Gold Coast, Nigeria and elsewhere. The International African Institute (IAI), established in 1926, sponsored a number of field studies funded by Britain and foreign governments.

Hailey saw little future for the training and employment of anthropologists in the field unless they were attached to a colonial administration, university or reputable foundation. He found a kindred spirit in Bronislaw Kasper Malinowski (1884–1942), a Polish-born physical scientist who turned his attention to social anthropology and wrote an account, based on published sources, of the family and kinship system of Australian Aborigines, which appeared in 1913. In the following year, Malinowski accompanied the Robert Mond anthropological expedition to New Guinea and had the good fortune to spend the war years among the Trobrianders, whose islands lie off the south-east tip of New Guinea. Here he invented a new kind of fieldwork for the anthropologist who, he wrote:

> must relinquish his comfortable position in the long chair of the missionary compound, Government station, or planter's bungalow, where, armed with pencil and note book and at times with a whisky and soda, he has been accustomed to collect statements from informants, write down stories and fill out sheets of papers with savage texts. He must go out into the villages, and see the natives at work in gardens, on the beach, in the jungle; he must sail with them to distant sandbanks and to foreign tribes, and observe them in fishing, trading, and ceremonial overseas expeditions. Field-work must come to him full-flavoured from his own observations of native life, and not to be squeezed out of reluctant informants as a trickle of talk. (cited in Gluckman, 1965: 28)

Appointed Reader in Social Anthropology in 1924 and Professor from 1927 at the London School of Economics, he became world-famous as the founder of modern anthropological field research methods, attracting aspiring anthropologists from different disciplines and countries.

The years between the global economic depression of 1929 onwards and the outbreak of the Second World War in 1939 were marked by widespread and often violent political controversy. It spread to British universities and penetrated Malinowski's classes, where left-wing students argued that anthropologists working for a government could not be objective, impartial observers in conflicts between the government and people. If so employed, their role should be clearly defined as that of a consultant, expected to advise, without strings attached to either side. Godfrey Wilson, the first Director of the important Rhodes-Livingstone Institute in Northern Rhodesia, was a rare example of an anthropologist who 'believed passionately in the possibility of an objective social science' (Brown, in Asad, 1975: 188).

I observed some of the debate at close quarters from the vantage-point of my dual role in the early 1930s as one of Malinowski's students and also a member of Hailey's team of writers employed (in my case for a weekly wage of £4.00) to write chapters on which he based his final version of the monumental work *An African Survey* (first published in 1938). In my opinion, almost all Wilson's colleagues preferred regular employment and the sense of power that went with a government job, often regarded as a stepping stone to a professorship with assured power, comfort and security.

The defeat of the Axis Powers, the formation of the United Nations, the ascendancy of the two superpowers, which for different reasons repudiated the old colonial system, and the consequent shift in the international balance of power put an end to the command structure in former dependencies. Colonies became sovereign states and in the United Nations outnumbered their former masters, who found it advantageous to negotiate with them on a formal basis of equality.

Britain's post-war government under Clement Attlee, looking to the former colonies for raw materials and tropical products, established the Colonial Development Corporation in 1948 to assist the growth of their economies and, in the same year, brought together in Lancaster House the first gathering ever held of black and white leaders from Britain's African colonies to prepare the ground for the expansion of the British Commonwealth to include the former colonies and consider the role of the Commonwealth Relations Office, the title adopted in 1947 for the old Dominions Office.

British social anthropology flourished in the post-war climate, unlike French and German colonial studies, which went into a severe decline. The Commonwealth Relations Office adopted a positive approach to the training and employment of social scientists able to give expert advice on the aspirations, capabilities and problems of former colonial subjects, who in many countries showed symptoms of strong national sentiment coupled with a rejection of white supremacy.

Budding anthropologists responded in growing numbers to the challenge and opportunities. The Association of Social Anthropologists of the British Commonwealth (ASA), formed in 1946, began with a membership of fewer than 20, which rose to over 150 in 1962 and about 240 in 1968. It was an elitist body of elected members, selected from the holders of a teaching or research post, a PhD or other postgraduate degree, or authors of a substantial numbers of publications.

Talal Asad (1975: 13–14), to whom I am indebted for the statistics, stated that social anthropology emerged at the beginning of the colonial era, became a flourishing academic profession towards its close, and throughout its lifetime was 'devoted to a description and analysis – carried out by Europeans, for a European audience – if non-European societies dominated by European coercive power and the African chief's ultimate dependence on it'.

There is substance in the complaint, but it overlooks the factors of time and place and raises several questions. Did anthropologists accompany Christopher Columbus to Cuba and Haiti in 1492, Pedro Cabral of Portugal who visited Brazil in 1652, Francisco Pizarro who conquered Peru in 1531–41, or Jan van Riebeeck who landed at the Cape of Good Hope in 1652. As Richard Brown observed (in Asad, 1975: 190–7), and as I shall discuss at greater length and breadth, anthropologists involved in surveys of the native population of Zambia in 1940–57 before it achieved independence, were obliged to contend with administrators, missionaries, settlers, racists, mineowners and municipal authorities while attending to their primary task of conducting fieldwork in villages, fishing hamlets, labour compounds, urban townships and Jehovah Witness communities.

Anthropologists who were employed in the colonial service or served it as consultants ran the risk of being regarded by Africans as common and garden *bwanas* employed to spy on behalf of their colonial masters. The strength of African nationalism and the probity of professional anthropologists generally preserved them from the odious reputation of Canadian anthropologists working in the Department of Indian Affairs, of whom it was said (Bowles et al., 1972: 42): 'Indians have been cursed above all other people in history. Indians have anthropologists.'

THE EISELEN LINE

The professional career of Dr W.M. Eiselen, who figured earlier in these chronicles, illustrates the effects on objectivity of a social scientist who accepts a senior position in the state's power structure. He had a wide and varied education, specialising in classical languages for his MA at Stellenbosch University in 1921, and studying phonetics and social anthropology at the Universities of Berlin and Hamburg between 1921 and 1924, where he received a doctorate for his thesis on the phonetics and syntax of African languages.

Back in South Africa he was appointed Senior Lecturer, and later Professor, in Bantu Studies at Stellenbosch University, where he taught until 1936, when he was appointed Chief Inspector of Native Education for the Transvaal. He insisted on mother-tongue instruction and strict equality between Afrikaans and English in teaching African pupils; and urged the government to transfer the control of the schools from the missionary societies to the Transvaal Education Department. He made his mark abroad in 1945–6 when the British government invited him to serve on the Basutoland Commission. In 1946 he accepted the Chair of Anthropology at the University of Pretoria.

The unexpected electoral victory of the National Party in 1948, its bold and aggressive declaration of an intention to segregate Africans, Indians and Coloured, and give the white minority total control of 87 per cent of the country's surface area, electrified Afrikaners of all classes. As members of the ruling race, they foresaw a prospect of obtaining good jobs and incomes in the immense task of rewriting the statute book and putting apartheid policies into effect.

Eiselen gave his version of apartheid in 1948 at a symposium arranged by the South African Institute of Race Relations (SAIRR) (1948: 69–86). He deplored the 'momentous decision to make the early colonists dependent upon the manual labour of a subordinate race and to import great numbers of slaves, when the aboriginals of the Cape were reluctant to enter their service':

> White people were here to stay. Separation was the only honest policy, as the leading liberal, Professor Hornlé, had pointed out, to achieve security. Fair provision should be made for Africans and Coloured, who could not with impunity be

kept in a state of subordination. Total separation would enable Africans to develop on their own without competition. Speculation about the way in which their customs might evolve served no useful purpose, but it was safe to assume that 'natural acculturation' would preserve many valuable traits which would disappear in any process of assimilation.

He was rewarded for such approval of apartheid by being appointed to head a Commission on Native Education (1949–51), an important strand in the expanding network of apartheid laws and practices. The Commission, after investigating education systems for Africans in South Africa and neighbouring states, acknowledged that Africans who gave evidence showed an extreme aversion to any education specially adapted to the Bantu, yet insisted that educational practice must recognise that it has to deal with a Bantu child, trained and conditioned in Bantu culture. Required by its terms of reference to formulate the aims and content of education for Africans as 'an independent race', the Commission under Eiselen's guidance understood the directive to mean the system of apartheid.

Schapera at least disagreed. Speaking at a meeting of the Institute of Citizenship in Cape Town in August 1949, he criticised the conception and practice of apartheid, claiming that the policy of a white South Africa was based on fear and increasing tension, since the whites had been told by successful government propaganda that the Natives were a danger. To some extent this tended to unite white South Africans, but it was also uniting non-Europeans in opposition to the whites, the more so as more and more restrictions were being imposed on the non-European peoples.

Schapera argued that an alternative policy was for South Africa, in common with the rest of the world, to decide that anybody who lives in a country is entitled to have a say in the running of that country (*Guardian*, 1 September 1949).

It was left to Dr H.F. Verwoerd, then Minister of Native Affairs, to spell out the political implications. He told the Assembly on 17 September 1953 that 'Bantu' education must conform to state policy, in terms of which there was no place for Africans in white communities above the level of 'certain forms of labour'. All doors were open to them within 'their own areas'. 'Education should, thus, stand with both feet in the Reserves and have its roots in the spirit and being of a Bantu society.'

The Bantu Education Act of 1953 transferred the control of African schools and training colleges from the provincial administration to the Department of Native Affairs. Eiselen, appointed Secretary of the Department on 17 October 1949, was forced to grapple with angry opposition to apartheid education. The African National Congress organised campaigns against the new school system, African teachers and churches protested, and the rest of the anti-apartheid lobby lined up with the resistance movement.

The greater the opposition, the more repressive was Eiselen's administration, and the further he leaned towards the crusade led by the Suid-Afrikaanse Buro vir Rasse-aangeleenthede (SABRA), formed in September 1949 to campaign for total apartheid, centred on the removal of African workers from so-called 'white areas' (Hugo, 1989: 6–11).

A beginning was made by declaring the Western Cape a labour reserve for whites and Coloured. Announcing this policy in 1953, Eiselen stated that Africans would no longer be issued with railway tickets for the southward journey beyond the junction at De Aar, which had spurs connecting it with the Transkei, a major source of workers for Cape western districts. This was the Eiselen Line. It remained in force until 1985, when the Abolition of Influx Control Act did away with pass laws restricting the movement of Africans into 'white people's country'.

After reaching retirement age on 12 June 1960, the architect of the Line became the Commissioner-General for Northern Sotholand, one of the eight 'national states' scheduled under the Promotion of Self-Government Act of 1959. Stationed at Turfloop near Pietersburg, he moved among people known to him from childhood on his father's mission station. In 1970 the University of the North appointed him its first Chancellor.

He was influential in shaping the legislation and policies of apartheid. In addition to administering the Department of Bantu Education, he had a hand in drafting the Bantu Authorities Act, 68 of 1951, Promotion of Bantu Self-Government Act, 46 of 1959, and the introduction of separate universities for blacks. In 1965 he gave evidence on behalf of the South African government before the International Court in the Hague on the issue of

separate development in Namibia, for which the Bantu Homelands were regarded as a prototype (Rogers, 1976 4–5).

His biographer (C.J. Beyers, 1987, vol. 5: 233–4) pays tribute
to Eiselen for his part in laying the foundations of the future
independence of black nations in South Africa, with the prospect
of a happy coexistence for all its peoples. That evaluation would
not be shared by people who regarded apartheid as a crime
against humanity.

Eiselen's adherence to apartheid dogma lowered the standard
of his scholarship in the field of race relations. The electoral
victory in 1948 was a watershed in the growth of Afrikaner
national consciousness. It demonstrated that the *Volk* had gained
the upper hand in the struggle against British imperialism and
black barbarism. Eiselen gave vent to this display of white
supremacy in a chapter which appeared in the first comprehensive work on South African history in Afrikaans by academics
writing for the general public and senior students (Van der Walt,
et al., 1951, vol. 2: 331–47). What follows is a short summary,
translated from the Afrikaans text, of his comments on the
Khoisan (pp. 331–5):

> The original inhabitants of South Africa in 1652 were Bush-
> men, Hottentots and Bantu. The Bushmen soon completed
> their role in the history of white settlement. The great majority
> became extinct and the small surviving remnants took refuge
> in the no man's land of the Kalahari, where they are virtually
> mobile museum pieces, living mummies representing the Stone
> Age. For our purpose it is not necessary to linger long with
> them.
>
> The Hottentots did not disappear from the scene in the
> same way. Many were exterminated by European dis-
> eases; some groups fled into exile across the Orange River; but
> if they vanished as a nation (*volk*) in South Africa, they lived on
> in the race mixture of the Cape Coloured, who in time
> grew into an important population group. As cattle owners
> of Hamitic stock they must have been particularly attached
> to their animals, but the infusion of Bushman blood was
> apparently so strong that they were willing to exchange
> their cattle for trinkets. As a result they became impover-
> ished vagrants, depending by lawful and unlawful means on
> whites.

If one considers the aptitude of these people for music, imaginative works, light-hearted enjoyment, humour and plea- sure, one can readily recognise the spiritual as well as the physical contribution of the Hottentot to the Cape Coloured.

This pseudo-ethnological approach, riddled with inaccuracies and racist concepts, violated the canons of scientific objectivity, but reinforced the bias of Afrikaans history writers and spread the notion that the Khoisan had only themselves to blame for the loss of their livestock, grazing grounds, water-holes and access to wild plants and game. In effect, Eiselen repeated Jan van Riebeeck's opinion that the chief qualities of the Khoi were joyous uncon- cern, laziness, dirt, robbery and dishonesty.

H.C. Bredekamp (1991: 7) considers that the Khoisan are a decor rather than a focal point of Afrikaans history writers. More widely considered, they saw the Khoisan as an element of the race problem with which European civilisations had to contend: how to satisfy the barbarians that it was to their advantage for whites to occupy and develop their land.

SLAVERY – A NECESSARY ELEMENT

Eiselen was quoted earlier as having said in 1948 that the introduction of slaves was an evil omen for the future course of South African development. He should have known and acknow- ledged that Jan van Riebeeck sent an urgent appeal to the Dutch East India Company (Verenigde Oostindische Compagne, VOC) in Batavia to ship slaves to the Cape settlement. The indigenous Hottentots and Bushmen, he explained, were unfit for continuous manual labour; and the Company's employees could not produce enough food for both the settlement and the ships passing through on the voyage to and from the Indies.

Chattel-slavery, the condition of a human who is the property of another, is as old as antiquity, having been practised on a large scale in ancient Egypt, Greece and Rome, and among Slavonic peoples in Eastern Europe. There was thus no moral objec- tion on the part of the VOC to the import of slaves into the Cape settlement, the injunction to van Riebeeck prohibiting any attempt to enslave the Khoisan being strictly a strategic decision.

Most African slaves came from Madagascar and Mozambique. They did 'the hard work in the vineyards, grain-lands, orchards and vegetable gardens of the settlers' (Marais, 1957: 1–2). Slaves were also imported from India, Ceylon and Malaysia. Many were Muslims, who quickly learnt the skills of almost all the trades practised at the Cape. When freed, many prospered commercially (Oakes, 1988: 50). Slavers on the way to the West Indies and America sold some of their human cargo to Company officials and private burghers in Cape Town. Van Riebeeck acquired 18 slaves within the first seven years of his stay at the Cape, an example that other whites readily followed. Census returns compiled in 1754 recorded a population of 6200 slaves and about the same number of colonists, including manumitted slaves and the children of white fathers and slave or Khoisan mothers, between whom and whites no official distinction was drawn.

WHITE RACISM: AN ACQUIRED CULTURAL TRAIT

Colour prejudice was scarcely known in the first 50 years of white settlement at the Cape. Dr Anna Böeseken, the senior editor of Archives Publications in Cape Town, told a conference of historians at the University of the Western Cape in February 1977 (*Rapport*, 6 February 1977) that manumitted slaves could marry whites in church, attend church services with whites, take part with them in communion and schools, live in houses side by side with top-ranking burghers and possess their own slaves. Some even owned farms in Jonkershoek at Stellenbosch.

An outstanding woman, Angela of Bengal, one of three women slaves who were among the first to be freed, had been transported with her husband and three children to the Cape, where they were sold to van Riebeeck. She looked after his children, and when he left on transfer to Batavia, he sold her to Abraham Gabbema, his second in command, who freed her and her children when he in turn left the Cape.

Poverty was unknown among the colonists during the first 15 years of the settlement when it was merely an administrative post. The introduction of free burghers in 1657 gave rise to a class of smallholders, artisans and tradesmen: fishermen, bakers, garment-makers and hunters. Some whites worked as labourers on the farms. Signs of poverty soon appeared. Smallholders complained that a scarcity of slaves prevented them from producing enough to supply their families' basic needs. The Council of Policy decided to provide funds to clothe the naked and provide relief for destitute children, pregnant mothers, widows, orphans and invalids (Marais, 1945: 1–71).

Poor relief services came from Holland, together with the Dutch Reformed Church, whose contribution, though subsidiary, was an important acknowledgement of the community's responsibility for its members' welfare. The Church's tradition of poor relief in local congregations for all members, both white and black, continued until the end of Company rule at the Cape in 1806.

All members of the Church, black and white, had the same rights of baptism, communion and participation in church services during this period, though signs of a growing racial consciousness appeared towards the end of the eighteenth century when non-white members were identified in church registers as 'bastards' and 'free slaves'. This tendency received a strong impetus with the introduction of mission stations for Khoikhoi and slaves. Segregation was more pronounced in rural villages, but the Church generally respected the terms of Ordinance 50 of 1828, which stipulated that there would be no discrimination on the grounds of colour.

Up to 100 slaves were freed in the seventeenth century, many after Commissioner Hendrik Adriaan van Rheede's visit in 1685. He issued instructions providing that slaves born of a white father were to be freed on reaching the age of discretion, 22 for women and 25 for men. Others born at the Cape were to be freed at the age of 40; those born elsewhere, after 30 years of faithful service.

Coming from many countries, the slaves commanded a wide range of languages and cultures and soon inter-married. Marriages between the colonists and free blacks who had white fathers were lawful and fairly common. Slavery begets promiscuity. During the settlement's first 20 years, at least three-quarters of children born of slave mothers were racially mixed. Of 90 children under 12 whose mothers were Company-owned slaves, 44 had white fathers. A census taken on 1 January 1693 showed that of Company-owned slaves, 29 school-children were of mixed descent and less than a third (32 per cent of wholly non-white stock. Among infants under three years the mixed descent group outnumbered those of non-white descent by 23 to 15 (Elphick and Shell, in Elphick and Giliomee, 1989: 195–6).

The Company housed its slaves of both sexes in filthy barracks under immoral conditions. The barracks also served as Cape Town's main brothel, which was patronised daily by whites, many of whom were sailors and soldiers from passing ships (Marais, 1957: 10; Heese, 1991: 3–4). Though sexual intercourse between colonists and slave or Khoikhoi women was a common practice in the early days of the settlement, few Afrikaans writers have ventured to describe these unions, which tarnished the image of Afrikaners as a people of pure European descent who regarded sex with black and brown women as repulsive. The furthest they, the writers, have gone in condemning slavery is to point out that it gave rise to the widespread South African notion of hard, physical, manual work being fit only for members of an inferior servile race.

Another debt owed to slaves and free blacks is the beginnings of the Afrikaans language in a pidgin Dutch spoken by slaves among themselves and in dealings with their masters. Armstrong and Worden (in Elphick and Giliomee, 1989: 121) noted that:

> The ethnic diversity of the Cape slaves meant linguistic diversity as well. Slaves from Angola, Dahomey, Madagascar, various Indonesian islands, India and the East African coast brought their own languages with them, and consequently had difficulty in communicating among themselves and with their masters. Not surprisingly a lingua franca emerged: in fact there were two. Some slaves used a form of creolised Portuguese . . . but it is clear that most masters and slaves conversed in an evolving form of Dutch which developed into Afrikaans.

Language and material culture went hand in hand. Slaves and Khoi acquired a taste for the colonists' diet of meat, vegetables, bread, rice, brandy and tobacco – tranquillisers more powerful than the *dagga* (*Cannabis sativa*) smoked or chewed by Khoi and San. The Khoi wore European-type clothes in urban areas, but in remote rural districts continued to dress in skins, grease their bodies and carry traditional weapons:

> In the trekboer regions the prevailing languages were Dutch and Portuguese, but otherwise the culture of slaves and colonists was a composite of European and Khoikhoi influences

appropriate to a livestock economy. Here the remaining cultural cleavages were between European, slaves, Bastards and a
few accultured Khoikhoi on the one hand, and the more
traditional Khoikhoi on the other. (Elphick and Shell, in
Elphick and Giliomee, 1989: 230)

VICTIMS OF COLONIALISM

The Khoikhoi soon lost their ecological heritage to the VOC and
the free burghers, who took possession of their grazing land,
water supplies and livestock by means of one-sided trading and
downright confiscation. A far greater disaster fell upon them in a
severe smallpox epidemic introduced in 1713 by a virus from a
visiting ship. The epidemic killed hundreds of colonists and
slaves, and an estimated nine-tenths of the Khoikhoi, who lacked
any natural immunity, in the south-western Cape. A second
epidemic in 1775 and another in 1767 completed the disruption
of their social cohesion. The survivors scattered, losing their clan
identity, and speeding the process of absorption in the colonial
social structure. They 'sank into the position of a landless
proletariat – labourers or vagrants on the lands of their ancestors'
(Marais, 1957: 7). Many took refuge in mission stations.

THE MISSIONARIES

The first mission station in the Cape was established in 1737 by
George Schmidt, a Herrnhuter or member of the reformational
Moravian Church, which came to the Cape with the approval of
the VOC and the Dutch Reformed Church, the only Church
previously allowed in the Colony. After living in a Khoi village
for some months, he moved to Baviaans Kloof, later known as
Genadendal. 'When he baptised five Hottentots in 1742, the
Council of Policy . . . decided to forbid Schmidt to baptize any
more converts.' He protested, and in January 1744 requested to
be allowed to return to his land of birth'. (Böeseken, in Muller,
1980: 69–70). The intolerance of the Governor, the Council of
Policy and the church ministers extended also to Lutherans,
whose request to set up their own church at the Cape was refused
by the Governor and Council in 1742. Only in 1780, nine years

after the death of Governor Ryk Tulbach, who had been a major obstacle, did the Lutherans succeed in building their own church at the Cape.

Three Moravians arrived in 1793 to revive the Genadendal station. 'Khoisan travelled great distances and defied hostile colonists in order to join the Missionaries.' Similar enthusiasm greeted the opening in 1803 of Bethelsdorp, a LMS station near Algoa Bay, which enrolled nearly 1000 people in the next six years. Most of them came from farms 'where the process of subordinating Khoisan was almost complete'. The converts committed themselves to radical culture change, described by one of them, Brother Boesak, in poetical imagery. 'The one heart . . . will do nothing but sing all kinds of Hottentots and Boscheman's songs and all that is bad and the other heart strives to sing the praises of Christ' (Elphick and Malherbe, in Elphick and Giliomee, 1989: 38–9).

In addition to spiritual enlightenment, residence on a mission station offered the material benefits of a disciplined, stable existence, regular meals, elementary education, the acquisition of manual skills and opportunities for a handful to become financially independent. For such reasons few colonists were well disposed towards mission stations. Some, fearing for their labour supply, put obstacles in the way of Khoisan wishing to proceed to Genadendal.

Trekboers closed their ranks in opposition to the missionaries' practice of treating Khoisans under their charge as friends and good companions:

> Their racial pride rebelled against such an attitude: to them the term 'Christian' meant European. They resented the attempts of the missionaries to educate the Hottentots while their own children were growing up in ignorance, neglected by both Church and State. . . . The missionaries reported that many of the Boers visiting Genadendal could neither read nor write. (Marais, 1957: 137)

Boer attitudes tended to change after Britain's annexation of the Colony in 1806. The new regime encouraged mission stations which, under the government's patronage, attracted a growing number of Khoi. Some nearby farmers began attending Genadendal church services, and for the first time admitted that Khoi converts were better than any they had yet employed.

Frontier farmers living beyond the reach of the VOC had a tradition of terrorism against Khoikhoi who challenged their authority. Leonard Guelke (In Elphick and Giliomee, 1989: 96–7) reported routine whippings, which occasionally resulted in death; the shooting by some of the offending Khoi in the legs; and outright executions. Yet conventional settlers took pains to foster their religious heritage:

> Regular devotional services, involving Bible reading and psalm singing, were a feature of orthodox frontier life. These services were usually conducted by the farmer himself in the presence of his family and Khoikhoi and slave dependants. The importance of religion in the daily lives of the majority of settlers is evident from the fact that whites often referred to themselves as 'Christians' and used this word to differentiate themselves from the slaves and the 'heathen' inhabitants of the country.

The London Missionary Society (LMS) – wrongly accused by Dr Eiselen of being the only cause of Boer antagonism to missionaries – began its activities in the Colony in 1799. Four years later it founded Bethelsdorp on a large, partly barren tract of land near Algoa Bay. The guiding spirit was a Hollander, Dr J.T. van der Kemp, who tried to practise what he preached, lived with the Khoi, married a slave's daughter, denounced slavery and condemned the government and colonists alike for neglecting the welfare of the Khoi and oppressing those in their employ.

His successor, Dr John Philip (1775–1851), though more conciliatory, was equally determined to remove the causes of Khoisan grievances. He came in 1819 to supervise the Society's large number of stations which were widely distributed throughout the Colony. His frequent tours by oxwagon and cart enabled him to acquire an exceptional knowledge of the country, which he used in replying to critics who accused him of being a political agitator who neglected his parishioners, a complaint of little substance.

> At Bethelsdorp hunters, sawyers and timber merchants, transport riders, salt collectors and stocking knitters could make a fair living. Also, the services of certain skilled residents at Genadendal (a cartwright, a blacksmith, a cooper, a miller, several masons and midwives) were in demand by farmers in the neighbourhood, and some became 'quite well-to-do' as a result. Cutlers trained by the missionary Christian Kühnel,

who had learned the craft at Herrnhut in Saxony, produced knives of the highest quality, which the colonists called 'herrn-huters'. Mission life gave a few Khoisan a measure of financial independence, but the shortage of suitable land on the overcrowded stations meant that most remained poor with no option but to hire themselves periodically to the farmers, or to enlist in the Regiment. (Elphick and Malherbe, in Elphick and Giliomee, 1989: 39)

Philip's biographer, W.M. Macmillan (1928: 107–8), put the case for his missionary zeal by linking it to wide national interests. 'Philip more than any man compelled reluctant statesmen to face the fundamental issue of Emancipation, and to concede that the coloured races were no longer to be regarded as slaves.'

It was John Philip and his fellow emancipators whose agitation brought about the enactment of Ordinance 50, 1828, which repealed laws passed by British governors in Cape Town during 1809–19, requiring Khoikhoi to be registered at the offices of the *landdrost* (magistrate) and carry passes when moving from their place of abode. Marais (1957: 116–31) argued at length that the labour laws protected the Khoi against ill-treatment by their masters, a conclusion strongly criticised by Dora Taylor, writing under the pen-name Nosipho Majeke (*circa* 1952: 18–19). She claimed that the Khoikhoi remained a landless people in spite of the 50 Ordinance, and that the farmers' outcry against 'vagrancy' after the passing of the Ordinance was 'an outcry for a controlled labour force'.

Dr C.F. Kotzé (in Muller, 1980: 137–8) argued that Ordinance 50 'increased vagrancy and theft', intensified the labour problem, further impoverished farmers harassed by Hottentot thieves and greatly increased the number of unemployed coloured vagrants. He went on to say:

It is worth noting that the Dutch colonists who remained in the Cape Colony and who did not take part in the Great Trek came to accept the concepts of British political liberalism, though never any form of social equality. The Fiftieth Ordinance was a turning point in the history of no-White legislation in the Cape Colony; thereafter Cape Legislation became 'colour-blind'. After 1828 there was no more discrimination on the grounds of race or colour, except in the case of Indians who were not considered an indigenous and assimilable element. The Cape Afrikaners, in time, came to accept this standpoint and in this respect the British anglicization policy had indeed been remarkably successful.

INDOCTRINATION

H.C. Bredekamp (1991: 7–11) pointed out that Afrikaans history writers stuck to the notions of white supremacy which shaped the thinking of generations of students in schools and universities. They learnt that the superior morality and social values of whites gave them a right to occupy and develop indigenous land. During the nationalist fervour that accompanied the celebrations of the 300th anniversary of van Riebeeck's landing at the Cape, and the electoral victory of the National Party on a platform of total apartheid, illustrated volumes of *Drie Eeue: Die Verhaal van ons Vaderland, 1952* portrayed Hottentots and Bushmen as murderers, robbers, arsonists and runaways, who occupied a small part of South Africa's history as hangers-on, henchmen and sometimes fellow travellers.

Inward-looking ethnocentrism, national glorification and disregard of the contributions and claims of non-Afrikaners seriously lowered the standards of scholarship among Afrikaner social scientists. Dr A.L. Müller (1991: 6–7) has drawn attention to the manner in which Afrikaans history writers tend to concentrate on the activities of Afrikaners, accompanied by much praise-singing of their achievements and belittling of the achievements and role of non-Afrikaners in a blatant attempt to attain political objectives. To illustrate his point he quotes a comment by Professor C.G.W. Schumann, Stellenbosch University's leading structural economist, who, to facilitate access to an international audience, published an English version of one of his major works in Britain (1938: viii). When contributing to an Afrikaans book on the cultural history of Afrikaners (van den Heever and Pienaar, 1945: 42) he wrote:

> The history of South Africa is mainly that of the Afrikaner, how a new volk was born and grew to maturity in an environment that made the highest demands on its physical powers, endurance, ingenuity and faith; a people who

struggled continuously among other population groups to remain true to themselves, to preserve what was theirs and to retain or conquer their rightful place in a world which constantly became more difficult and imposed new demands on those who wanted to survive and maintain their identity.

Books written in English with a similar slant towards the *Volk* and its nationalist aspirations were acceptable to Afrikaners and an important source of information before an Afrikaans history and social science took shape. This kind of service was provided by the Canadian-born George McCall Theal (1837–1919), whose prodigious literary output, based mainly on archival records, vindicated by and large the triumph of colonial and imperial expansion over barbarism.

Christopher Saunders (1988: 29), in a penetrating probe of Theal's work, observed that he wrote at times as though blacks did not exist in South Africa. They were inferior in his eyes and their history was less significant than the history of white settlement.

No other major historian – at least before the 1970s – had more personal contact with Africans, or more to do with their administration. Yet Theal, the pioneer, the father of South African historiography, did more than anyone else to establish a tradition of strongly pro-colonialist, anti-black historical writing, and to create the racist paradigm which lay at the core of that tradition and which served to justify white rule.

Even slavery, in spite of its importance in the Colony's social and economic life, was a neglected subject in early Afrikaans writings, its only significance for them being the effect of its abolition on the Great Trek of 1854. In 1834, the year of emancipation, the Colony's slave population numbered 39 000, the great majority of whom were held in Cape Town and its rural countryside. The farmers who took part in the Trek came largely from prosperous districts in the Western Cape. They objected less to the amount of compensation paid by Britain for the loss of their slaves than to the concept of equality between black and white. They left the Colony for the vast regions north of the Orange River, carrying with them 'the old inherited belief that it was the function of the Hottentot and bastard and now of the

Bantu and freed slave to serve the white man' (Edwards, 1942: 203–4).

From 1950 onwards Afrikaans writers tended to take a more realistic approach to slavery and its abolition. Van der Walt et al. (1951, vol. 11: 188–91) wrote that though the compensation money paid by the British Treasury was only half the estimated market value of the emancipated slaves, amounting to £3 million, and the financial loss to the owners was serious, the overall results were beneficial. The rise in wages of free workers barely exceeded the cost of maintaining slaves, who were not indispensable. Emancipation was not a serious obstacle to economic growth in the following years; and the main receivers of benefit were the colonists who had been demoralised by the system, which encouraged idleness, comfort and luxury among the masters. They looked down on manual work, regarding it as degrading, an attitude which hindered the growth of a white artisan class. Skilled as well as unskilled labour was carried out by slaves, while Afrikaners learnt to consider that only the learned professions and land ownership were worthy of whites. Emancipation forced the colonists to work and contribute to making the Boervolk the most energetic and enterprising people in South Africa.

Afrikaner writers were less broadminded when discussing the racial makeup of the *Volk*. An outstanding exception was the historian Johannes Stephanus (Etienne) Marais (1898–1969). Born on a farm and educated in Paarl, he majored in classics at the University of Cape Town and studied history at Oxford. Returning to Cape Town as a senior lecturer in the University's history department, he wrote the *Cape Coloured People 1652–1937*, in which he pioneered neglected aspects of inter-racial relations, among them the Bastards (Saunders, 1988: 115–17).

BASTARDS

The dictionary definition is a person born out of wedlock, but in early Cape practice the word was applied also to offspring of white fathers and slave or Khoi mothers. 'Baster', meaning half-caste and hybrid, is deeply embedded in the Afrikaans language. A popular Afrikaans–English dictionary (Bosman et al., 1936: 64) lists about 25 words of which baster is a component, as in basterras, baster taal, basterhottentot and bastermeid.

When trekboers drove their cattle and sheep into the remote north-western Cape, some had sex with Khoi servants who accompanied them or with Khoi women whom they encountered during their travels. A permanent conjugal relationship between a white man and Khoi woman was strictly taboo:

> A Boer who took a Hottentot wife lost caste among his own people nor could his children hope to join Boer society. By the second half of the eighteenth century the Bastards were becoming a people apart from both Boers and Hottentots. They were already tending to intermarry only among themselves, and since they had large families, were rapidly increasing in number. Thus did the Boers keep their own race pure and bring into existence a nation of half-breeds. (Marais, 1957: 11)

The Bastards, who usually adopted the surnames of their Boer fathers and Christian religion, lived with their flocks and herds at a good distance from their white kinsmen. When the trekboers caught up with them, they summarily expelled their relatives of mixed descent. Some retreated to the Orange River to form in later years the nucleus of the Griqua, one of the Coloured subgroups listed under the Population Registration Act of 1950. Another group moved further north, blending with the Nama, a Khoikhoi clan thought to have been in Namibia for centuries. Peter Carstens (1966: 230–5), who researched the social structure of a Coloured reserve in Little Namaqualand, described their culture as being a synthesis of Afrikaner and Khoikhoi traditions. Proud of their white ancestral strain, they accepted the name Baster as a badge of honour which gave them a moral right to lord it over pure indigenous people, with whom they shared a maternal lineage (Wellington, 1967: 155–7).

Parties of trekboers followed the trail into 'Bushmanland', a desert-like region south of the Orange River, on the north side of which lies Professor Carl Boshoff's envisaged Afrikaner Republic. Willem Charles Scully, the Civil Commissioner for Namaqualand in 1892 (*circa* 1898: 2–4), wrote that the average trekboer of Bushmanland was

> a being *sui generis*. He is usually ignorant to a degree unknown among men call civilised. He is untruthful, prejudiced, superstitious, cunning, lazy and dirty. On the other hand he is extremely hospitable. . . . The usual lack of fresh meat and the

absence of green vegetables as an item in his diet, has reacted upon his physique and made him listless and slouching in gait and deportment, as well as anaemic and prone to disease. This is especially true of his womankind, who being extremely short-lived have, as a rule, lost nearly all pretension to beauty of face or form.

The trekboer's family house, like that of the Khoi, was a portable beehive-shaped hut made of pliable stakes bent inwards and fastened at the top. The framework was covered with rush mats made by the women, the whole being 'a form of architecture adopted from the Hottentots'.

Though Namaqualand's trekboers assimilated a large slice of Khoikhoi material culture, they never forgot that they belonged to a master race. With few exceptions, they clung to their racial identity and Christian faith, observed the Sabbath, baptised their children, married in church and faithfully attended communion services when a Dutch Reformed Church minister visited his scattered and far-flung congregations.

The Khoikhoi lost the support of their traditional institutions in colonial wars and white man's diseases. The survivors 'sank into the position of a landless proletariat – labourers or vagrants on the lands of their ancestors' (Marais, 1957: 7). They found employment with trekking farmers whose mode of subsistence did not differ much from their own, which involved a constant search for water, game and grazing. But the Khoi resented their masters' attempts to enslave them and revolted when a opportunity came their way. This happened in 1795 when Graaff-Reinet Boers rose in arms against British rule. Khoi troops were sent to suppress the revolt. After they had carried out their mission, the British commanding officer decided to disarm them, fearing that they would be returned to the Boers' service. The Khoi fled to join Xhosa impis who had invaded the Colony. Attempts to detach the Khoi from their new allies led to the issue of South Africa's first labour laws (Marais, 1957: 113–15).

THE NOBLE SAVAGE IMAGE

George Fredrickson (1982: 132), wishing to spell out differences between the social conditions of the Khoikhoi and the American

Indian, agrees that the Coloured of South Africa 'are for the most part descendants of the early amalgamation of Whites, Khoikhoi, and slaves that preceded the main black–white confrontation'.

American Indians also blended, physically and culturally, with whites and other stocks. When Christopher Columbus (1446– 1506) landed in South America in 1498, thinking it was India, the estimated North American Indian population numbered 1.25 million. Today there are perhaps 500 000, few of whom are of unmixed descent. Like the Khoikhoi, they suffered greatly from the spread of white man's diseases – smallpox, tuberculosis, syphilis, alcoholism – and the slaughter of bison, their main source of meat. When they ceased to be a military threat or source of servile labour, they were elevated to the status of the 'Noble Savage' image, a symbol of natural virtue imagined by Jean-Jacques Rousseau (1712–78) in his discourse on *The Origin of Inequality* (1753) and by Friedrich Engels (1820–95) in the *Origin of the Family, Private Property and the State* (1884).

The inclusion of the Khoikhoi in the 'Noble Savage' simile was ruled out, according to Fredrickson (pp. 39–40) for two reasons: 'the degradation and barbarism of Africa' and the outlandish appearance of the Khoi in their primal state: the hollow back, the protruding buttocks, the 'peppercorn' hair, and even some alleged deformities of the female sexual organs. The element of race determinism in these passages is offensive, inaccurate and inconsistent with the author's aim of debunking the myth of 'white supremacy', which 'suggests systematic and self-conscious efforts to make race or colour a qualification for membership in the civil community' (p. xi).

The survivors and descendants of the Khoikhoi have no reason to regret their exclusion from the 'Noble Savage' myth. Their claim to fame rests on the more solid foundation of active participation, during 400 years, in the rise and growth of the Coloured population, now estimated at 3.27 million, and in the creation and growth of South Africa's social and economic structure.

THE SAN

The San, once the only human inhabitants of South Africa, are Stone Age people of the kind describes by Fagan and Phillipson as having lived in Central Africa between one and two million years ago. The San were nicknamed 'Boesman' by Dutch settlers and 'Bushmen' by some English speakers who prefer it to San, in the same way as racists use 'Hotnot', the Afrikaans version of Khoikhoi. The two peoples are closely related and share the compound word Khoisan, as well as click consonants which are confined to a small part of the continent stretching formerly from the southern Cape through the Kalahari and Namibia to southern Angola (Wellington, 1967: 130–1).

The San are of small stature with a long and low skull, tight yellow skin stretched and glossy over high cheek bones, sparse facial and body hair, and fatty tissues in the buttocks, especially in the women. Before the white invasion, men wore a strip of triangular skin which was passed between the legs and tied round the waist. Women were clothed in long skin wraps. They lived in low huts made of reed mats, used few roughly made utensils and carried water in ostrich eggshells.

Their primary social unit was the hunting, food-gathering band, consisting of a few related families, usually monogamist and small, as it is difficult for a woman to rear more than one small child at a time and carry a youngster on long marches in search of food. D.F. Bleek (in Duggan-Cronin, 1942: 9–10) observed that:

> Every group of families owns several springs or water-holes at long distances from each other and moves from one to another according to the season. The buck drinking at these holes is the property of the group. Men from other parts shooting this game are poachers, and it is the owners' right to attack them. Hence the feuds that have sprung up everywhere when intruders, yellow, black or white, have penetrated into Bushman territory. The invaders have occupied their precious water-hole, have shot or frightened away the game; the Bushmen robbed and ruined thereby have attacked the people and carried off their stock. Thereupon the invaders, unconscious of any aggression on their part, have dubbed the original owners thieves and murderers, and have done their best to eliminate them. The end was only a matter of time.

William Scully (*circa* 1898: 15) also doubted the ability of the San to survive. He wrote that 'The Bushman was the true Ishmaelite; he was bound to be eliminated. As a matter of fact there is no room for a Bushman and anyone else in any given area, no matter how large.'

Hunting and gathering wild plants were the only way of life known to ancestors of the San until about 2000 years ago, when cattle herders, ancestors of the Khoikhoi, came with long-horned Afrikander cattle, the only breed indigenous to South Africa, and fat-tailed angora-type sheep. The herders competed with the San for wild plants, game and water-holes. The San tamed no animals except the dog, and lived mainly by hunting with a simple bow and poison-tipped arrows, gathered plants and ate anything edible: meat, roots, bulbs, insects, snakes, frogs, lizards, honey and ants' eggs.

About 1700 years ago Iron Age Africans who kept cattle and raised crops began moving through the Transvaal and Natal to the eastern Cape where Khoikhoi and San lived. The Xhosa-speaking chiefdoms fraternised with San and Khoi, but overran their hunting and grazing lands, making it impossible for them to continue their traditional way of life. The arrival of Dutch settlers from 1650 onwards threatened the very existence of all indigenous peoples. The settlers seized land for farms and grazing, used firearms to kill large numbers of game, and conducted wars of colonial conquest against Khoikhoi, San and African chiefdoms.

At the time of the white invasion, the Khoikhoi were mainly coastal dwellers while the San, driven out of the well-watered lowlands, lived on the high veld and mountain slopes. Candy Malherbe wrote (1986: 7, 18–20, 38–40) that they traded skins, honey, ostrich-shell beads for clay pots, metal goods and factory-made beads. Some San worked as herders and soldiers for Khoikhoi; some resisted the invaders, raiding the herds of Khoi, Xhosa and trekboers. The San's resistance delayed the advance into the Northern Cape of trekboers, who resorted to wars of extermination, which peaked in the second half of the eighteenth century. The San fought back with bows and arrows in an untutored guerrilla war. The struggle sharpened the Boers' race consciousness and belief in white supremacy. Marais (1957: 15) concluded that:

> The incoming Boers do not seem to have attempted to come to any sort of accommodation with the Bushmen whose hunting grounds they invaded, killing off their game and depriving them of their *veldkos*. . . . The tradition early took

root among the men on the then frontier that the Bushmen were no better than wild animals and that it was justifiable to exterminate them like so much vermin. On their side the Bushmen became fiercer and more predatory as their means of subsistence disappeared before their eyes.

Commandos of Boer militia were called up as early as 1715 for punitive action against the San. A force of whites, Khoi and Coloured, under a commandant appointed by the government, scoured the northern frontier, killing 503 and capturing 239. Between 1786 and 1895, the last decade of Company rule at the Cape, the office of the landdrost in the magistracy of Graaff-Reinet recorded 2504 San killed and 669 taken prisoner. Women were often killed as well, while children were taken alive and distributed as apprentices, who were held in virtual slavery, together with adult prisoners.

To pacify the Boers, the north-east frontier was extended to the Orange River in 1834, thus enabling them to obtain legal title to the land they had already seized and occupied. The concession did not stop them from driving their flocks and herds into the driest of the dry lands, known as Boesmanland, the last part of the Colony in which the San retained a foothold.

Traditional San society was a sharing, and within the narrow limits of related bands, a caring society. What follows is a shortened summary of Candy Malherbe's description (1986: 35–52). Adult San spend between 12 and 33 hours a week in getting food, which they share so that no one goes hungry, and to unite people by creating dependence on one another. Women walk up to 2400 kilometres a year, carrying small children and personal possessions, weighing less than 11 kilograms each. To prevent conflict in closely knit bands, members share, exchange gifts, practise good manners and if necessary leave the band to avoid quarrelling. Children are taught to live in peace with one another.

There are no specialised craftsmen. The raw materials used are wood, reeds, bone, leather, sinew, ostrich eggshell and vegetable fibre. A family's stock of goods can fit into two or three leather bags. Carved pipes, bead necklaces, thumb pianos and musical bows are freely given, thus avoiding jealousy and bad feeling.

Most San believe in a Great God living in the east, who works through a sly and vengeful god in the west. They approach the

Great God through a healer. Almost half the men and, in some groups, a third of the women become healers. Their healing power comes in a trance, which occurs in a dance that starts at dusk and goes on until morning. The healers, more correctly called medicine-men, claim to see images during the trance, probably induced by chewing or smoking dagga, the only plant the San cultivated. Its effects are similar to those experienced by American Indians, who also go into a trance after observing prescribed rituals and eating peyote, a spineless cactus.

SURVIVAL

Some city dwellers with a taste for adventure might envy the San's style of life, but it cannot endure in overcrowded countries where space is at a premium. The San have been forced by more powerful invaders to brace themselves for major changes in their customs and traditions.

Nowadays, after the expulsion of the San from their hunting grounds, whites are inclined to view them with respect for their hardiness, ability to live in harsh, semi-desert regions, acquire an intimate knowledge of their environment, its animals, insects and plants, and how to cope with its adversities. Antiquarians have drawn attention to the historical and artistic merits of the San rock paintings, which depict animals and people in the act of hunting, marching, dancing, fighting and digging. The culture of hunting and gathering reflected in these works of art have gone from most parts of Southern Africa, but the San live on in the Kalahari, Caprivi Strip and Namibia.

The Odendaal Commission on South West African Affairs, 1960–7 (Wellington, 1967: 384–5) estimated that there were 12 000 San in Namibia in 1960, when they formed 2.24 per cent of the country's total population of 526 000. Some San worked on white-owned farms, others were able to continue hunting and gathering in Ovamboland and arid regions in the south, but government regulations issued for the protection of wild animals prevented the San from hunting at will. They were considered to be in a state of transition and unqualified for the kind of limited self-rule granted to other ethnic groups.

Candy Malherbe estimated that between 40 000 and 50 000 San were living in Botswana and the Kalahari at the time of writing. Their numbers were increasing but cattle-herding farmers who moved into their hunting grounds about 60 years ago had forced them to change their mode of production.

A.A. Anderson (1888: 21), a celebrated traveller in the second half of the nineteenth century, came across a dejected, poverty-stricken group of people called Masarwa. Theal (1919: 21) considered they were of 'mixed Bantu and Bushman blood, the latter preponderating'. Photographs of Masarwa (in Duggan-Cronin, 1941: Plates XXIII–XXV) show a pronounced 'Bantu' strain in members of a San group. Their descendants are very likely the Sarwa 'serfs' described by Schapera (1955: 32, 251–3). They hunted, herded cattle, ploughed and did domestic work for their owners, against whom they had no right of action for wrongs inflicted on them. 'If ill-treated, as they often were, they had no other remedy than to run away if they could, and were often followed up and brought back forcibly' (p. 252). Proclamations issued in 1936 declared that 'slavery in any form is unlawful and that the legal status of slavery does not exist'. A labour law was introduced, setting out the conditions under which Africans could be employed as servants by African masters.

The San learned to adapt the hard way. Some became mercenaries, employed as trackers and spies by the South African Defence Force in the war against SWAPO (the South-West Africa People's Organisation) in the 1970s and 1980s. They were drafted into two separate battalions, one based in the Caprivi Strip, the other in Namibia. Employed as trackers and intelligence agents, they were highly praised by their commanding officers. The battalions were disbanded after Namibia won its independence on 1 April 1989. Candy Malherbe anticipated in 1986 (p. 64) that when the war stopped, San servicemen might lose their jobs and the ability to buy things they took for granted in the army: clothes, radios and basic foods.

NAME-CALLING

There is magic in names, perhaps more so in racially divided South Africa than elsewhere. Jon Qwelane (*Cape Argus*, 16 May 1991) traces the consequences in a biographical note, which summarised reads:

I was born a Native . . . in a Native Reserve. The official policy guiding all Natives and their reserves was called apartheid. I was also . . . a Problem and a Question. . . . As I was growing up I became a burning question, or a pressing problem. . . . From Native I developed into a Bantu, and my habitat into a bantustan. The official policy also changed, developing from apartheid into separate development. . . . From Bantu I suddenly became a Plural, and my habitat changed from bantustan to homeland. The policy became known as plural relations. But before the latest change could sink in I changed from Plural to Co-operative . . . I became a black, my habitat became a national state, and the policy became Development Aid.

Sometimes the magic is 'black', involving witchcraft or demons, or undiluted racism, as in a criminal law case reported in the *Cape Times* (21 March 1991). Eugene Marais, a member of the Afrikaans-Weerstandbeweging (AWB), murdered seven black men and attempted to kill 27 others in an attack on a passenger bus in 1990. He claimed to be a member of a sect called the 'Gemeente van die Verbondsvolk'. Mr Carl Pieter Liebenberg, the assistant Town Secretary in Richards Bay, stated that he had tried to save Marais's soul and get him to renounce the AWB. It was his personal opinion that blacks were 'wild animals of the veld who did not have redeemable souls'. The right-wing religious sect to which he belonged did not spread this doctrine; but he had never tried to save the soul of a black person because paradise was reserved for whites only.

NAME-CALLING FASHIONS

The fashions change, as Jon Qwelane noted. Some names were discarded because they offended, causing resentment, the most notorious of these being Kaffir. This is derived from a Muslim word meaning 'infidel' and applied to non-believers who rejected Islam, but were compelled to accept it in 1895 after centuries of resistance. The Portuguese appear to have brought it to South Africa and used it to describe Xhosa-speaking chiefdoms of the Eastern Cape. Leading historians, including Macmillan (1928: xiv–xv and passim) and Marais (1957: 132) used the term as a matter of course, though it was not until 1850, when the eighth 'Kaffir' war was fought, that the word received official recognition by Sir Harry Smith, the Governor of the Colony and British High Commissioner, who administered the territory between the Keiskamma and the Kei, the territory known as British Kaffraria (Peires, 1981: 165–9).

The Xhosa never used the term, which was foreign to them and imposed by strangers. Many regarded it as a term of contempt, as did the Supreme Court in June 1976 when it awarded an African damages of R150 from a white who called him a 'kaffir'. Jean Branford (1980: 124–9) lists 46 words of which 'kaffir' is a component; and asserts that most black and white South Africans regard it as offensive (p. 125).

Another imported word which gives rise to problems is Afrikaan (-ane), which is derived from Dutch. It is much too close for comfort to Afrikaners, the plural for Afrikaner. The word Afrikaan (-kane), meaning a native of Africa, is acceptable, but when referring to white persons, the adjective 'Suid' is invariably added. A South African is a white person.

There is no Afrikaans equivalent of the African National Congress. It is commonly referred to in Afrikaans as the 'ANC' or with the full title in English. The emergence of the Black Consciousness Movement in the 1970s contributed to an ideological climate which excluded whites in principle from the movements of the oppressed, and encouraged the apartheid regime to substitute 'black' for 'Native' and 'Bantu' in the titles of laws and administrative bodies.

POPULATION REGISTRATION

The Population Registration Act of 1950 was repealed on 17 June 1991. Said to have been the 'cornerstone of apartheid', it was repealed by the tricameral parliament. Only the Conservative Party opposed the repeal, because, said Dr Treurnicht, the repeal of this and other apartheid laws 'touched the roots of own community life' and the 'self-determination of nations'. The government explained that population registration would be retained for election purposes until a non-racial constitution had been negotiated. It was pointed out that the Repeal Act did away with race classification only for South Africans born after its enactment. The state president, Mr F.W. de Klerk, acknowledged that in the meantime, the constitution would be based on race because the tricameral parliament continued to function and Africans still did not have the vote (Race Relations Survey, 1991/2: 457).

According to the Urban Foundation (quoted in Race Relations Survey 1991/2: 1–3) South Africa's total population in 1991, including the ten homelands, numbered 21 589 000, of whom Africans accounted for 12 265 600, whites 5 068 100, Coloured 3 271 100 and Asians 984 200 though this must be considered a gross underestimate. The estimated population in the year 2000 would be 47 592 400, consisting of 37 260 000 Africans, 5 427 700 whites, 3 782 600 Coloured and 1 122 000 Indians.

IN DEFENCE OF AFRIKANERDOM

Harrison M. Wright (1977: 108) has criticised South African historians, right, left and centre, with some arrogance as though he alone has the correct story of the past. He singles out opponents of apartheid who trace Afrikaner racialism to the days of the trekboer, 'the most "illiberal" of the Afrikaners, who, with little or no qualification, then serve as the general type for all' (p. 40). Radical liberals and 'Marxist revisionists', he argues, fail to face up to the evidence that the frontiersmen treated their black servants better than did the British settlers.

He cites, among others, John X. Merriman, a leading Cape liberal member of parliament, who wrote to his mother in 1900: 'Perhaps the Dutch know how to manage native servants better. . . . The patriarchal method, which certainly involves great harshness at times, is also compatible with a good deal of laxity. It is more human though less humane' (p. 38). The Commissioners of Enquiry, who were sent by the British government in 1823 to report on the conditions of the Khoikhoi, found that they preferred service with the Boers to that of the English settlers who paid more but exacted more labour. Wright sets much store by this comment, which is dealt with at greater length by Marais (1957: 12–30).

Wright failed to note that what he called Dutch 'patriarchy' was an offshoot of white supremacy under which no black could with impunity put forward claims to equality, whether in status, social behaviour or decision-making. This outlook, known in Afrikaans as *baasskap*, is a major obstacle to the adoption of a constitution in which the universal franchise will be extended to Africans with the same rights as whites, Coloured and Indians in a multi-party parliament.

The vast majority of the Khoi were quite unfit for hard agricultural work. They wanted and were best fit for looking after cattle, whether as herdsmen or as wagon-drivers. The Commissioners, who left the Colony in 1826, were told by Genadendal missionaries that 'in their dealings with the farmers the Hottentots, from ignorance of the value of money, and from habitual carelessness and indifference, entered into agreements that secured no adequate remuneration for their labour'. They could not learn the value of money from their employers, who themselves obtained little more than the bare necessities of life. They rarely handled money and often paid their servants in food, clothing and cattle. Nearly half of the Khoikhoi in the interior worked only for their food and clothing. Having lost their land, flocks and herds to the settlers, they had no choice but to work for the trekboers who spoke a patois which they understood even though their masters would, on occasion, give vent to their frustrations in violent assaults, like the one recorded by Stephen Watson (1991: 58) in a book of /Xam poems.

LAMENTS OF THE SAN

The poems are derived from three members of a group of Bushmen sent from the Northern Cape to serve sentences of hard labour on the breakwater in Cape Town's harbour. Dr Watson explains in an introductory note that Dr W.H. Bleek, a distinguished linguist, persuaded Sir Phillip Wodehouse, the Cape Governor from 1862 to 1870, to grant him custody of some of the convicts and house them in the garden of his house in Mowbray. Bleek learned their language, reduced it to a written form and recorded the information they provided in phonetic script, which Watson used for his own 'double translation'. Most of the transcribing was done by Lucy Lloyd, Bleek's sister-in-law. Without the three /Xam storytellers and the two linguists, the oral traditions of South Africa's oldest culture would have been lost forever.

The Story of Ruyter

Ruyter, brought up by white men – Ruyter died amidst white men at a place Called Springkaan's Kolk. He was bound to a wagon with straps from the oxen; they tied him face down because of herding the sheep. The Boer who was master, the Boer began beating him with the riem that they used for tying a beast. He said Ruyter, the herder, had not herded well.

This happened, this beating that led to his death. The Boer hit him and hit him; the other Boers too. When at last they unloosed him, Ruyter he fainted. Those who were there – they all must have known, they must have known then, when picking him up, that Ruyter, the herder, was near beaten to death.

This happened. He, Ruyter, said to those people, he said white people did not believe he felt pain; they would not believe he felt half-beaten to death. But to him, to himself, it did not seem he could live. He kept whispering, repeating, 'I looked after the sheep. I, Ruyter, looked after the sheep'. He kept saying the pain was such, so bad, he could not last long.

It was he, Ruyter, who told the white people there that his body's middle, here, ached badly, very bad. It was he who tried still to walk without help. But the Boer, his master, the one whom he served, had trampled his body while beating his body. And Ruyter, before dying, the white men around him, Ruyter said: 'the Boer has broken my body's middle'.

Song of the Broken String

Because
of a people,
because of
others,
other people
who came
breaking
the string for me,
the earth
is not earth,
this place is
a place now

changed for me
. . .
Because
of this string,
because of a people
breaking the string,
this earth, my place
is a place
of something –
a string broken –
that does not stop
sounding,
breaking within me.

The Name of My Place

You have not heard,
I have not told how I,
a convict at that time,
first went travelling in a train,
how I would have fallen out
had not a woman dragged me back,
and how nice it was to sit in it,
the two of us then seated there:
I and one black man.

You have not heard
nor have I yet said
how his face was black,
how his black man's mouth
was also black:
how the white men are those
whose faces are red,
they being to me
the handsome men.

You have not heard
and I have not yet said
how it was this black man
who asked me then:
'What is your place, its name?'

How I replied, 'I come
from that place called home.'
How he asked again,
'Tell me, what is its name?'
And how I, called Kabbo, said:
'My place is Bitterpits.'

What is Your Name?

Your name, your real /Xam name,
What is it? Call it for me
say it out loud for me
that I may hear once more
its sound – what it is like.

Tell me, what is your name,
your true /Xam name?
Call it, say it for me.
I long to hear it now,
the sound that it will make.

And do not tell me stories,
Do not now deceive me.
Talk only your own /Xam
that I can truly hear you,
how you speak our only tongue.
But you, a /Xam like us
you do not tell us plainly.
The country that is yours –
what is its name? I say again
tell me where you come from.

Your people are at what place?
Tell me where your people live?
Pronounce the place's name for me.
And tell me now, what is your name,
your only name, your true /Xam name!
                    (in Watson, 1991: 57–65)

2 The Colonial Conquest of Zambia

WHITE SUPREMACY IN THE SOUTH

White supremacy, firmly entrenched in Southern Africa by the end of the nineteenth century, was conspicuous in the British war of 1899–1902 against the Boer Republics. Both sides refrained from recruiting blacks to fight their battles. They participated, if at all, only as non-combatants. Africans took advantage of the breakdown of social controls to ignore taxes, forced labour and other exactions, but for the most part continued to work on farms whose owners were away on commando. British troops burnt farms and crowded the occupants into concentration camps which, at the end of the war, had 200 000 inmates, including 80 000 Africans segregated in separate camps (Walker, 1964: 498).

Oakes (1988: 258–9) has recorded scattered but significant signs of revolt among the Kgatla, Venda and Pedi of the northern and western districts of the Transvaal Republic, spreading fear among the owners and their families, some of whom abandoned their homesteads. In May 1902, during the last month of the war, a commando seized Zulu cattle near Vryheid, capital of the Boer New Republic proclaimed in August 1844, and challenged the Zulu to recover them, which they did with spears and firearms, killing 56 Boers for the loss of 52 of their own men.

When Coloured and Africans in the Cape Colony, many of whom were parliamentary voters, asked for arms to protect their lives and property, rural Afrikaners threatened to rise in revolt. The danger was real enough. Boer commandos which invaded Cape districts compelled blacks and Coloured to supply them with livestock and products without the payment of compensation. Abraham Esau, leader of the Coloured in Calvinia, organised a defence force in defiance of the magistrate who feared an Afrikaner mutiny. On 10 January 1901 an OFS commando with Cape rebels, headed by Commandant Charles Niewoudt, rode into the town, shot and beat resisters, threw Esau and local officials into jail, and ordered him to be flogged for speaking against the Boers and attempting to arm his supporters. The assault was repeated during the next two weeks. 'Finally, on 5th February, he was placed in leg irons, tied between two horses and dragged for about a kilometre out of town, where he was shot.' A few weeks later Niewoudt's commando left Calvinia.

The Vereeniging Peace Treaty of 31 May 1900 provided an amnesty for most rebels, guaranteed that none of those tried would be sentenced to death, and contained a clause which kept blacks off the electoral rolls in the two former republics. This gross piece of racial discrimination gave rise to the election of an all-white male parliament in 1910 under the South Africa Act passed by the British parliament. Africans responded to the betrayal by forming in 1912 the South African Native National Congress, forerunner of the African National Congress (ANC).

The centres of African power shifted from chiefdoms and segregated reserves to urban townships and slums, where the remnants of the old, traditional society mingled with Western forms of religion, family, politics, economics, sport and art (Simons, 1987: 1–88). These drastic changes, Leonard Thompson noted (1969: 5), were distorting and eliminated living traditions at an extremely rapid rate. A systematic recording of oral evidence from competent informants might add much of value, but could not compensate for the study of societies undergoing change.

LIGHT FROM THE NORTH

Northern Rhodesia under colonial rule provided opportunities for such a study. The Rhodes-Livingstone Institute, founded in 1937, had as its Director Godfrey Wilson, an anthropologist, 'a word which aroused the greatest possible apprehension in the minds of government officials and settlers at the time' (Audrey Richards, in African Social Research (ASR), 1977: 277).

The Institute operated during Zambia's transition from the status of a Protectorate to that of an unwilling partner in a Federation and from there to the position in 1964 of a sovereign independent state. The anthropologists who directed the Institute and conducted its fieldwork were alive to the contradictions and conflicts between the professed aims of the colonial administrations for the 'moral uplift' of the African population and the harsh realities of migrant labour, broken homes, starvation wages, colour bars, race discrimination, uneven growth, neglect of village communities and conflicts between rulers and ruled, officials and people, employers and workers (Simons, 1977; Richards, 1977: 259–73)

This awareness was seldom allowed to side-step the invisible, internal censorship of the anthropologist. A stranger in a strange land, working on sufferance from the colonial authority, dependent on it in one way or another for his income and research costs, he tended to observe an unstated convention that made colonial policies and structures marginal to his main concerns. Godfrey Wilson formulated the guiding principle in 1940: anthropologists were fact-finders, not decision-makers; their function was to supply relevant information rather than to suggest policies. Given this mandate, the most socially minded scientist could, in good conscience, stick to the facts and steer clear of crusades for social reform.

The response of the administrator to the researcher's project depended less on the objectivity and accuracy of his findings than on their bearings on policies, strategies and institutions. Much depended on the terrain and themes selected for research. Max Gluckman (1911–75), writing about Lozi law, government and social structures, produced outstanding treatises that dovetailed neatly with the policy of giving the Lozi state the privileged position of a protectorate within the Protectorate (Colson and Gluckman, 1968: 56–7). In contrast, Godfrey Wilson (Brown, in Asad, 1975: 187–96; Wilson, in ASR, 1977: 279–83) fell foul of the administration and mining companies by undertaking research on the Copperbelt, the hub of the economy, main source of surplus value, centre of class conflict and the preserve of great transnational mining companies. His research, recorded in *Essay on the Economics of Detribalisation in Northern Rhodesia* (1941–2), showed that African urbanisation had begun. Growing numbers of Africans were taking up long-term residence on the Copperbelt.

ECONOMIC DEPRESSION

The world-wide depression which began in 1929 with the collapse of the Wall Street share market and ended in the arms race leading to the Second World War, shook the confidence of mining companies and the government in the country's prospects. Copper prices fell, most mines stopped producing for two or three years, public expenditure outstripped revenue and the Governor, Sir Hubert Young, recommended the adoption of the South African system of rotating migrant workers. They would be paid a single man's wage, their families would remain in villages and feed off the land, the administration would be spared the cost of educating, housing and welfare services for urban families, and the rotating miners would not be able to complete with white miners and artisans. There was no complaint of bias, distortion or insufficient evidence against Wilson, but the companies denied him access to the mine compounds on the trivial ground that he was hobnobbing with the miners and their families. The ban forced Godfrey Wilson to resign the directorship of the Rhodes-Livingstone Institute after only three years in office.

His was not the only case of intolerance on the part of a mining company towards a competent anthropologist. A.L. Epstein, a research officer attached to the Rhodes-Livingstone Institute (later the Institute for African Studies), was treated in much the same way by the management of the Roan Antelope Copper Mine near Luanshya, at the southern extremity of the Copperbelt. He carried out research between August 1953 and June 1954 in the town, but 'as a result of a series of unfortunate misunderstandings' was denied access to the mine compound (Epstein, 1958: xvii–xviii). It would seem that the mining companies and government of Northern Rhodesia had something to hide from the scrutiny of independent, trained investigators.

Their treatment at the hands of the colonial oligarchy shocked the small, tightly knit band of anthropologists who were thinly scattered in Central and West Africa, but there was a war on, and some were being drawn into its whirlpool. With the Institute under fire and its future in the balance, Gluckman, who took charge when Audrey Richards turned down the offer of the directorship, set out to repair the damage and restore good relations with the Government and Board of Trustees, consisting of the Governor, ex officio chairman, civil servants, representatives of the British South African Company, mining companies and an unofficial member of the legislative council.

South African-born, trained in anthropology at Witwatersrand University, and with a successful spell of fieldwork in Zululand, he knew the risk facing social scientists in a white-dominated, racially divided society. His Zululand experience had led him to conclude that the district commissioner, though an instrument of oppression, might be also a social worker, advising African communities on their welfare, and forming a bridge between whites and blacks. With this background, he gained the approval of the authorities without compromising the Institute's integrity as a centre of scientific studies.

Its driving force came from his great energy, organising skills and sense of public responsibility. Almost single-handed during the war years, he completed Wilson's draft programme and in 1943 presented a seven-year plan for research in Central Africa which extended the Institute's sphere of influence beyond Zambia's boundaries. He opened the Institute to the public and launched a journal, *Human Problems in Central Africa*, to which civil servants, missionaries and other people with relevant knowledge contributed. Their participation and the practical value of the research monograph published by the Manchester University Press on behalf of the Institute won the confidence of the Trustees and the Colonial Office, which made it a prototype of similar bodies founded after the war at Ibandan and Makerere.

Elizabeth Colson (1977: 289–90) called it a programme of the impossible. It included Wilson's emphasis on industrialisation and labour migration, the interactions between village and town, and widened the scope to cover population growth, land tenure, law, economics, sociology and social welfare. The funds needed to employ the demographers and other specialists were not forthcoming; much of the programme had to be put in cold storage; but the guidelines it laid down were faithfully followed in the following years. Gluckman's vision, drive and commitment had much to do with the high quality of the books, monographs and papers presented by anthropologists and published under the auspices of the Institute between 1942 and 1958 (Colson, 1977: 285–307).

DEFEAT OF THE NGONI

It was a remarkable – perhaps unique – intrusion by social scientists upon rural and urban communities at an early stage of colonisation. Colonial rule was imposed on the peoples of Northern Rhodesia before the anthropologists took up their posts between 1939 and 1952, but the change from customary societies had taken place within the living memories of the older inhabitants and could be observed at first hand in some aspects of the social structure. There were many variations in the response to alien institutions and also some constant features, one being the acceptance with little resistance of the white administration and its body of laws.

A notable occurrence of this kind was the rise and fall of the warlike Ngoni state which emerged from the breakup of Shaka's Zulu kingdom. Zwangendaba, a minor chieftain, led his followers in a bid for independence through Delagoa Bay into Mashonaland in about 1820, crossed to the north side of the Zambezi River in 1835, and settled in 1842 along Lake Tanganyika, where the warlord died in 1848 (Omer-Cooper, 1966: 64–9; Barnes, 1967: 7–6, 212–13). The Ngoni state split into rival segments which survived as separate entities until the end of the century, when they clashed with Arab and European invaders.

Zwangendaba's nominated heir was Mpezeni, who became chief after the death of the regent. He led his segment of the Ngoni to what was later called Fort Jameson district, a compact area surrounded by sparsely inhabited country. His chiefdom grew by recruiting prisoners of war. Unlike the Lozi, Bemba and Lunda, who entered into treaties with Cecil Rhodes' British South African Company (BSAC), the Ngoni refused to yield their sovereignty and chose to run the risk of the armed conflict. This was bound to take place, as the Company and other Europeans 'were determined to take over Ngoniland, which some believed was rich in gold; they also wanted to recruit Ngoni as labourers for plantations in Nyasaland' (Roberts, 1976: 168). Nsingu, son of the chief and commander of the Ngoni soldiers, mobilised a large force employing traditional weapons and tactics, which were ineffective against machine guns and cannons. Nsingu was captured and tried by court martial for murder and raiding in British territory. He was found guilty and shot on 9 February 1898 in the presence of his captured lieutenants. Ngoni cattle seized by the Nyasaland troops were treated as loot, some going to the troops and the rest to the Company.

Crippled by the defeat and seizure of cattle, Mpezini surrendered. The Ngoni State was crushed and reduced to the level of a rural district council in a backward area. 'But in the eyes of his people, the Paramount Chief still belongs to the Ngoni, and not to the Administration' (Barnes, 1967: 172). Chiefs' courts were formally recognised in 1929, together with judicial review by district commissioners and the appointment of literate court clerks. An Ngoni Native Treasury was introduced in 1938 under the management of an African treasurer. At the same time a Native Authority, consisting of the chief, councillors and officials, was constituted, forming together with the Native Court and Native Treasury a single system of local government. Christianity took the place of the Ngoni's traditional beliefs in the power of ancestral spirits and the need to appease them.

The suppression of Ngoni and Lunda resistance cleared the way for the invasion of the Copperbelt by BSAC agents. One of them, 'Chirupula' J.E. Stephenson, described the planting of the British flag among the Lala people which cleared the way for the seizure of the Copperbelt: 'We made no treaty; we referred to no treaty; we complied with no treaty!' We walked in; and 'fresh from conquering the Angoni, we forthwith started to "administer" the country.' To make the conquest a harsh reality in the lives of villagers, the Company's officials imposed taxation, forced labour and conscripted porterage (Mushindo, 1973: x–xiii).

Coercion was used to obtain the underpaid workers demanded by colonists on farms, mines and works. Sir Harry Johnstone, the Commissioner in Nyasaland, instructed district officers to destroy the huts of defaulters the day after taxes fell due. Huts and whole villages were put to the torch. This ruthless collection of taxes drove thousands of men to the mines of the Copperbelt, Southern Rhodesia and South Africa. At the same time, white farmers bought the land of dispossessed villagers for two or three pence an acre and destroyed their villages if they refused to move.

MISSIONARIES AND IMPERIALISTS

The first Europeans to establish a presence in the North-Western region were missionaries. They came in the last quarter of the nineteenth century and were welcomed by the victims of aggressive Bemba rulers and their associates, the gun-running Arab slavers. Dr Henry Meebelo (1972: 31) explained why there was no widespread resistance to the colonial conquest:

All in all, because of missionary influence, the fear of the Bemba, and the economic benefits derived from their early contacts with European traders, the Namwanga, the Mambwe, the Lungu and others do not appear to have shown any opposition to the establishment of colonical rule. It was only the Bemba, with something to lose – their empire, and a flourishing trade in slaves and guns – who, in spite of internal dissensions, showed protracted and aggressive antagonism to the establishment of white rule.

Mission stations spread throughout Zambia between 1882 and 1909. Among them were those established by the London Missionary Society, the White Fathers, the United Free Church of Scotland, the Dutch Reformed Mission, Primitive Church Mission, Primitive Methodists and Wesleyans. They set out to convert pupils and families to the Christian faith and its moral code, teach reading, writing and arithmetic, and 'secure their own area of influence', by warding off rival missions among whom intense competition was common (Mwanakatwe, 1968: 12–13).

The Barotse National School was established in 1907 under an agreement between Paramount Chief Lewanika and the British South African Company. It undertook to set aside 10 per cent of the tax collected from the Lozi for their education, but failed to provide direct financial aid to the school, unlike the support it gave for the education of white pupils in separate schools, which set the pattern of racial segregation in the schools of both Rhodesia.

Lozi children were educated in schools administered by the Paris Evangelical Mission, a Protestant society headed by François Coillard, who founded a mission at Sefula, near the capital at Lealui in 1886. Many chiefs and councillors, though polygamists and not members of the church, attended its services and claimed to be good Christians (Gluckman, in Colson and Gluckman, 1968: 57). They supported the mission school wholeheartedly and contributed to its excellence, which gave educated Lozi a distinct advantage in competition for posts in the public service. In 1984 the Western Province, the Lozi stronghold, with only 13 per cent of Zambia's population, contributed 61 cabinet ministers, permanent secretaries and departmental heads, ranking second only to the Bemba's quota in 31 per cent of the population (Lungu, 1985, ASR).

A rapid growth of missionary activity and white settlement came at the end of the nineteenth century in the wake of explorations publicised by the renowned missionary David Livingstone, who died at Chitambo on 1 May 1873. Fifteen years later another Briton with a very different kind of mission appeared on the Central African stage. This was Cecil John Rhodes, millionaire, gold and diamond magnate, politician and arch-imperialist, who aspired to obtain control of mineral resources as far north as Katanga and extend British rule 'from Cape to Cairo'. His partner, Charles D. Rudd, aided by Charles Helm of the London Missionary Society, wangled a concession from Lobengula, king of the Ndebele, which enabled Rhodes to obtain from Queen Victoria, on 29 October 1889, a Royal Charter, giving his British South African Company the powers and authority of a sovereign state, ruling over a vast region extending from the borders of British Bechuanaland and the Transvaal Boer Republic to the limits of Portugal's colony of Angola. (Davidson, 1988: 176–81).

Southern Rhodesia acquired its title in 1895 when the countries once held by Ndebele and Shona were amalgamated. The Colony, formally annexed to Britain in 1923 under a constitution granting it responsible government, went the way of South Africa towards racial discrimination and white supremacy rule. It was the apple of Rhodes' eye, the place where he chose to be buried in 1902.

Northern Rhodesia stretched from the Zambezi River to the Belgian Congo in the west and to Nyasaland in the east. Under Company rule Northern Rhodesia was mainly valuable as a labour reserve for mines in both Katanga and Southern Rhodesia:

It had a major stake in the mines of Katanga, since these provided much traffic for the railways which ran through the Rhodesia, and these were owned by the Company. In Southern Rhodesia the Company had a still more direct interest in the mining industry, whether as shareholder or royalty owner, while as the governing power in the territory it taxed mining profits. The Company was thus anxious to see that mines in both Southern Rhodesia and Katanga obtained African labour as cheaply as possible. In Northern Rhodesia it was very well placed to do this, for there it ruled over about a million people and these could be compelled to pay taxes in cash. For nearly all Africans in Northern Rhodesia the only way of obtaining cash was to engage in wage-labour outside the territory; there was very little opportunity to sell local products for cash. (Roberts, 1976: 177)

UNDER MISSIONARY RULE

The BSAC began administering Northern Rhodesia in typical colonial style only in 1901, by which time most missionary societies had settled down in their respective sphere of influence and expanded their stations to include a network of village churches and schools. Most missionaries were appalled by the beliefs and practices of the surrounding indigenous people whom they regarded as being steeped in darkest heathendom. Few shared the outlook of D.C. Scott, Alexander Hetherwick and their associates who managed the stations of the Free Church of Scotland and the Blantyre Mission in 1875–6, fifteen years before Nyasaland was declared a British Protectorate in 1891.

The Scottish missionaries saw the paramountcy of African interests as being the key to any future development because they believed that Africans, individually and collectively, had a latent capacity for positive development towards a civilised Christian society based upon the traditional African culture. They opposed the intrusion of Rhodes' BSAC which, in their opinion, was a threat to African development, alongside that posed by Arab and Portuguese slavers. They argued that 'a Chartered Company is not a government and never can be. To be ruled by such is to be ruled for commercial ends by absentee directors and shareholders whose real interests are only served by tangible dividends' (Ross, 1966: 334–40).

In the absence of a colonial authority, missionaries in Northern Rhodesia 'became the unquestioned rulers of a large part of North-Eastern Rhodesia', none more completely so than representatives of the London Missionary Society. They began by building stockades and introducing other methods to protect Mambwe and Lungu families from Bemba and Arab slavers, and gradually proceeded to impose total control over converts and neophytes. Robert Rotberg, the main source of information in this section, cites correspondence between James Hemans and R. Wardlow Thompson, two LMS missionaries, in November 1898, explaining that:

Without full control of the villages the children would not come to school; the people would not attend Sunday services; the villages would be thoroughly corrupted; missionaries would often be, as in the early days, without servants; if called upon hurriedly to go on a journey it would be impossible to get men [as carriers]; in cases of emergency . . . it would be impossible to get them [to help] . . . (Rotberg, 1965: 59–60)

The reasons given for 'complete control' indicate a serious state of alienation on the part of the villagers, whose resistance to the missionaries' decrees was overcome by imposing a strict disciplinary code. It required them to clean huts and enclosures, prohibited the possession of loaded firearms and punished failure to attend school and church services, and to commit common law crimes such as drunkenness, adultery, theft and homicide. Breaches of regulations were punishable by flogging, manual labour without pay or the confiscation of tools and weapons. Corporal punishment was administered by the *chikoti*, a long whip made of hippopotamus hide cut into strips.

THE COLONIAL STATE

Missionaries ceased to exercise the powers of secular government when colonial authorities took charge in stages. In 1899–1900 the two segments of Northern Rhodesia – north-western and north-eastern – were placed by Order-in-Council under the control of the Chartered BSAC. In May 1911 the two territories were amalgamated under the name of Northern Rhodesia, administered by the Company through an official, styled Administrator. Legislation was by proclamation of the High Commissioner for South Africa. For reasons of economy, the Administrator of Southern Rhodesia also became Administrator of Northern Rhodesia, but the government of the two territories differed in important respects. Southern Rhodesia followed Roman-Dutch law, whereas Northern Rhodesia had always been under the English legal system. Southern Rhodesia recruited its civil service mainly from the Cape Colony, whereas Northern Rhodesia was served in the main by officers from British public schools and universities. On 1 April 1924, Northern Rhodesia passed from the BSAC to the direct control of the Crown with a constitution that followed existing Colonial Protectorate models (Pim and Milligan, 1938: 148–9).

Northern Rhodesia's first Governor, appointed on 1 April 1924, was Sir Herbert Stanley. He had previously served in Southern Rhodesia and South Africa, firmly believed in white supremacy, encouraged European immigration and set aside blocks of land available for exclusive European use. The first reserve had been delimited in 1907 for the Ngoni. African land rights in Barotseland, covering 29.5 million acres, were secured by treaty. By 1938, according to the Pim Report, native reserves outside Barotseland numbered 38 and occupied 34.5 million acres. The system underwent a radical change in 1947, when the Northern Rhodesia Native Trust Land Act Order was issued. It did not affect existing reserves but vested the trust lands, amounting to 109.25 million acres, in the Secretary of State, whose authority was required to secure rights in trust lands (Hailey, 1957: 767–8).

Some missionaries defended African land rights which were under threat of dispossession by settlers; but their demand for land was largely confined to tracts along both sides of the railway line from Livingstone to Ndola and in the remote Fort Jameson district, the scene of the defeat by British forces of Mpezeni's Ngoni. The missionaries generally welcomed the BSAC's presence, regarded it as a system of benevolent colonial rule, looked to it for support and believed that association with it gave their evangelical efforts an added attraction to Africans. They helped the administration to collect taxes which, when levied on huts, tended to reduce the incidence of polygynous marriages and demonstrated their solidarity with whites. Rotberg (1965: 101) considers that:

> This solidarity of purpose was natural: administrators and missionaries were both European, and were mutually occupied with the implementation of a kindred social system. In following their mutual callings, they were faced alike with conservative and often unwilling tribesmen. They were, in sum, united by the desire to transform indigenous authority wherever it interfered with their own.

The solidarity was neither natural nor inevitable. The Scottish missionaries of Nyasaland and Blantyre showed that there was another way of developing an African community of Christians.

THE CASE OF THE GWEMBE TONGA

Missionaries settled in most parts of Northern Rhodesia, often before the administration opened a *boma*, its district or provincial headquarters. The Tonga of the Gwembe Valley was no exception. Methodists, Jesuits, the Pilgrim Holiness, Salvation Army and others competed for sites on which to build churches, schools, boarding houses and staff quarters suited to their means and lifestyles. Most of their income came from parent bodies overseas, which influenced their policies and relations with white governments and local inhabitants.

> As late as 1957 the mission could claim few converts in the villages, although some schoolboys had been baptized, a few had gone on to become evangelists who would later work in Gwembe, and others were beginning to query aspects of their own religion as they noted that schoolteachers and missionaries seemed to thrive through they made no offerings to shades or 'basangu' and spoke only of God or iLeza: (Colson, 1971: 233)

The people of the Valley were subsistence farmers who grew millet, sorghum and maize as their staple food and many subsidiary crops for use as relish or for sale. They relied on traditional skills and rituals to grow and harvest the food crops. In spite of their hard and skilful work, they often experienced food shortages, amounting at times to famine, because of drought, flood or pests. When the rains failed and the plants burnt up on the river banks and plains, they made no attempt to water them from the nearby Zambezi River, but relied instead on rain shrines and a leader who co-ordinated stages in the agricultural cycle (Scudder, 1962: 26, 30–4, 111–29).

Their beliefs and practices were shattered, their villages destroyed, not by supernatural agencies but by the political ambitions of the Federal government which represented the two Rhodesias and Malawi. Sir Godfrey Huggins, the Federation's prime minister, announced in 1953 that a hydroelectric dam would be built along the Zambezi River on both sides of the Kariba Gorge. It would be one of the world's largest man-made lakes. Owned jointly by the two Rhodesias it would be a monument to the triumph of white supremacy in Southern Rhodesia: 'Besides, the power station, a highly strategic point, was sited on the south bank, thus symbolising the predominance of Southern Rhodesia in Federal planning' (Roberts, 1976: 213).

An estimated 34 000 people in Northern Rhodesia and 23 000 in Southern Rhodesia, with their flocks, herds and game animals would have to be removed and relocated. Opponents of the scheme denounced it, saying that this was another plot to advance the interests of settlers at the expense of the Valley people. The African National Congress of Northern Rhodesia called on the Tonga to resist, which they did in June 1958. A village headman and his people refused to move, saying they had never been consulted. An attempt to arrest him sparked off a riot in which the villagers attacked the District Officer and his officials, who beat a hasty retreat. In September the Governor, Sir Arthur Benson, took a hand, visited Chisama village where the resisters had gathered and, after the failure of negotiations, ordered the men to board lorries for their evacuation. They refused and rushed the police, who fired, killing 8 and wounding 32.

The forced removal and resettlement of thousands of villagers with their possessions in bush country caused much hardship. They had to clear the ground for huts and kraals, prepare gardens and adapt to strange conditions. On the positive side, the process of displacement and resettlement speeded up a process, long underway, of men and women leaving the isolation of the Valley which they loved for a wider world, driven there by the need to pay taxes and the scarcity of arable ground. In 1956, before the forced removals were carried out, more than 40 per cent of taxable men were absent from the Valley for periods of three months to over a year. Some stayed away for as long as four years or settled permanently in urban centres (Scudder, 1962: 156–8). The discovery and mining in 1966–8 of coal deposits at Nkandabwe in Gwembe Valley near Lake Kariba provided opportunities for employment close at hand. The Valley Tonga tended to avoid working in the mine, but many took jobs in domestic service, commercial firms and the informal sector.

THE MATRILINEAL NDEMBU

At the northern end of Zambia, in the Mwinilungu district of the North-Western Province, live the Ndembu, a small population of

17 000 at the time when Victor Turner, a Research Officer of the Rhodes-Livingstone Institute, researched their village life in two periods of fieldwork: 1950–2 and 1953–4. (Turner, 1957: xv). Like the Gwembe Tonga, the Ndembu are remnants of a large kingdom before the colonial conquest, which divided the Lunda–Ndembu–Mwinilungu territory between Portugal's Angola, Belgium's Congo and Britain's Northern Rhodesia. The Ndembu live in all three countries, but Dr Turner confined his research to the Ndembu of Northern Rhodesia, whose lives were disrupted by imperialist invasion and colonial aggression.

In 1905 the King of Italy settled a dispute between Portugal and Britain over the north-western boundary. His decision created the 'Katanga pedicle', a narrow, tapering strip of land between Northern Rhodesia and the Congo. The British South African Company, which governed Northern Rhodesia, introduced a repressive regime and imposed taxes in 1913. The harsh measures resulted in large-scale migration of Ndembu into Angola and the Congo. Many trickled back into villages sited near the district officer's *boma*, or clustered around the Kalene mission station built in the pedicle in 1906 by the Christian Mission of Many Lands.

A trading store, farm and schools were established, each under the control of whites who employed domestic servants, labourers, clerks, teachers and nurses. The regular wage workers attracted kinsmen and dependants; refugees from Angola settled in the pedicle, the number of African traders multiplied in the thriving cash economy; in short, 'The pedicle area exhibits the highest degree of disruption of the traditional social system seen in the Ndembu region' (Turner, 1957: 9). In the 1980s, 30 years after Turner's departure, the pedicle was a notorious outlet for stolen cars, maize and other contraband from Zambia into poverty-stricken Zaire, where customs officials and soldiers complained of not being paid their salaries.

The total Ndembu population at the time of Turner's survey was 18 346, with a density of 6.13 to the square mile. The pedicle chiefdoms accounted for 11 519 people with a density of 16.19, the remaining 6827 had a density of 2.92. The lower the density, the greater was the capacity of the traditional Ndembu culture and economy to survive. Turner's fieldwork was carried out for the most part in an area of low density, where men cut trees, cleared the bush and hunted, while women planted, weeded and harvested. Beer was laid on for members of working parties invited to clear the bush for the laying out of gardens, which were owned and worked individually. If a man had two wives, they usually cultivated on opposite sides of his cassava patch in the middle of the clearing.

The men, who traced their descent from their mother's lineage, were the binding element in an Ndembu village. Girls left it soon after reaching sexual maturity to marry men belonging to a matrilineal line of descent different from their own. Their place was taken by brides drawn from other villages. Men needed the alliance of both sisters and wives to keep the village structure together and support the claims of individual men to the village headmanship. A child belonged to its mother's lineage and looked to her male relatives – brothers, sons, and the sons of daughters – for a home in the event of dissolution of marriage by reason of death or divorce.

People brought up in patrilineal society with patriarchal family heads often find the Ndembu pattern somewhat odd. Yet there is no great difference between its rules of descent, marriage and residence and the corresponding institutions of the patrilineal Xhosa-Zulu or Sotho-Tswana in South Africa. Males dominate in both systems. The patriarchs represent wives, sons and daughters while they remain within the family fold, arrange their marriages, represent them in court, teach them skills and instruct them in customs and law, in both patrilineal and matrilineal societies.

Turner sets out the Ndembu arrangement in some detail (ch. 1, pp. 61–81), and concentrates his account on a small population of fewer than 7000, among the most conservative section of the pedicle's inhabitants. His analysis, based on material collected in the field 40 years ago, no longer reflects the lives of even those Ndembu who were most opposed to change. They too have been sucked into the money economy by taxation, labour migration and the purchase of traders' goods and contraband. This is the condition of most Ndembu who live near government and commercial centres.

Forty years ago two-thirds of unmarried Ndembu under 20 years of age in the region studied by Turner lived with both parents in the father's village and about a quarter with their mother only. Ndembu marriages were 'brittle'. Older divorced women usually lived at the village of their nearest male matrili-

neal kin until remarriage. Children usually went with their
mother on divorce. After widowhood or divorce mothers rejoined
their sons, and daughters their mothers. For such reasons Turner
suggested that 'The mother–child bond is perhaps the most
powerful kinship link in Ndembu society' (p. 62).

This might well have been the case, but the validity of the
statement cannot be easily assessed because of insufficient information about the court system and the settlement of conflicting
claims to the custody of children. Turner mentions both factors
in an account of Ndembu slavery, which the BSAC outlawed at
the beginning of the twentieth century. Slaves were exchanged to
put an end to feuds, compensate a village for the loss of a
member killed unlawfully, settle debts and reward a chief for
using the poison oracle to acquit a person accused of slavery (p.
187f).

The handing over of a slave might be ordered by a chief's court
or council of elders, or agreed to by direct negotiations between
the parties to a dispute. In the absence of a slave, a debtor might
hand over a sister's child to compensate for a homicide. For
example, wrote Turner,

> the mother's brother of one of my informants went to my
> informant's father about thirty years ago in Angola and tried
> to take his daughter to pay her as compensation for a debt of
> long- standing. But my informant's father became angry and
> told his brother-in-law to remove himself from the village
> forthwith. The latter replied: 'You are a bad brother-in-law.
> You have no right to keep your children from me.'

Anecdotal evidence of this kind, supposedly describing events that
took place in the first quarter of the twentieth century, is hardly
reliable and certainly falls far short of evidence required by South
African courts to determine disputes between husbands and wives
over the custody of children (Simons, 1958: 338–9).

More credible is Turner's contention that Ndembu still clung
to aspects of slavery in the 1930s, in spite of the institution having
been formally abolished by the BSAC in the early years of this
century. It lingered on in secret for many years afterwards in
village communities, who were restrained from enforcing it only
by the knowledge that the colonial administration applied sanctions against Ndembu caught attempting to keep and exchange
slaves. Most people accepted the new situation in course of time

and came to regard the former slaves as free people. New settlements inhabited by former slaves grew up all over Mwinilungu district: 'Former slaves and free Ndembu intermarry freely and the children of former slave women are regarded as free' (pp. 196–7).

The administration made accusations of sorcery, like slavery, a punishable offence, but it flourished in villages under strict precautions to prevent the practice from coming to the notice of the *boma*. Accusations of witchcraft made in anger at beer parties were regarded as slander, to be settled by elders who might order the offenders to pay small sums as damages to the aggrieved parties. Quarrels often arose from old rivalries between men competing for the position of a village chief, which conferred great prestige and the prospect of receiving fruits of office.

Ndembu society, 40 years ago, was rent by recurring disputes. 'Misfortune, illness and reproductive troubles among Ndembu, if severe enough are associated with the activities of spirits, witches and sorcerers (p. 301). Women and men were believed to possess familiar spirits, those of the women being different and the more dangerous. They took the form of little men (like the Xhosa belief in *tokoloshe* in South Africa), who made demands on their owners to kill husbands or junior matrilineal kinsfolk.

Rituals of affliction were performed to relieve patients who complained of misfortune and were diagnosed as having offended ancestral spirits by failing to honour them with offerings of drink and food, or by persistent quarrels among close relatives, or by violating kinship rules. Women suffering from serious physical ailments or mental disorders were treated by traditional healers who had themselves been treated and cured for similar afflictions. A patient, if cured, was admitted into the ranks of qualified diviners.

Ndembu society had few opportunities for ambitious persons to improve their status and rise to positions of authority. Turner suggested (p. 297) that

> the status differentiation within each cult and the exclusion of uninitiated persons, whatever their rank or standing in other contexts, from its central mysteries, provides some compensation for the frustrations of ambitious urges, or for the occupation of an inferior status in secular life.

THE LUNDA OF LUAPULA

The Lunda empire spread through conquest and colonisation along the Luapula valley and established the kingdom of Kazembe in about 1740 at the south end of Lake Mweru, from where the Luapula River flows for about 90 miles through a broad valley, much of which is permanently under water and rich in fish. Cassava, an American root crop, reached the Luapula from the west, to become the principal cultivated plant around Kazembe's capital by the end of the eighteenth century (Roberts, 1976: 94–6).

The lands inhabited by the Lunda are situated on the east bank of the river before it joins Lake Mweru, and on a narrow strip of swamp and hard soil, about 140 miles long on the Lake's south-east shore. The river is the boundary between Zambia and Zaire and adjoins the pedicle in Mwinilungu district where Turner studied the Ndembu in 1950–4. Ian Cunnison (1959: ix) worked in 1948–51 among the Lunda of Luapula who, like the Ndembu, are Bemba-speaking and matrilineal, though succession to the position of village headman is usually patrilineal.

The economy of the Ndembu in the northern part of the pedicle is similar to that of the Lunda, who like money, the business of making it and the pleasures of spending it. Kazembe, the capital, has dance halls, beer houses, hotels and prostitutes. It attracts men and women of pleasure from neighbouring chiefdoms, who are distinguished by name, territory and allegiance. Shops in the bigger villages along the main road stock most of the goods sold in African markets in Copperbelt towns. Tea-rooms and beer-houses blare forth loud music from gramophones, radios and guitars to attract cyclists and bus or lorry passengers travelling along the highway.

Luapulans' staple foods are fish and cassava. Other crops grown for domestic use include maize, millet, palm oil kernels, pumpkins and sweet potatoes. Fishing is the main source of wealth; money-making the chief concern of fishermen. The only government tax is a levy on fish nets, imposed to conserve the fish and payable once a year to the local authority.

Young boys accompany their fathers on fishing trips from an early age. An adolescent might aspire to setting up a store in his village, selling tea, bread, bananas and second-hand goods. A successful fisherman might invest in a motor boat, or build a camp in the swamps, well away from his village to discourage relatives from begging for fish or disturbing his money-making. Most fishermen prefer to take their fish to the market in the capital, where they get a better price than in their village and where women congregate to barter cassava, root-beer (*munkoya*), firewood and fruit. Some men transport dried fish by bicycle to the Copperbelt, more than 200 miles away, with a view to making a good profit. An aspiring capitalist might run a bus service to the Copperbelt and build a two-storey house along the main road.

Fishing in the lake and swamps is hard and sometimes danger-ous. Many Luapulans would prefer to have a regular job with a monthly wage for unskilled work. At the beginning of the twentieth century they looked for work in the Congo copper mines, and by 1910 in Southern Rhodesia. Since 1924 they have contributed substantially to the Copperbelt's labour force. Almost a quarter of taxable men were working away from home in 1949.

The Luapula way of life retains its hold on people who leave the Valley to work abroad. They need not fear returning home, for work abroad provides an opportunity to make money and enjoy Copperbelt pleasures in their home environment. 'And men of substance, knowledgable on native affairs, likewise return to offices of importance. In spite therefore of the great change in material conditions, the interest remains in the kingship in tribes and lineages, in history, custom, ceremonial and ritual' (Cunni-son, 1959: 29).

The villagers are volatile. They often move from village to village in search of headmen under whom people prosper, live long in peace and free from sorcery. Chiefs and headmen welcome strangers and gladly allocate building plots to them and their followers. The more subjects a chief has the bigger is his income from tribute and the local Native Authority.

Kazembe's capital, the country's largest settlement, is situated on a hill about 20 miles south of the lagoon, and has 12 sections, each the size of a substantial village. The royal fence in the middle of the capital surrounds the king's house, the houses of his wives and the royal kitchen. Outside the fence is an open space in which the Native Authority offices are situated. The king occupies a dual role, being the head of the Lunda Native Authority which stretched from village headmen to the Northern Rhodesia Administration and from there to the Colonial Office.

The country is a proclaimed Native Trust Land, not to be settled by whites or used for pecuniary gain by outsiders. At the time of Cunnison's visit, the white population resident on the east bank numbered 140, most of whom were members of the staff and families of the Administration's Luapula Leprosy Settlement and five mission stations serving the Lunda: African Methodists, Jehovah's Witnesses, London Missionary Society, Seventh Day Adventists and White Fathers (Cunnison, 1959: 5, 204–5).

JEHOVAH'S WITNESSES

The religious sects which settled in Luapula from 1879 onwards respected one another's sphere of influence. Serious competition came from a more radical course, the Jehovah's Witnesses, a society of marked Adventist view, which was founded in Pennsylvania in 1884. The movement is highly organised, with decentralised control from Brooklyn, New York:

> Doctrine comes from the headquarters in Brooklyn, through a sole European representative in Northern Rhodesia. From him, control is delegated to Africans in their home areas who themselves organize their country into various orders of districts for preaching. The movement spread quickly, gaining many converts from religions already established, until now perhaps half of those professing Christianity on the Luapula are Jehovah's Witnesses. Seven thousand of them gathered from the Valley and surrounding districts to a convention which took place at Kazembe's capital in 1950. (Cunnison, 1959: 206)

The challenge to the older churches was much the same as that presented by the nonconformist Wesleyans, Methodists and Baptists to the Anglican community in the nineteenth century. The Witnesses stood out by being better dressed, more organised, seemingly prosperous and avowedly resistant to political involvement. When going to meetings the men line up with bicycles and cycle in single file to church. They meet twice a week to worship, receive reports on work done for the church, and come together from time to time in large gatherings.

Norman Long (1968: 1–2) conducted intensive fieldwork in Serenje district, in Zambia's Central Province in 1963–4, among

the Lala in the administrative parish of Kapepa. Active Witnesses
in Zambia numbered about 28 000 in 1963, the year before the
country's independence from colonial rule. They published and
sold journals and books in English, Bemba, Nyanja and Lozi, met
twice a week in church halls for worship, to study the Bible and
attend literacy classes. Long's detailed account (pp. 202–7) of the
church's planned activities leaves an impression of great commitment, strict discipline and hard work by dedicated members. The
parish is part of 'a highly bureaucratized religious organization'
with a ranking system of office-bearers. Only members of good
standing with an approved record of preaching, recruiting converts and knowledge of Watch Tower publications qualify for the
position of ministers. Promotion comes, not from academic
studies, but by diligent attention to the duties and interests of the
Church.

Unlike Max Weber's conception of Protestant Calvinism,
which he derived from first-hand observations of religious in-
fluences in the United States (Garth and Mills, 1948: 302–13), the
Witnesses do not consider worldly success a sign of divine grace.
Their expectations centre on a belief in the battle of Armaged-
don, a final struggle between God and Satan. 'Only those who
have been faithful to Jehovah God will survive the onslaught and
inherit the new paradise on earth' (Long, 1968: p. 207).

It is a God-given duty to acquire skills by training for a
particular occupation such as the building trades, tailoring,
woodwork, joinery and carpentry, and all kinds of metalwork and
engineering. These skills will continue to exist in the New
Kingdom on earth, whereas the unskilled will remain labourers
throughout eternity. Money should be used to house, dress and
feed the family, not to buy beer and cigarettes. The simple family
of parents and children is better than the customary polygamous,
extended family of the Lala. A man with more than one wife is
not fit to be a Witness, and adultery is strongly condemned.

The Lala of Serenje, like the Lunda of Luapula and the
Ndembu of Mwinilungu, are matrilineal, tracing descent through
the mother's lineage, while marriage is virilocal. Women, 'on
whom the social continuity of villages depends, reside at their
husbands' villages after marriage' and succession to chiefs and
headmen was traditionally through the matrilineal descent group
(Turner, 1957: xviii, 323). When a Luapulan man dies, members
of his lineage appoint a successor who inherits his name, position

of office and the widow with her children. 'This then is a form of widow inheritance in which the successor becomes a husband to the wife and a father to the children of the deceased. It is part of "positional succession" and the successor adopts the *persona* of the dead kinsman.' Some Christians refuse to comply with the custom, saying that it is adulterous and bigamous (Cunnison, 1959: 98, 102).

This view is held more emphatically by Jehovah Witnesses in the Kapepa Parish of the Lala in Serenje District. Matrilineal kinship is a major determinant of residential affiliation. The core of the village is the headman and his female uterine siblings with their immediate matrilineal descendants, but the social ethic preached by the Witnesses

> places important emphasis on the nuclear family as a Christian grouping, disapproves of matrilineal forms of descent and inheritance and puts a ban on polygynous marriages. Such an ideology can serve both to legitimize the repudiation of ties with matrilineal kin and can sanction the furthering of close bonds with fellow Jehovah's Witnesses. Hence farmers who utilize links with fellow churchmen to solve problems of farm management and labour have a ready-made ideological justification for their actions. (Long, 1968: 78, 91–2)

A larger proportion of Witnesses, as compared with other people, lived in small settlements outside their matrilineal villages and moved from a subsistence to a cash economy. The Witnesses of both sexes were better educated than other Lala, and were expected to dress more smartly. Men wore jackets and ties when preaching or attending meetings, and often carried briefcases to indicate their status.

These marks of distinction were less conspicuous in a town, where literacy and manual skills were seldom enough to enable a rural work-seeker to find a good job in the face of competition from permanent urban residents. A high proportion of Witnesses in towns were domestic servants, gardeners or marketeers who returned to their parish where they could use their skills and experience to better advantage. A returned Witness usually lived in his wife's village for some years, performing customary services for her maternal relatives. Most men eventually established independent settlements away from relatives on both sides.

Witnesses claimed that all members were of equal status and entitled to become ministers if suitably qualified. Women also received training in the Theocratic Ministry School Servant before going out to preach to housewives, who were told to pass on the good message to housewives, who in turn passed it to husbands, read the Bible and taught them to read and write. Some women with school education and experience of urban life joined the Society on their own initiative, but most were influenced to do so by their husbands. By and large, equality of treatment between men and women was more of a reality among Witnesses than others in Serenje (Long, 1968: 213, 233–4)

Witnesses who lived by the Society's book of rules were almost certain to fall foul of the United National Independence Party (UNIP) and its government by asserting their constitutional right and God-given duty to keep out of politics. They were active in trade unions, but refused to vote, sing the national anthem or salute the Zambian flag. Their non-collaboration policy resulted in clashes, much violence and cases of house-burning in Luapula Province (Roberts, 1976: 250; Tordoff, 1974: 86–8, 359, note).

THE LABOUR MARKET

Northern Rhodesia was a Protectorate, governed by the British South Africa Company until 1924, when Britain took charge. It introduced a constitution providing for a Governor, an Executive Council of four officials and a Legislative Council of nine officials and elected unofficial members. The franchise effectively excluded Africans who, among other disqualifications, were 'protectorate subjects' and therefore not eligible for the vote, which was available only to British subjects (Hailey, 1957: 290).

The Protectorate's African population in 1931 was estimated at nearly 2 million as compared with 14 000 whites, the ratio being 94:1. Sir Herbert Stanley, the country's first Governor, had previously served in Southern Rhodesia and South Africa. He believed firmly in the principle of white supremacy and tried to promote it by opening the door to white settlers. Under his guidance the government set aside blocks of land for them at the expense of the plateau Tonga in the south, the Lambawa and Mambwe in the north, and the Ngoni and Chewa in the east. Overpopulation in the areas reserved for Africans resulted in a steady flow of work seekers to farms and urban centres (Roberts, 1976: 183–5).

The small trickle of men who left their villages at the beginning of the century to find jobs in Southern Rhodesia and South Africa grew into a large and steady stream. By 1920 about 50 000 Zambians were working outside their country. Ten years later 113 000 had entered the labour market, 78 000 of them within Zambia.

Tax collectors, labour recruiters, traders and missionaries gave the movement a big push in all provinces. Villagers in the railway belt could combine wage-earning with the sale of surplus food; those in distant areas depended more on wages earned in towns. Villagers were drawn into the market system in one way or another.

Capital needed a growing market and created one by killing the demand for the products of village craftsmen. Cotton cloth took the place of bark cloth; ironware took the place of earthenware; factory-made hoes, axes and knives, imported from overseas, replaced tools made by village blacksmiths. Shop goods – tea, sugar, salt, paraffin, candles, clothing and blankets – had appealing use-value and became necessities in many villages. Missionaries encouraged people to wear European-style dress, attend church and schools, buy books and pay dues and fees. Money for the goods and service came mostly from wages.

E.A.G. Robinson, the economist on the J. Merle Davis team which inquired into the effects of copper mining in Northern Rhodesia on Africans and the work of Christian missions (Davis, 1933: 135), made the point that a balance between receipts and expenditure was a necessary function of a market economy. Labour migration was a factor in the balance of trade relations between villages and towns:

Having nothing else to sell, the Native has sold himself. The need to find the money to pay his taxes, his mission or education dues, and to buy the products of the store, has led him to seek work in the towns, on the farms, at the mines both in Northern Rhodesia and the surrounding countries. For the time being, this method of payment may suffice. But the drift to the towns and to the neighbouring territories has already thrown strains both upon the organisation of the Native agriculture, and upon the social and political structure, which these are at present ill-equipped to bear. There is almost certainly some upper limit, and it may well prove to be comparatively low one, to the number of workers who can without harm be absent at any time from the village.

Villagers who were only slightly exposed or responsive to the agents of social change might carry on with their traditional occupations. Apart from seasonal food shortages and occasional droughts or floods, they could satisfy their needs for food, clothing and shelter from their own resources. They could not as easily escape the demand of tax collectors who, from 1905 onwards under the administration of the British South African Company, commonly burnt huts and flogged defaulters to enforce demand for tax and labour.

FORCED LABOUR

Colonial taxation took the place of tribute given to traditional rulers and demonstrated the power of the colonial authority. Company officials, backed by police or army units, moved from village to village registering the men and collecting taxes in tours that brought them face to face with people, many of whom had never before set eyes on a white person. Taxes had to be paid in cash, except in remote areas where men could earn a tax receipt by working for a month at the local *boma* or in road-making and construction.

The yearly tax in 1930 ranged from 7s 6d, in the north-west to 12s 6d along the railway belt. African taxes yielded £148 000 in 1931–2, more than the income tax paid by expatriates and contributing one-sixth of government revenues (Simons, 1976: 9–10; Turok, 1979: 7–8). Audrey Richards (1977: 22–3), who worked among the Bemba in 1930–4, found that between 40 and 60 per cent of adult men left their villages to find work which would enable them to pay the tax of 7s 6d and buy the shopkeepers' goods. Most of them worked in the Copperbelt, but many went to Katanga, Southern Rhodesia and South Africa. They usually moved to and fro between their villages and employment centres, settling down for good eventually in their home district.

In 1927 about 8500 Africans were employed on mines and concession stores in Northern Rhodesia. The number increased twofold by the end of 1928 and reached a peak in September 1930, with a total 32 000 (Berger, 1974: 13). Underground miners were paid 1s a day, surface workers 15s a month, the same rate as that paid to Africans employed in the few urban industries existing at the time. The tax formed only a small part of the worker's cash needs, but it had to be paid and therefore made wage-labour unavoidable for thousands of men.

The white settlers generally approved of this arrangement. It was proper for blacks to circulate between village and town until sickness or old age forced them to retire. Wives and families were not wanted in towns. They ought to stay in the village, raising crops, looking after children and supporting their families from the fields and what their men gave them out of wages. Sir Ernest Oppenheimer, Chairman of Anglo-American, sympathetically remarked in 1941 that the natives might suffer increasing exhaustion after 18 months on the job. Moreover, the cost of feeding and housing a miner's wife was 12s 6d a month, almost as much as a labourer's wage. The company should not have to bear the cost of housing and management of long-term employees (Berger, 1974: 69–70).

A Native Labour Association was formed in March 1930 to recruit villagers for work in Copperbelt mines. It introduced the same kind of organisation as the Native Recruiting Corporation and Native Labour Association established by South African mining houses towards the end of the nineteenth century (Simons and Simons, 1987: 6–13). There was an important difference. Only men and boys were allowed to enter and occupy rooms in South Africa's segregated labour compounds, whereas villagers recruited by the Northern Rhodesia NLA were allowed to bring wives and young children with them and occupy huts in the married quarters of the mining location.

The economic slump of the 1930s had a depressing effect on the copper mining industry. Recruitment came to a standstill. Six mines had stopped production by the end of 1931, leaving only two with more than a skeleton labour force, and the companies repatriated those workers with their families who wanted to go home to their villages. Others who preferred town life were told to find accommodation in municipal townships and locations supervised by white municipal councils or district commissioners.

These segregated ghettos were situated at distances of a mile or
so from the commercial centre and further than that from the
low- density, high-cost white residential suburbs. The standards
of housing, water supply and sanitation in the municipal locations
were atrocious, and wages of the residents correspondingly low
(Saffrey, 1943; Coulter, in Davis, 1933: 61–5, 78–80).

The Pim-Mulligan Commission of 1937–8 (1938: 29–55) reported that villagers had serious difficulties in meeting their tax
obligations. A district officers conference in 1937 concluded that
they could not afford more than 3s a year, or 2s 6d, according to
the Pim Report (p. 117). The government was committed to a
migrant labour system, expanded it through the pressure of
taxation, and rejected the opportunity on the Copperbelt to
promote a stable African labour force, along the lines of the policy
adopted by the Union Minière in Katanga, where the proportion
of white employees to Africans was 1:14, as compared with 1:8 or
1:10 on the Copperbelt. The Commission concluded that Africans
had a wider sphere of employment on the Belgian mines (p. 43).

The average monthly wage on Northern Rhodesia mines in
March 1937 was 18s for surface workers and 31s 6d for men
working underground. Employers were obliged by statute to
provide their African employees with adequate housing and
sufficient rations. The average monthly cash wage at the mines
in 1935 was 23s 6d. Workers on the railways received 13s 6d and
farm workers 5–10s a month. The differences caused a steady
drift of work- seekers to the mines.

With an adequate supply of workers, employers could keep
wage rates at a level well below a family's minimum subsistence
needs. A. L. Saffrey found in 1943 that an average-sized family
needed £6 11s 7d a month for a decent living, whereas earnings
ranged from £2 5s 10d in secondary industries to £4 14s 7d in
mining. The wage rates were related to the assumed basic needs
of an unlettered man who wore a blanket when off duty, slept on
an earthen floor and ate mealie meal porridge (*nshima*) with relish.
Malnutrition diseases and tuberculosis were rife.

WOMEN GO TO TOWN

Men led the way from villages to mine compounds and urban
locations. Those who came with wives and children, or acquired

them in the town, were expected to build their own houses in the absence of accommodation provided by employers. Zambia's 'shanty towns' and 'squatter compounds' emerged in the early days of urban growth. The administration tried to prevent women from joining their menfolk by instructing chiefs and headmen to stop them leaving their villages without a pass (*chitupa*). The courts could order a women living in town without a male guardian to return with her children to the village. On entering a town in search of work, men had to report to the *boma* and obtain a *chitupa*, containing details of the bearer's chief, headman, village work record and reasons for discharge from employment. Convictions under the pass laws averaged about 10 000 a year.

Few white-dominated governments in Southern and Central Africa conceded that African women had a moral right and social reasons for joining their menfolk in industrial and urban centres. The Belgian Congo was a rare exception. The Union Minière wanted to reduce recruiting costs and the number of whites employed as supervisors; while the Belgian authorities rejected the South African and Rhodesian practice of giving white workers sheltered employment behind colour bars. A 'stabilized labour system' had the advantage of a permanent industrial African working class living in urban areas with family housing and basic services. The company could draw on successive generations of urbanised workers committed to wage-earning and becoming increasingly efficient to the extent of undertaking advanced technical operations far surpassing those entrusted to men in Northern Rhodesia's copper mines (Hailey, 1957: 583, 1391–3).

In the early days of copper mining in Northern Rhodesia, the government also wanted to encourage labour stabilisation, but the slump in copper prices and strikes in 1935 by African miners against tax increases, during which troops fired on protestors and killed six, caused a sharp swing among company and government officials towards the familiar migratory system. An important contributory factor was the policy of Sir Hubert Young, the newly arrived Governor, transferred from Nyasaland in 1934. A year later the publication of the report of the Nyasaland Committee on Emigrant Labour drew general attention in British colonies to the harmful effects on village life by the absence of men for long periods at distant labour centres (Hailey, 1957: 1381–2).

Young insisted on the repatriation of African mine workers to their villages every two years to preserve and enrich the customary society (Berger, 1974: 35-7).

White settlers approved his policy. They foresaw that a permanently urbanised African population would press for political rights and entry into the skilled trades. Copper prices rose after the war from an average of £62 a ton in 1941-5 to a peak of £332 in 1955. High outputs and profits made it the most prosperous decade in the industry's history. More work seekers came to town, adding to the chronic housing shortage. Senior officials admitted at long last that a permanently settled working class, properly housed with their families, might offset costs by improved standards of skill and labour discipline. Legislation introduced in 1948 obliged local authorities to build family houses for Africans with subsidies from the central Treasury.

Sir Ronald Prain, Chairman of the Rhodesian Selection Trust, argued that the size of the capital outlay needed to house the rapidly growing African urban population was a daunting prospect. It might make Copperbelt mines high-cost producers and was already inhibiting the growth of secondary industries (Prain, 1954: 308). Officials complained that real improvement in the living standards of urban Africans would swamp the towns with an influx of villagers. Swamping was another word for urban stabilisation, which had already gone a long way, as was shown during the war by the anthropologists Godfrey Wilson and A.L. Epstein.

The issue was settled, not by cost accountants and company promoters, but by villagers. They marched into towns, in defiance of pass laws, to take possession of what was theirs by right of birth and claims to the fruits of their labour. In spite of appeals by the ruling United National Independence Party (UNIP) and the government to go back to the land, Zambians continued to vote with their feet for the towns. Between 1963 and 1974 the country's urban population grew 21 times faster than the rural population and four times faster than the national population. Of every 100 Zambians, 35 lived in an urban area, a far higher proportion than in most African countries (Simons, 1976: 1-3).

Sir Hubert Young, during his term of office as Governor in Northern Rhodesia in 1934, had agreed to the permanent settlement of a small number of Africans on the Copperbelt provided that the great majority went back to their villages at

regular intervals. The rural districts had few prospects of economic progress except by the circulation of wages earned in the
urban economy. Wages remitted to rural families enriched the
villagers and enabled them to pay taxes and buy manufactured
goods.

His policies had an adherent in William Watson, one of
Gluckman's team of anthropologists. He conducted fieldwork in
1952 among the Mambwe, a patrilineal, cattle-herding people
who practised hoe cultivation on a plain on the south side of Lake
Tanganyika. Their staple diet was *nshima*, a porridge made of
millet; they seldom killed their cattle for meat, and bought dried
fish from hawkers and canned meat from shops (Watson, 1958:
20–4).

He fell in love with the Mambwe and their country. Like
Rabelais's Pantagruel, he found it the best of all possible worlds.
He had the outlook of a structuralist resembling Talcott Parson's
conviction that any social system had an internal mechanism for
adjusting to social change without losing cohesion and the
enduring relations between the parts.

It is this thesis that I need to explore by examining the effects
of the movement of Mambwe villagers to employment centres.
All able-bodied men in the 'working age group' of 18 to 45 took
part in the exodus. The number from this group who were absent
at any one time was seldom less than 50 per cent of the total.
Experience in Southern and Central Africa shows that this high
degree of absence has a disturbing effect on village life and on
women in particular. For a reliable survey of the consequences I
have used the findings of the ILO/JASPA *Basic Needs Mission to
Zambia* (1981: 17–27):

> Where migration is seasonal, traditional farming systems have
> been less disrupted than in areas of more or less permanent
> migration, such as the Northern and Luapula Provinces . . .
> In these less favourable and peripheral areas with permanent
> out-migration, agriculture is generally stagnant or in decline.
> For a period before 1974, Luapula Province experienced a
> net decrease in population due to out-migration, and
> elsewhere the rate of out-migration, though slowing, remains
> significant. The scale of urban–rural remittances is difficult
> to assess but the balance of informed opinion suggests
> that they have declined. The absence of able-bodied men in

these areas has often dislocated family life, work-sharing, farming systems and other interdependent relations which sustained the rural economy of the past. The removal of male workers has made farm management much more difficult. For example, where the fire climax, bush fallow system of *citimene* is practised, it is the men who cut and lop the trees for burning to provide the ash bed for the staple millet. With fewer men to cut the trees, the area under *citimene* has declined. The alternative practices of cultivation, crop mixes and crop rotations, are more labour-demanding – in weeding, hoeing, ridging and mound-making. The result has been a decrease in the variety of garden types and crop mixes, and greater reliance on cassava and other starchy crops such as sweet potatoes.

A large population of small, weak and poor households has arisen. Many are headed by women who struggle to combine the work of farmer, water-carrier, woodcutter, mother and housewife. Few are able to use adequately the facilities provided by the government for schooling, health clinics and rural extension services.

Yet the cash needs of rural people have increased. During earlier, less penurious times, they became accustomed to purchasing a range of goods. At the same time they lost skills, such as making clay pots and to some extent mat-making, and now need to be able to buy substitutes. Moreover, from their earlier experiences and from their urban visits they know what they are missing. All need to buy clothes and other basic goods; children need to be educated, and men and women alike desire money to spend on basic needs like improving their homes and local travel, as well as the important small things which enhance daily life. (p.19)

Watson carried out fieldwork among the Mambwe in the 1950s. Twenty years before the economic slump that afflicted Zambia, caused largely because of the fall in world copper prices which reduced Zambia's real GDP in 1974–80 by 52 per cent he claimed, in a concluding remark, that the Mambwe society had inbuilt shock absorbers and was so constituted as to insulate it against such setbacks (p. 228):

The effects of industrialism and wage-labour on the Mambwe suggest that in the process of social change, a society will always tend to adjust to new conditions through its existing social institutions. These institutions will survive, but with new values, in a changed social system.

Dr Wim van Binsbergen (1979: 338–9) comments that:

> Watson's essentially functionalist outlook, which gave priority to institutions and values over relations of production (i.e. patterns of expropriation and control), made this conclusion fairly inevitable . . . . However, in the paradigm of the articulation of modes of production Watson's conclusion would appear to be much less self-evident. We would rather look at these surviving institutions as devices which an encroaching capitalism (of which Watson's book provides numerous examples) allowed to survive, and actually furthered, for its own benefit: because these institutions maintain a setting for the reproduction of cheap labour and the accommodation of discarded labourers, in pre-capitalist, neo-traditional pockets of the world system.

Watson (1958) explained that the Mambwe had a long history of labour migration, going back even before the British South Africa Company began to rule the country in 1893. Its first representative, called the Collector of Revenue and Postmaster, required the men to pay tax, which imposed their first compulsion to work outside their own economy. The London Missionary Society set up a station on the shores of Lake Tanganyika in 1883, and moved to the plateau in 1890. Their mission was soon flooded with refugees from the Bemba war. They made their first acquaintance with a stable European society, whose religion and material culture had a deep effect on the converts. The missionaries looked upon the villagers as naked barbarians and made them aware of their backwardness:

> Today, after more than sixty years of European contact, the pressures to work are much more complex. Wage-labour is now an accepted part of a man's life; he is expected to go out and earn wages in the same way as most men in our own society. The Mambwe can get money only by working, and they need money for taxes, marriage payments, court fines, bicycles, bus fares, clothes, sewing machines, and household

goods. Young men need large sums for marriage payments
before they can marry. 'Wage-labour is the most important
school for all Mambwe, much more important than the formal
schools of the missions and the Native Authorities.' (Watson,
1958: 44)

Women put much pressure on the men to go out to work and
often went with them to the towns. Of 40 men from eight villages
who were absent on wage labour, 29 took their wives with them,
mostly to the Copperbelt (ibid.). Watson claimed that the system
maintained the required level of production, in spite of the high
level of migrant wage-earners, because of the work-party, for
which beer was provided as refreshment, and the principle of
reciprocity. 'A man who attends another's work-party obliges the
other to work in his own fields in return.' The villagers arranged
these work-parties among themselves, but the headman supervised the arrangements in the general interest (ibid.: 107–8).

Admittedly, the absence of 50 per cent of active men might be
expected to disrupt the subsistence economy. To get over this
hurdle in his argument Watson entered into an elaborate comparison with the Bemba, a matrilineal people whose husbands are
required to spend the first few years of marriage in their wives'
villages. The comparison in no way enables Watson to solve the
problem of the absent migrants, the large number of women who
go to town with their husbands or on their own account, and
cease to take part in the communal mode of production. The
consequence is bound to be a decline in the Mambwe population
and variety of garden crops, and the emergence of a large
number of small households headed by women who, in the words
of the *ILO/JASPA Mission* (1977), struggled to combine the work
of farmer, water-carrier, woodcutter, mother and housewife.

Political and religious conflicts also disturbed the even tenor of
the traditional society. When Watson arrived among the Mambwe
in 1953 he found they were upset by the proposal to include
Northern Rhodesia in the Federation of Central Africa. They
feared that they might lose their land to whites, and could not
escape the effects of a growing African nationalism or the challenge by Jehovah's Witnesses to the London Missionary Society.
Some Mambwe migrant workers joined trade unions, took part in
demonstrations against colour bars, struck work with fellow dissidents and defied the government's fishing and agricultural controls.

TOWARDS INDEPENDENCE

In the 1940s Northern Rhodesia's small white community favoured a close association with the settler regime in Southern Rhodesia and welcomed the formation of the Central African Federation in 1953. It joined the two Rhodesias with Nyasaland and brought them close to white-dominated states in Southern Africa. The main African objection was that whites would rob them of the land.

The advent of Federation stimulated the growth of African nationalism in Northern Rhodesia. Its spokesman was the African National Congress (ANC). Formed in 1948, it appointed a Supreme Action Council in 1952 to rouse public opinion against Federation. Simon Zukas, the only white on the Council, was deported for advocating a general strike, and the campaign fizzled out because people thought that Federation was inevitable. The ANC's stand was an important stage in the growth of African nationalism. Zambia achieved independence in 1964, Zukas returned to his adopted country, joined the Movement for a Multi-Party Democracy (MMD) 27 years later, was elected to parliament in the general election of November 1991, and served as a junior minister in the President's Office.

Africans were allowed to form trade unions after the Second World War. A Labour government was in office in Britain and an anti-colonial left wing wanted action to be taken on the labour front. The Colonial Office sent William Comrie, a Scottish trade unionist, to assist Africans to form trade unions. Shop assistants on the Copperbelt were the first to organise. Their union was set up under Comrie's supervision from members of welfare societies, clerks and leading hands on the mines. In March 1949 a number of mine unions formed the African Mineworkers Union (AMU). It made its first wage claim at the end of the year when its declared membership was 19 000 out of an African labour force of 35 000.

AFRICAN ADVANCEMENT

White miners had struck work in March 1940 after the outbreak of war, and won most of their demands through arbitration. African miners at Nkana and Mufulira came out in the following month. The Nkana strikers were fired upon by police and soldiers, who killed 13 men and wounded 71, four of whom died later. A committee of African miners demanded 10s a day, half the wage paid at the time to the lowest paid white worker on the mines. They said that 'the White men had learned the work from them and did no work. The natives did all the work' (Berger, 1974: 57).

The first three years of Federation had been beneficial. Living standards and job opportunities improved. Africans ceased to fear Federation and in time often thought that it was too firmly entrenched to be broken down by the boycotts, agitation against chiefs and support for dissident religious sects on which the African National Congress relied to mobilise mass resistance (Mulford, 1967: 38–40).

Migrant workers who, like the Mambwe, joined trade unions were probably more impressed by their struggles for skilled jobs and a rise in wages. These were 'for the most part, insufficient to support the worker and his dependants in the towns where the cost of living was very much higher than in rural areas' (Perrings, 1977: 42–3).

Capital wanted a low wage-scale for unskilled workers and a high turnover of labour, 'marked by short-term engagements designed to secure the cash requirements of a population compelled to depend primarily on subsistence agriculture as a result of their exclusion from the main agricultural produce markets, and the very low wage ceiling fixed for industrially unskilled labour'.

The immediate cause of the 1935 strike, referred to earlier, was an increase in the taxes imposed on Africans in urban areas. It was a deliberate attempt to force those who were considered surplus to industrial needs to go back into the villages. African taxes on men from the north-east went up by 50 per cent and in rural areas went down by 25 per cent (Perrings, 1977: 33–5). The mining companies and the government had responded to the depression by increasing the unskilled component in the workforce and diluting the more skilled component. Starting wages were low enough to ensure an overall saving even with the cost of short- term training.

African claims to promotion to higher grades of work were put on hold during the war. They again came to the fore in 1955 and 1960 during a period of booms and slumps in the industry, strikes by white and African miners, and indications that the Central African Federation might collapse. 'With the prospect of independence being granted to Northern Rhodesia in the near future uppermost in many people's minds, the Europeans realised that their present status would soon be untenable and were therefore prepared to negotiate compensation for any loss incurred' (Burawoy, 1972: 29).

White miners gave up their monopoly of more than 60 low-grade jobs and took steps to share the 'golden handshake' given to civil servants who retired to make way for Africans. Complete Zambianisation in the copper mines was not to be achieved in the next 25 years, but enough progress was made to justify a comparison made in 1987 (Simons and Simons, 1987: 71):

> On Zambian copper mines the job of blaster is a middle-range occupation commanding a wage similar to that of plumbers and carpenters. In South Africa, blasting may be carried out only by a scheduled person holding a blasting certificate, the hallmark of a professional miner. Unlike the artisan who is a craftsman working in a trade that gives him access to a wide range of industries, the miner is bound to his occupation within a narrow field and cannot easily find employment for his skills outside the mining industry. This high degree of specialisation goes far to explain the tenacity of the certificated miner in defence of his monopoly. Commenting on this dependence on job colour bars the Wiehahn Commission explained that White miners were accustomed to protection from African competition in the work place. Their anxieties clustered round the blasting certificate, the key to job status and income.

3 Patriarchal Rule

THE FAMILY

The African family in South Africa's customary societies was patriarchal and polygynous. Though the head had wide powers over the wives, children and dependants in his household, it cannot be said – as was said of early Roman law (Bodenheimer, 1940: 20) – that the law 'stopped on the threshold of the home'. He administered any property they acquired, was held responsible for their civil wrongdoing and arranged the marriages of his children.

Marriages were privately arranged without the intervention of a public authority, resembling in this respect the position in Roman and early European society (Ellis, 1928, vol. VI: 429). The negotiations were conducted on behalf of the family heads. If they reached an agreement, marriages were brought about by the observance of rituals and the transfer of cattle, or their equivalent, to the guardian of the bride.

Divorce was also a private matter. Either husbands of wives could have their marriages dissolved without reference to the courts, which were called on to intervene only if the parties disagreed about the custody of children or the amount of bride-wealth, which I call *lobolo* or *bogadi*, to be restored to the husband. If a man died first, his widow was expected to remain with his family, continue serving it and bear children in the name of the deceased. If she refused, or left his family with the intention of not returning, she might be held to have deserted them, thereby giving grounds for divorce.

Women neither owned nor inherited property. They were perpetual minors, subject to male tutelage, no matter what their age or marital condition might be. They could never be the guardians of their children. Girls married men selected or approved by the family heads who received the *lobolo* handed over by the bridegroom's group and had a strong material interest in the maintenance of the marriage tie.

Men could marry more than one wife and usually aspired to do so. African polygyny was not associated with anything like the purdah found among Hindu women of rank or the veil worn by

Muslim women partly to hide their face from strangers. African women were often outspoken and self-assertive, but with rare exceptions, of which the most notable were the Transvaal Lovedu (Krige and Krige, 1943), had no part in public life. They were not chiefs, headmen or councillors, and did not speak in assemblies or courts of law.

The co-wives of a polygynist were ranked according to rules which varied from one cultural cluster to another. A wife's position in the household determined that of her children in the household. Concubinage and prostitution were unknown. Most women married soon after puberty, and always belonged to a family group. No woman and, for that matter, no man, could live independently of a family:

> The choice for a woman lay between marriage and life-long dependence on a father, brother or other male kinsman. Since there were more marriageable women than men – because the women married at an earlier age and lived longer – the adoption of monogamy would have left some women in a state of permanent spinsterdom, for which condition the customary society contained no arrangements.

By reason of polygyny and the associated practices of the levirate (ukungena) and sororate (isisu) every girl, widow and divorcee had a reasonable certainty of entering into a fully sanctioned marital union and of bearing children throughout their reproductive years. The sharing of a husband may not have seemed too great a price to pay for the advantage of being a wife and mother in a society where other careers were not open to women. The co-wives also benefited from the companionship and security that a large establishment provided. Where homesteads were scattered and relatively isolated, as among the Nguni, life would have been lonelier and more vulnerable in a small, monogamous family. Co-wives shared the burden of work and of bearing children. A form of family planning operated in tribes whose customs prohibited intercourse during the period of breast feeding, which might extend over two or more years. Such birth controls would have been less effective if the man had been limited to one wife. A major gain from polygyny was that it preserved women from the excessive childbearing which had harassed working class wives in monogamous communities. (Simons, 1968: 81–2)

Little is known about the feelings of women themselves in pre-colonial times about the merits of polygyny. They may have been merely submissive, as some missionaries alleged, or they may have preferred polygyny, but co-wives certainly did not bewail their fate. Though jealousy, strife and plotting occurred in joint households, there is no firm evidence that they had more marital discord than monogamous families experience in present-day societies. From all accounts, it appears that a first wife rarely opposed her husband's decision to take a second wife. Theophilus Shepstone told the Cape Government Commission on Native Laws and Customs of 1883 (Evidence: 29), 'It is a matter of pride to native wives that they belong to a large establishment; they have rank among themselves, and they prize very highly the privileges attached to their position.'

The division of labour in the customary society conformed to a pattern found throughout Africa south of the Sahara before the colonial invasion. The men hunted, fished, herded cattle, made war, cleared the ground of bush, assisted women in building houses and attended to public affairs and courts of law. Women bore and raised children, cultivated gardens, harvested and stored produce, cooked, cleaned and carried water in containers on their heads sometimes for a mile or more. The workload might not have been excessive by standards in other peasant societies before the industrial revolution, yet it was severely condemned by white settlers and colonists. Anxious to force the men into the labour market, they said that polygynists battened on the labour of their wives, who also made available to them an 'increasing means of sexual indulgence' (Natal, 1852–3: Report 46).

An extreme case of this kind was the report and proceedings of the 'Kaffir' Commission of 1852–3 (Natal, 1852–3), appointed to inquire into the past and present state of the kaffirs in the District of Natal. The Governor, Benjamin Pine, who appointed the commissioners, gave them the cue in the statement issued in 1853 (Natal, 1852–3: 22–3). He reported that his predecessors had blundered in allowing tribal remnants to occupy 'immense tracts' where the power and tyranny of chiefs were increasing and polygamy was gaining strength. 'The wives of a man are practically his slaves, and the more a man has the richer he is.' Polygamy enabled the tribal peasant to compete with the immigrant farmer or gardener, and destroy his market. 'How can an

Englishman with one pair of hands compete with a native man with five to twenty slave wives?'

Among the commissioners were Theophilus Shepstone, diplomatic agent to Natal's chiefdoms, John Bird, the surveyor-general, Walter Harding, the crown prosecutor, and J. N. Boshoff, the court registrar (many years later a president of the Orange Free State), with 19 other members, of whom some were old-time colonists and some recent immigrants of only 5 years standing or less. They published the evidence seriatim, and issued the most intemperate and prejudiced report to come from a public inquiry in South Africa. None of the public servants on the Commission had a hand in drafting the report, and Shepstone, after he had left the service, pointedly disclaimed responsibility for it (Cape G.4, 1883: Minutes of Evidence, 11); but no member dissented from its findings at the time of publication (Simons, 1968: 21).

Superstitious, warlike, cruel, bloodthirsty, crafty, indolent, servile, debased, sensual, deceitful, immoral – such were the epithets that the commissioners hurled indiscriminately at their servants and neighbours. Yet there had not been a single case of murder or attempted murder of a white person in the colony during the preceding ten years. Africans did most of the work on the settlers' farms. They cooked, nursed infants and children, laundered lingerie and were entrusted with intimate domestic duties in white households. There was, asserted Magistrate Peppercorn, 'great mental obliquity' in anyone who denied the general honesty of people so trusted. To call them 'unreclaimable savages', he added, 'is the libel and pretext of those who seek to rob them of their birthright as human beings'.

The commissioners aimed some of their fiercest broadsides at polygamy, 'female slavery' and 'bartering cattle for women' which, they claimed, 'mould the whole life of the kaffir, degrade the positions and wound the feelings of the older or first married wives'. Daughters were 'systematically trained and reared as an article of sale, and from the chief circulating medium of the Kaffir in the purchase of cattle'. A wife became the property of her husband to a great extent. Compelled to labour for him in a condition resembling slavery, she enabled him to spend his life in indolent sensuality.

The Commission recommended that polygamy and *lobolo* should be prohibited by law after an early given date. Also:

All Kaffirs should be ordered to go decently clothed. This measure would at once tend to increase the number of labourers, because many would be obliged to work to procure the means of buying clothing; it would also add to the general revenue of the colony through Customs duties. (Natal, 1852–3: Report, 37–8, 47)

The eminent historian Eric A. Walker (1964: 274–5) was less than fair to the Commission when he wrote that the 'only results of its labours were to kill the wilder schemes for breaking up the reserves and to change . . . "Diplomatic Agent" into "Secretary for Native Affairs" '. It was actually Lord Grey who insisted on a change in the title! At least one other recommendation came into effect. A proclamation ordered all the Zulu to wear European clothing in Durban and Pietermaritzburg. Shepstone proudly reported that on the stipulated day – only a month after the issue of the proclamation – every Zulu appeared dressed as ordered. All men making the journey to the towns carried trousers ready to be put on when they entered the borough (Natal, 1864: 8).

LEGAL IDENTITY IN THE REPUBLICS

The history of their legal institutions yields no support for this version.

The burgers of the small, isolated republics did enforce a rigid segregation, but only in the form of an inequality of civic status between white and black. They began with an assertion of principled non-intervention in the internal affairs of self-contained chiefdoms, but failed to enforce territorial separation. A large and persistent land-hunger, a never-ending demand for low-paid manual workers and the search for security defeated attempts to isolate the chiefdoms. The republican constitutions began by applying the Roman-Dutch law to all inhabitants.

The Orange Free State Volksraad never recognised customary law as a valid system. The Raad hardly did more in this regard than to sanction the customary law of inheritance of monogamists who lived together as husband and wife and kept aloof from polygyny. Two proposals concerning African marriages came before the Raad in May 1876 (Notulen van den Volksraad, van den Oranjevrijstaat, 1876: 408f). One, submitted by 102 memorialists, urged the government to stop the evils arising from customary marriages: the exchange, amounting to slavery, of women and children and the theft of cattle for *lobolo*. The moral sentiments, coming from a community whose members raided African villages for child- labour (Orpen, 1909: 426–7), were largely a pretence; but the alleged link between marriage and cattle-stealing must have carried weight. It cropped up again in the debate on the second motion which proposed that predicants, other than missionaries, should not preside over African marriages. They went together with extravagant and costly festivities and the theft of livestock to provide meat for guests. Some members argued that if Dutch Reformed Church ministers refused to solemnise the marriages, Africans would turn to the English church. The Raad did not approve of their living in sin. What it wanted was a simple, monogamous marriage, performed by a separate minister in a separate church, out of sight of white congregations and without noisy festivities which kept people away from their work and gave them a large appetite for meat.

CUSTOMARY MARRIAGE REJECTED

Of all the South African states, only the Transvaal Volksraad actually outlawed African customary marriages. Law 3 of 1876, which provided for the appointment of chiefs and administrators, declared that 'In furtherance of morality the purchase of women or polygyny among the Coloured races is not recognised in this Republic by the law of the land.'

The annexation of the Transvaal Republic by Britain in 1877 enabled Shepstone to introduce the Natal policy of recognising African customary law and setting up separate courts for Africans. There was much delay in giving statutory effect to his proposals. The Enabling Act, Ordinance 11 of 1881, was passed after the armistice and three weeks before the restoration of independence to the Republic. The Ordinance was largely a reproduction of the Natal Law 26 of 1875, which in turn had been derived from the Royal Instructions of 1848. The Volksraad repealed the legislation introduced during the British interregnum, but re-enacted the main provisions of Ordinance 11 of 1881 in Law 4 of 1885.

The wording of the text and its translation into Dutch had an important bearing, as we shall see, on judicial decisions affecting African customary marriages and the position of African women. The Natal Law 26 of 1875 stated that 'all matters and disputes in the nature of civil cases between natives shall be tried under the provisions of this law and not otherwise, and according to native laws, customs and usages for the time being prevailing, so far as the same shall not be of a nature to work some manifest injustice, or be repugnant to the settle principles and policy of natural equity'.

Section 2 of Law 4 of 1885 stipulated that 'The laws, habits and customs hitherto observed among the natives shall continue to remain in force in this Republic as long as they have not appeared to be inconsistent with the general principles of civilisation as recognised in the civilised world.' E. R. Garthorne (1924: 27) suggested that the content of section 2 should have followed the wording of the Natal Law 11 of 1881, from which is was derived. In such case the law should be construed as follows:

> The laws, customs or usages hitherto prevailing among the Native population, save and except in so far as they may be repugnant to the general principles of humanity as recognized throughout the civilized world, shall continue to be of force and effect in this Republic.

Had this view been before the Court it seems feasible that the validity of Native marriage and other customs would not have been so emphatically negative by the dicta of judges.

With respect, it might be argued that the substitution of 'civilization' for 'humanity' was intended rather than inadvertent. Humanity (*menslikheid* in Afrikaans) is more comprehensive than civilization (*beskaving*). The Volksraad might have preferred the less inclusive term which would shut out *kleurlinge* (all blacks!) from its vision of a community of nations (*volke*).

The Transvaal's administration persisted in looking at chiefdoms in terms of military security. The Commandant-General of the armed forces was, until 1896, also the superintendent of Natives, who heard appeals from the courts of Native Commissioners. Appeals from his judgments went to the state president and the Executive Council (van der Walt et al., 1955: 462–3). The Superintendent instructed the courts in 1895 that the 'purchase of women for money or cattle' was contraband on which they could not pronounce judgment. Natal's courts had not difficulty in finding that customary marriages were compatible with the principles of humanity and natural justice. The Republic's courts, in contrast, refused to sanction potentially polygynous marriages. Some of the reasons for this unbending stand appeared in the Volksraad's debates in 1895–7 on the Coloured Persons Marriage Bill which would allow *kleurlinge* (the term used to describe Africans, Coloured and Asians) to enter into marriage under the Roman-Dutch law.

The Republic's first marriage law, No. 3 of 1871, provided for the marriage of whites only and promised that a separate law would be made for the marriages of *kleurlinge*. Pending this event and because of the refusal to recognise customary marriages, Africans could not marry lawfully in the Republic. The 1895 Bill was meant to cure this defect. It met with much opposition from the burgers, many of whom petitioned for its complete rejection. After turning it down in two previous sessions, the Raad opted a revised version by 13 votes to 12.

The opposition argued that the proposed measure would encourage equality between white and black people, something which the constitution prohibited. Africans would marry in churches, bring their divorce suits to the Supreme Court and use the same offices and courts as whites. Another line of attack was to allege that Africans were not civilised enough to appreciate Christian marriages, and that any action taken to discourage *lobolo* would have an adverse effect on the supply of workers, since men obtained cattle for bride-wealth by means of farm labour.

Members who favoured the bill did not want it thought that they were pleading for the Natives, yet it was no more than the Raad's duty to encourage the spread of civilisation. How could the Natives become Christians if their marriages were not recognised as lawful? Under existing conditions, they persisted in taking more and more wives, selling their children for high prices and living in indolence. President Paul Kruger agreed that the *Volk* wanted neither equality nor polygyny, and claimed that the proposed measure would discourage both evils (Notulen van den Eersten Volksraad der Z.A. Republiek, 1895: 167–8; 1896: 186–91; 1897: 384, 447).

This early attempt to assert white supremacy by means of strict racial discrimination in an integrated economy dependent on low-paid black workers caused some confusion of aims in the administration and courts of law. The directive of 1895 barring them from addressing claims to *lobolo* was issued to discourage, on moral grounds, the practice of polygyny which, farmers said, allowed men to stay idly at home instead of entering the labour market. The rejection of the *lobolo* institution, which validated customary marriages, weakened the family structure and lowered moral standards. The chiefs continued to settle *lobolo* disputes, but could not enforce their decisions by legal process. Native commissioners complained that the absence of legal redress was driving women into prostitution (South African Native Affairs Commission, 1903–5: Minutes of Evidence, vol. 5, 185, 229f, 297). This was probably an overstatement. There were many factors that contributed to marital and family instability, but the warning had been given. Yet it did not deter the Milner regime, installed after the defeat of the republics in the 1899–1902 war, from repeating the former Transvaal Republic's policy of denying *lobolo* claims in a bid to discourage polygny. In 1902, W. Windham, the Secretary for Native Affairs, reissued the Republic's circular of 1895 instructing the courts to regard *lobolo* as forbidden traffic, and therefore not adjudgeable (S.A. Native Affairs Commission, 1903–5: Minutes of Evidence, vol. 5, 303).

Justice J.G. Kotzé, the Judge President of the Republic's High Court, was more broad-mined. He rejected the argument that a customary marriage had no validity under the Republic's constitution. Tribal marriage, he said, was not a state of concubinage. The second wife of a polygynist was as much his wife by customary law as his first wife. The proper test to apply was whether a marriage, though potentially polygynous, was in fact monogamous. Section 2 of Law 4 of 1885 did not invalidate a *de facto* monogamous union entered into under tribal law. 'The recognition of a "Kaffir" marriage, where it appears that the Kaffir has the accused as his only wife, is not *contra bonos mores* or in conflict with civilized practice, which is something that the Court may not assume' (*The Queen* v. *Sepana* [1880] (Kotzé 172); *The State* v. *Marroko* [1893] (Hertzog 110)).

The Transvaal Supreme Court established after the 1899–1902 war was less tolerant. It ignored the historical antecedents of Law 4 of 1885, identified marriage with the institutions of Christian monogamists, and closed its eyes to the social implications of the conflict between the common law and customary law. Innes, C.J.

defined marriage as 'the union of one man with one woman, to
the exclusion, while it lasts, of all others' (*Ebrahim* v. *Essop* [1905],
T.S. 59). This describes marriage of a European kind, and not a
Muslim or African marriage, which has as much moral claim to
judicial recognition as monogamous unions. He ruled in later
cases that a customary African marriage, whether actually or
potentially polygynous, was 'inconsistent with the general principles of civilization recognized in the civilized world', and therefore fell outside the scope of the recognition contemplated in
section 2 of Law 4 of 1885 (*Nalana* v. *Rex* [1907] T.S. 407; *Rex* v.
Mboko [1910] T.S. 445). But the civilised world is wider than the
countries of Christeadom; and if the legislature had wanted to
nullify customary marriages, why did it not make its intention
explicit?

The Supreme Court refused to recognise the validity of customary marriages in criminal cases in which the admissibility of
a wife's evidence against her husband was in question, and could
hardly adopt a more favourable view in suits between Africans.
In the leading case of *Kaba* v. *Ntela* ([1910] T.S. 964) a Commissioner's Court granted a husband married by customary law the
custody of his children and the return of *lobolo*. The Supreme
Court reversed this decision on appeal. De Villiers, J.P. concluded that though Law 4 of 1885 had repealed Law 3 of 1876
which outlawed polygyny, the Volksraad had not intended to do
away with the principle. He followed judgments of courts in
regions of the Cape where customary law had not received
statutory recognition, and ruled that *lobolo* was 'a consideration
given for future immoral cohabitation', which could not be
recovered in a court of law. The children of a customary
marriage were illegitimate and their mother was their natural
guardian.

It might be argued that in handing down such decisions, the
courts liberated African women from the bondage of patriarchal
domination. Indeed, the Transvaal Supreme Court explicitly
declared that the custom under which they remained perpetual
minors for life could not be enforced, but women might well have
rejected an emancipation reducing them to the condition of
concubines with illegitimate children. Wessels, J. remarked in
Meesedoosa v. *Links* [1915] T.P.D. 357) that by rejecting customary
marriage with *lobolo*, 'we have so undermined the fundamental
native customs that there is very little left'. Judges with a better

understanding of the customs and complexities of a diversified cultural society would have hesitated to be so destructive. They might have criticised laws made to uphold white supremacy at the expense of a conquered people who had no voice in their country's government and no members of their race among the judiciary.

INTEGRATION

Judges and lawyers seldom mentioned the findings of social scientists who conduct research among the people from whom litigants and lawbreakers. The legal fraternity prefer to take their cue from statutes, decided cases and authoritative textbooks based on these sources. In what follows in this section I draw heavily on my paper on the reform of marriage and family law in South Africa (Simons, 1991).

Customary marriages, both actually and potentially polygamous, are valid throughout South Africa in proceedings between Africans. If non-Africans are involved, as in claims for damages, the common law courts formerly refused to confer legitimacy on such marriages because of the element of polygamy. Parliament removed this obstacle by 31, Act 76 of 1963 which enables the parties to a customary marriage to claim damages for loss of support from any person who unlawfully caused the death of a spouse.

The Appellate Division ruled in *Nkambula* v. *Linda* ([1951] (1) SA 377 AD) that customary marriages were not lawful in terms of the common law and did not constitute a legal impediment on a civil marriage between one of the partners and a third person. Either party to the customary marriage could lawfully during its subsistence marry another person by civil rites.

Such difficulties persisted for as long as Africans could switch from customary marriages to civil marriage and back again. The possibility arose from the inferior status of customary marriages. A first step towards achieving parity is to introduce formal procedures for validating customary marriages, which are in a state of confusion similar to that of common law marriages in Europe before the Church Council of Trent's decrees in 1563. A ceremony is not prescribed for the conclusion of customary marriages nor are they registered, except in Natal.

The Natal Code of Zulu Law of 1987 confers majority status on women at 21, provides for the registration of customary marriages, the issue of marriage certificates and the recording of *lobolo* agreements. Polygamy is declared valid in customary marriages, which are defined as civil law contracts binding for life unless annulled of dissolved by a court. Men are prohibited from entering into a customary marriage during the subsistence of a civil marriage contracted in accordance with the Marriage Act, 25 of 1961.

At one time leading authorities argued that 'under the law of the land, the union is an illicit cohabitation' (Seymour, 1960: 171) and 'not a valid marriage in our law' (Hahlo, 1953: 436). Firoz Cachalia (1991: 21) has the same opinion. He writes that 'the monogamous marriage of Roman-Dutch law is the only form of marriage recognised under our law. . . . Marriages in accordance with Muslim (or Hindu) rites are denied recognition on the basis that they are "potentially polygamous" unless solemnized by a marriage officer in terms of Section 3 of the Marriage Act 25 of 1961, in which event a valid *civil* marriage arise.'

I queried the validity of these assertions (Simons, 1968: 152) in a passage reading: 'African law is recognized by the constitution, regulates, in part, the lives of a majority of South African citizens, and regarded from their point of view, is as much "our" law as the Roman Dutch.' This contention has been strengthened by the Matrimonial Property Law Amendment Act, 3 of 1988, which puts the civil marriages of Africans on the same footing as those of other people.

THE DECLINE OF POLYGAMY

Polygamy, a major reason for the refusal of common law courts to recognise the validity of customary unions, had drastically declined during the twentieth century. The oldest set of figures available were recorded in Natal, where marriage regulations of 1869 imposed a registration fee of £5 for every African marriage. Of the customary marriages registered between 1871 and 1880, 43 per cent were polygamous. The proportion was 36 per cent in 1894–1903. One fifth of married men in the Transkei at the beginning of the twentieth century had more than one wife. Of the married men counted in the 1921 population census, 14 per cent were polygamous. A conservative estimate based on the 1951 population census returns indicate that between 5 and 10 per cent of South African-born men were polygamists (Simons, 1968: 78-9).

The African family system is undergoing a revolutionary change from patriarchal, polygamous, joint family communities to the monogamous, simple family units of urban-industrial societies. Important causes are the market economy, industrialism, urban growth, school education and Christianity. The change cannot be halted, let alone reversed, if Africans are to continue their advance to progressive and enlightened social forms of development. Women especially will lose much by being forced back into the mould of patriarchal rule along the lines laid down for an orthodox Hindu wife by the Indian Laws of Manu (Campbell, 1985: 56):

> A woman is never to be independent. She must not attempt to free herself from her father, husband or sons. She shall obey as long as she lives with him to whom her father (or with her father's permission, her brother) has given her; and when he is dead, she must never dishonour his memory.... Even a husband of no virtue, without any good qualities at all, and pursuing his pleasures elsewhere, is to be worshipped unflaggingly as a god.... In reward for such conduct, the female who controls her thoughts, speech, and actions, gains in this life highest renown, and in the next a place beside her husband.

The South African parallel to Hindu patriarchy is bound up with *lobolo*. It is a necessary element of customary marriages; accompanies most civil marriages among all social classes; figures prominently in divorce suits; and has survived the many big changes in African life.

FUNCTION OF LOBOLO

Before the abolition of the Special Courts for Africans in 1986, they insisted that *lobolo* was the 'keystone' of customary marriage which remained in force as long as the wife's group retained all of some of the bride-wealth. If she deserted her husband and refused to return, her people had to refund the equivalent of one head of cattle to dissolve the marriage. She could not enter into a second customary marriage until this had been done. If she took a lover, any children she had by him belonged to her husband, who was entitled to claim damages from their father. The court might allow her to obtain a divorce without refund of *lobolo* if she suffered extreme neglect or cruelty at the hands of the husband, but in nearly all cases it preferred to uphold the patriarchal power (*Mokoena* v. *Mafokeng* [1945] NAC (C & C) 89).

Lobolo enabled a woman's natural guardian to keep a close grip on her domestic life after her marriage. He can press claims to unpaid bride-wealth to the extent of breaking up her marriage. Commissioner W. Carmichael, in *Sipoxo* v. *Rwexwana* (4 NAC 205 [1919]), dissenting from a majority judgment upholding the patriarchal power, called it 'the essentially slave laws of parental divorce', and argued that a customary marriage should be dissolved in life only by the will or act of either spouse.

ALWAYS MINORS

The now defunct Native Commissioners' courts held that in the customary African law women were perpetual minors. They could not own property, inherit and be guardians of their own children. They could not make contracts, sue or be sued without the aid of their male guardians. At all ages and without regard to social or marital status, they were legally obliged to submit to the patriarchal authority.

This interpretation rested on faulty premises and a misreading of traditional African culture. Women had more rights than those conceded by alien courts. Common law terms such as ownership, contract and status are saturated with western concepts of individualism unknown in the traditional society before the colonial invasion. It was the family unit, rather than individuals, which had full legal capacity. It was both a producing and consuming unit, and undertook a wide range of activities performed by private enterprise or public agencies in capitalist and socialist societies.

Today more than a million African women, forming 65 per cent of those who are economically active, work for wages and salaries outside their homes in professions, offices, factories, shops or farms in South Africa. Many are market traders, herbalists, diviners or make and sell goods in the informal sector. Many are actually heads of families and assert individual claims to property.

WITHOUT PROPERTY

Customary law had not kept pace with these changes. White judicial officers, who are outside the communities whose laws they administer, are only slightly exposed to the pressure of African opinion, and tend to stress the qualities of authority, certainty and uniformity. They draw a sharp line between 'majors' and 'minors', credit the patriarchal authority with the 'ownership' of all property acquired by members of the household, and repudiate customs that enable women to own cattle and arrange marriages on their own behalf, as is done among the Transvaal Venda and Lovedu (Simons, 1968: 92). The Native Commissioners ignored regional differences, devised stereotypes which lacked the flexibility of unwritten law, and yielded to the opinion of African assessors who served the interests of creditors by allowing them to attach cattle belonging to a wife in settlement of her husband's debts.

A woman sued her husband for cattle she had earned in doctor's fees (*Nomtwebula* v. *Ndumndum*, 2 NAC 121 [1911]). The Assessors said that if a wife makes a mat or basket it belongs to her husband. 'Even if she acquired a knowledge of medicine, the medicine belongs to her husband's kraal. She cannot claim cattle earned by her during the subsistence of the marriage.' On such a slender basis the courts ruled that a wife had no proprietary capacity. Customary marriage, said Young, P. (*Mondlane* v. *Magcaka* [1929] NAC (C & O) 89) did not create a partnership between husband and wife. Her position 'is assimilated to that of a child and, with certain exceptions, she cannot hold property, either in her own right or in partnership with her husband'.

Household goods and personal effects given to her as wedding gifts belong to him. He is entitled to keep them on the dissolution of the marriage. Her earnings and anything she buys with them accrue to her house and come under his control (*Mpantsha* v. *Nkolonkulu* [1952] NAC 41).

LEGAL CAPACITY

A person has full legal capacity when he may legally exercise the maximum amount of power permitted in his society. Acting in his or her name and without assistance, he and she can make contracts, acquire and own property, sue and be sued, and enter into other transactions. If sane, solvent and over 18 years of age, men and women – other than wives who are subject to their husband's marital power – have full legal capacity under the common law.

In the customary African society, a woman shared the rank of her father and husband, did much of the hard work in the household and fields, not for an employer but for the family to which she and her children belonged. The product of her labours formed part of the joint family estate which the patriarch managed, not as 'owner', but in the capacity of head and senior partner. Women were junior partners and occupied a subordinate position in home affairs. They acquiesced in the superiority of the man's authority because it was customary and sanctioned by the division of functions. Each sex had its own sphere of activity. Women did not contend with men for rank, power, office or wealth because their roles were incompatible rather than competitive.

The idea of a *femme sole*, a women of independent status, could not take place in a society in which there was no class war or battle of the sexes. People belonged to kinship and local groups and were not aware of themselves as individuals with rights, interests and claims detached from their group affiliations. To emancipate women from the patriarchal authority, the family must cease to be the main productive unit and lose it self-sufficiency. Women must receive school education and take part along with men in productive activity outside the home before they can assert claims to equality of status.

MAJORITY STATUS

The Natal and Transvaal Native Appeal Court turned its attention in the 1930s to the uneven rate of social change. Women in big urban centres who had adapted the standards and outlook of enlightened classes should fall under the common law and be allowed to sue in their own name, said Stubbs, P. (*Monaheng* v. *Konupi* [1930] NAC (N & T) 59: 61). He added that he had come to this conclusion with great reluctance because it would involve the court in 'innumerable fine distinctions and complications'. Such doubts were repeated with growing emphasis in subsequent judgments. Eventually, the court rejected the plea that individuals should obtain relief from customary law in 'hard cases' and on grounds of 'equity'.

Claiming that the Native Administration Act of 1927 established a 'new outlook in native policy', McLoughlin, P. said (*Matsheng* v. *Dhlamini* [1937] NAC (N & T) 89) that its effect was to restore without modification the rule of perpetual tutelage over women. He considered that the rule was wholly consistent with the principles of civilisation and natural justice, and should be enforced also in proceedings under common law. It was not easy to draft tests of fitness for relief from male tutelage, and the court should not speed up the disintegration which set in when women broke away from the restraints of customary law and undermined their family life and institutions.

THE CONFLICT OF LAWS

Section 11(1) of the Native Administration Act, 38 of 1927 gives the Native Commissioners' Courts a discretion to apply African customary law in civil cases involving tribal customs, subject to two limitations. The relevant rule of law must not have been repealed or modified or 'opposed to the principles of public policy or natural justice'. To place the legality of *lobolo* or *bogadi* or other similar custom beyond doubt, a further proviso stipulates that it 'shall not be lawful for any court to declare that it is repugnant to such principles'. These provisions brought to a successful conclusion the long-sustained battle to give customary law a recognised and uniform status throughout the country. *Lobolo* had at last found its way on to the statute book in terms that are unique and record a great deal of South Africa's legal history. No other colonial legislature has found it necessary to entrench the custom of bride-wealth by statute, or to affirm that it is neither immoral nor opposed to natural justice.

The Commissioners' Courts had two opposing precedents to guide them. One, inherited from the policies of the Cape,

Transvaal and Orange Free State, gave priority to the common law. Natal, in contrast, made customary African law the primary system in civil suits between Africans. The Natal tradition gained the upper hand over the years.

The Southern Division originally held that the common law should be primarily applied. Customary law ought to be followed only in matters peculiar to tribal law. In an action arising out of a loan of money the Roman-Dutch law would be suitable (*Nganoyi* v. *Njombeni* [1930] NAC, C&O, 18). The Northern Division disagreed when dealing with an action for the repayment of a loan of cattle (*Moima* v. *Matladi* [1937] NAC, N&T, 40). McLoughlin, T., who delivered the judgment, argued that though parliament had adopted the 'Transkeian formula' in s. 11 (1), it had not adopted the Cape approach, but wanted the Natal rule to operate throughout the country. Later, when President of the Southern Division, he imposed his version also on the Cape. He rejected, in *Sawintshi* v. *Magidela* ([1944] NAC, C&O, 47), the notion that the court, when in doubt, should apply the common law. The buyer and seller in a reserve must be assumed to have contracted under customary law, the system 'familiar and peculiar to them': 'it is common sense and natural to expect the Natives, who are parties, to think and act under their system rather than the European, whose pitfalls are unknown to them and, therefore, not in contemplations.'

Justice McLoughlin was a champion of what he called the 'Shepstonian conception of legal segregation', which he interpreted 'by the spirit rather than the letter of the law' (*Matsheng* v. *Dhlamini* [1937], NAC, N&T, 89 at p. 91; *Yako* v. *Beyi* [1944], NAC, C&O 72 at p. 76). He was also a stern patriarch where African women were concerned, and insisted on reversing the process of emancipating them from male domination. He ruled that the court must uphold the law under which a woman remained a perpetual ward, even to the extent of refusing a widow the right to sue unaided in an action under the common law (*Matsheng* v. *Dhlamini* [1937], above).

In *Yako* v. *Beyi* (above, at p. 77) he applied his subjective method of interpreting statutes and doubted if a woman should be allowed to claim damages under the common law for seduction. In any event, she should not receive more than her guardian would be entitled to claim under customary law. In a later case (*Lebona* v. *Ramokone* [1946], NAC, C&O, 14) the court denied a woman's claim under the common law to lying-in expenses and to maintenance for her minor child. The effect of these judgments was to offset the advantage that women gained from the legitimacy of customary marriage.

Parliament intervened to undo the harm and, in so doing, showed that the Commissioners' Courts had misinterpreted the legislature's intention. Section 5, Act 21 of 1943 amended s. 11 of the Native Administration Act, 38 of 1927, by providing that the capacity of an African was to be determined as if he were a white person, unless the right or obligation in question fell under tribal law. In this event it determines the capacity of the parties to the suit. Women obtained an additional measure of relief from the Appellate Division of the Supreme Court (*ex parte* the Minister of Native Affairs; *in re Yako* v. *Beyi*, [1948] (1) S.A. 388 (A.D.)). It ruled that an African woman was not barred from succeeding in an action under the common law for seduction. If she succeeded, her damages were not necessarily limited to the amount that her guardian was entitled to claim under customary law.

Because the common law is generally more favourable to the emancipation of African women than their customary law, they stand to gain from a policy that allows them a free choice of law. But the decisions of the common law courts have not always been to their advantage. By refusing to acknowledge that African customary law is an integral part of the country's legal structure, and by denying the validity of its marriage customs, the courts have barred the wives of customary marriages from obtaining compensation from non-Africans who unlawfully caused the death of their husbands. The courts persistently refused a right of action in such cases. Parliament reversed these decisions by enacting s. 31, Act 76 of 1963, which gives women a right to claim damages under the common law for personal injuries resulting from the unlawful killing of a breadwinner, or assault and defamation (Simons, 1968: 153–5, 192).

UNDER APARTHEID

Dr Verwoerd, when Minister of Native Affairs, agreed that polygyny, 'now rapidly disappearing', must be discouraged (Senate Debates, 4 June 1952, col. 3844–5). Generally, it was his government's policy to conserve tribalism and make it work. He took 'liberalists' to task for replacing, by underhand means, trial customs with the Roman-Dutch law. The African should 'develop his own law according to changed circumstances but starting from a system of law that is his'. The Minister of Bantu Administration and Development, de Wet Nel, expressed great concern at the plight of African women who, through past mistakes, had not been given their due place in social life. It was time to restore to them 'the status they enjoyed in the old traditional society' (House of Assembly Debates, 10 April 1962, col. 3637).

This is not what forward-looking women want. They ceased to be junior partners in a joint family enterprise. It no longer exists. They ought to take their place on an equal footing with men in the building of a new life. They will lose much and gain nothing by being forced back into the framework of 'tribal' law. Yet this is what Parliament appeared to contemplate in s. 50 (2)(b) of the Transkei Constitution Act of 1963. It directs that:

> in all suits or proceedings between parties involving or based on questions of Bantu custom the Court shall apply the Bantu Law applicable to such custom as far as is practicable in deciding such question, except where such custom is opposed to the principles of public policy or natural justice: 'that the custom of lobolo or bogadi or any similar custom is repugnant to such principles'.

The peremptory nature of the directive leaves the court with no choice. It must apply customary law 'as far as is practicable' and subject to the conditions of the repugnancy proviso. In 1927 Parliament chose the more flexible formula of Transkeian legislation for incorporation in s. 11 (1) of the Native Administration Act 38 of 1927, and extended it to all provinces. In enacting s. 50 (2) (b) of the Transkei Constitution Act, Parliament in effect reverted to the narrower and more rigid approach expressed in s. 80 of the Natal Courts (Native) Act of 1898, which stipulated that 'All civil Native cases shall be tried according to Native laws, customs and usages save so far as may be ... repugnant to the settled principles and policy of natural justice.'

TRANSKEIAN INTERLUDE

The Transkeian Annexation Act of 1877 gave the Governor power to legislate by proclamation for the Territories. No Cape statute was to operate in them unless especially extended. The magistrates were to follow colonial law, 'except where all the parties to the suit or proceedings are what are commonly called Natives, in which case it may be dealt with according to Native law'. (Proclamations 110 of 1879, 112 of 1879 and 140 of 1885). The courts applied Roman-Dutch law when the parties had abandoned tribal custom, or when the claim was unknown to tribal law, and refused to uphold a custom that was 'repugnant to justice and equity' or 'contrary to good policy and public morals' (Simons, 1968: 32–3).

The Transkeian General Council, known widely as the Bhunga, was a singular and strictly localised exception to the South African practice of excluding Africans from the process of shaping their personal laws and regulating their own affairs. Most members of the Bhunga were traditionalist headmen. White magistrates dominated the executive and select committees, where the basic work was done. The Council could not legislate. It recommended action to the Native Affairs Department, but had the merit of giving Transkeian an annual forum for ventilating grievances and drawing the people into discussions by referring contentions motions to district councils and ward meeting. The reports of the Council's proceedings, which extended without a break from 1903, were an unrivalled source of information on African opinions and aspirations.

Men only sat on the Council. Most of them upheld the principle of patriarchal rule, but a more advanced section, to which some of the magistrates belonged, defended Christian marriage, the emancipation of women, the claims of widows and spinsters. When hard-pressed, the traditionalists resorted to the delaying tactic of referring the issue to the district councils and the mass of peasants. The Council adopted this procedure in 1920 on a motion to restore the traditional law of male guardianship over unmarried women.

Councillor Hlangeni, who introduced the motion, said that a girl was her father's inheritance, and asked why his bread should be taken from him. Most of the councillors who spoke supported him. What they objected to was that girls over 21 should be free to marry by civil rites without their fathers' consent. A magistrate reminded them that there were advanced councillors among them who year after year called for the repeal of colour bars and one legal system for black and white people. To give effect to

Hlangeni's motion would result in discrimination between African and white women!

Councillor Mandela rejected the argument. White women, he said, were not liberated. They did not hold office as magistrates or sit on the Council as rulers. If they were liberated, how was it that natives were not allowed to be in love with them? 'Many Natives were shot for being in love with European girls, therefore European girls were not free' (Transkei, 1920: 70–7).

G.B.M. Whitfield, a magistrate and official member of the Bhunga, whose book on South African native law (1929) was a pioneering work, urged the Transkei to follow Natal's example by giving priority to tribal law in civil suits. He said that it was wrong to force the Roman-Dutch law on hundreds of thousands peasants who were neither willing nor ready to receive its principles. He moved that 'Native law and custom, where both parties are Natives, shall form the rule of decision.' Civil and Christian marriages should have the same consequences as a customary marriage. Persons wishing to abandon tribal customs should be able to obtain exemption and place themselves under the common law (Transkei, 1921: 3; 1922: 153–9).

The motion, he explained, was aimed at restoring the customary law and removing the anomalies of a legal dualism. His fellow magistrates disagreed, and the motion was heavily defeated. They wanted elasticity, and looked forward to the abandonment of customs which, though not highly offensive, should lapse into disuse.

It was Whitfield's view that prevailed 40 years later in s. 50 (2)(b) of the Transkei Constitution Act of 1963 and the Transkei Marriage Act, 21 of 1978, which goes much further than any other legislation in Southern Africa in the degree of recognition given to customary marriage. In terms of the Act, a woman is subject to her husband's guardianship in both a customary and civil law marriage. If a polygnist marries one wife under customary law and another under civil law, the latter will be regarded as a customary marriage wife. Her status and legal capacity, and those of her children, will be determined in accordance with the customary marriage law.

The Act legitimates polygyny. A husband may enter into a second marriage without dissolving the first. A customary and civil marriage can coexist in a hybrid relationship; but if the man has entered into a valid civil marriage in community of property, he is not allowed to marry another woman under customary law.

Professor Carmen Nathan has warned people to 'Think carefully before you let your daughter marry a man domiciled in Transkei!' (1983: 164).

The Transkei is the only state with a marriage system that equalises customary and civil marriages and stipulates that the marital power can never be excluded. When a polygynist marries more than one wife, of whom one is married by civil rites, they are subject to his marital power.

Of the ten Bantu Homelands, four have been declared sovereign and independent. They are the BCTV territories: Bophuthatswana, Ciskei, Transkei and Venda. The other six announced in a joint statement that they had no intention of 'opting for so-called independence and the loss of South African citizenship'. They did not want to abdicate their South African birthright, nor forfeit their share 'of the economy and wealth we have jointly built' (S.A. Institute of Race Relations, 1977: 3–4).

HIGH COMMISSION TERRITORIES

Once known as 'Protectorates', Lesotho, Botswana and Swaziland were taken over by Britain at different times, administered by a High Commissioner, and scheduled for eventual absorption in South Africa's body politic, after consultation with their inhabitants. The small white communities strongly favoured the transfer, whereas Africans vigorously opposed the move. The dispute was finally settled by changes in the South Africa Act of 1909 and the Act of Union of 1910, the loosening of South Africa's ties with Britain and the Commonwealth and the introduction of segregation policies by the Nationalist Party Government, Lord Hailey cautiously concluded that 'a refusal by the United Kingdom to hand over possession of the Territories must, from a practical standpoint, be regarded as decisive' (1957: 182).

South Africa's legal dualism strongly influenced legal development in the High Commission Territories. The uneasy relationship between customary and common law is still largely left for the courts to unravel but the dualism has been modified. 'Nowhere is the separation of the two forms of marriage as rigid and complete as in South Africa and nowhere is the customary marriage treated with the scant respect it receives in South Africa' (Bennett and Peart 1983: 156–8).

LESOTHO

Britain annexed Lesotho in 1868 at the request of King Moesheshwe who was being harassed by the Orange Free State Boers, and incorporated it soon afterwards in the Cape Colony. The British government resumed control of the territory in 1884 and issued a proclamation stating that Lesotho's law should be the same as that in the Cape. Roman-Dutch law has since then formed the substance of the common law, but the proclamation of 1884 and another of 1889 recognised the authority of the traditional chiefs and authorised them to judge any cases in which the parties were Sotho.

A Basutoland National Council became the officially recognised mouthpiece of the Sotho people in 1910. One of its earliest activities was to issue the Laws of Lerotholi, a code of rules based on Sotho custom. All chiefs, of whom there were 1340 in 1938, could try customary law cases, the main source of income of many minor chiefs. The number of chiefs' courts was reduced to 134 in 1946 and to 63 in 1953. Appeals went to the court of the Paramount Chief and from there to Judicial Commissioners, who could grant leave for an appeal to the Lesotho High Court (Hailey, 1957: 505–9).

A Marriage Act, No. 10 of 1974, allows polygyny, lays down the formalities of civil/Christian marriage and defines the capacity of the spouses. Traditional Sotho custom determines these issues in a customary marriage, and might apply also to such matters as matrimonial property and intestate succession in a civil and Christian marriage. When deciding which system to apply, the courts follow a rule-of-thumb test based on living standards, which in practice amounts to income and wealth. Roman-Dutch law is applied to the rich and well-to-do, while the majority of rural women are assumed to be traditionalists, who are subject to customary law (Stewart and Armstrong, 1990: 48–50).

BOTSWANA

Britain extended its jurisdiction over Bechuanaland, the former name of Botswana, in 1885, mainly to prevent the Transvaal Republic from closing the 'road to the North'. The Colonial Office was less interested in administering the country, most of which was considered 'unsuitable for European colonization'.

The first Assistant Commissioner sent to Bechuanaland Protectorate in 1887 was instructed 'not to interfere with Native
Administration; the Chiefs are understood not to be desirous to
part with their rights of sovereignty, nor are her Majesty's
Government by any means anxious to assume the responsibilities
of it' (Hailey, 1957: 498–502).

The policy of preserving Sotho customary law and the authority of chiefs remained in force for the next half-century but
traditional usages changed considerably. Christianity was a
powerful instrument of change. The first mission stations were
founded in 1846 and spread to all the major tribes by 1870.
Christianity is the official religion of nearly every tribe. Converts
were forbidden to practise polygamy, the inheritance of widows,
initiation into age regiments, bride-wealth (*bogadi*), magic and
witchcraft (Schapera, 1955: 43). The great majority of church
members are women who find attendance at services, prayer
meetings, catechism classes and other church activities a welcome
relief from the daily domestic round.

Women are socially inferior to men and always subject to male
guardianship, take no part in government and never hold a
political office. A wife who bears only daughters is held to have
failed in her most important duty to her husband. Modernisation
is a saving grace. Females far outnumber males in formal
education, as in church membership. Many more girls attend
school because most boys spend the greater part of their youth
at cattleposts far from villages and schools (Schapera, 1955:
p. 28–9). The cumulative effects are visible in a measure of
economic independence, greater freedom from patriarchal domination and access to employment in teaching, nursing and
secretarial work.

Recent studies show that the emancipation of Tswana women
is still far from being a reality. Athalia Molokomme (1987: 183–5)
explains that Tswana customary marriage is patriarchal. Marital
power is vested in the husband. He is the household head,
decides the family's place of domicile, has the final say in
domestic matters and is the guardian of the minor children
subject to the rule that their interests override other claims.
Customary law governs matrimonial property rights and intestate
succession in both kinds of marriage, but the parties to a
civil/Christian marriage can exclude this provision by a written
agreement.

A husband has the right to administer the joint property if the marriage is in community of property, and the wife's separate estate in a marriage out of community, unless this aspect of the marital power has been excluded by a prenuptial contract. The Married Person's Property Act excludes community of property from marriages after January 1971, unless the spouses declare before the marriage that they want to be married in community. 'The marital power can never attach to a marriage out of community of property, but will still attach to a marriage in community. Thus a wife married out of community of property after 1971 is only subject to the personal aspects of her husband's marital power' (Molokomme, 1987: 185).

SWAZILAND

The scene of bitter rivalries between the Transvaal Republic, Britain and traditional chiefs, Swaziland is the only High Commission Territory which was never conquered by Bantu, Boer or British. At one time a Protectorate of the Republic which constantly tried to absorb it fully, it came under British rule in 1903 in terms of an Order in Council which stipulated that the government should 'respect any Native laws' regulating the civil relations of chiefs, tribes and people. The Native Administration Proclamation of 1950 had the same general purport. It declared that the Paramount Chief in Council was the sole Native Authority and had the power to make rules for the 'good order and welfare' of the Swazi (Hailey, 1957: 514–15).

More than 90 per cent of the country's population are Swazi. As in Lesotho and Botswana, the common law is based on South Africa's Roman-Dutch rules. The parties to a civil or Christian marriage can choose between marriage in community of property, marriage with a prenuptial contract excluding community of property and the marital power, and marriage excluding community of property but not the marital power.

In the absence of a written agreement before marriage applying Roman-Dutch law, Swazi customary law regulates the property rights of the spouses and the husband's marital power. Section 24 of the Marriage Act 47, 1964 states that if both parties to the marriage are Africans, the marital power of the husband and the proprietary rights of the spouses shall be governed by Swazi law and custom, subject to the terms of section 25. This enables Africans to exclude customary law provisions and accept the common law consequences of a civil marriage by declaring their preference to the marriage officer, who should endorse their decision on the marriage register.

Thandabantu Nhlapo (1987: 39–43) considers that the provisions have given rise 'to massive problems in practice'. Only the highly educated Swazi make the declaration required by section 25. Others simply assume that when they marry with a civil or church ceremony the Roman-Dutch law applies. Marriage officers do not, as a matter of course, warn spouses of the effect of section 24. Thousands of couples discover with shock that in spite of their attempt to enter into a civil marriage, the customary law governs their proprietary capacity and the marital power.

Under Swazi customary law the husband is the head of the family and has the final say in all matters pertaining to his household and its property. A wife must have his permission to work for a wage. If she makes a profit out of a home-based industry, it is with his sanction. A widow has no claim on her late husband's estate and unmarried women have almost no proprietary capacity except for such personal items as clothing. A customary marriage debars the wife from having a real stake in profitable enterprises such as land, housing, business, banking and shares. The question is whether 'a woman who acquires these (or assists her husband in doing so), during the marriage must stand by and watch her in-laws divide these among themselves on the death of her husband' (Nhlapo, 1987: 44–5).

ZIMBABWE

A legal dualism exists also in Zimbabwe. Its domiciled residents have a choice between a 'general' law and African customary law, but the distinction was blurred by section 13 of the Native Marriages Ordinance of 1917, which provided that marriages between Africans under the general law would not affect the property of the spouses. It 'shall be held, may be disposed of, and unless disposed of by will shall devolve according to native law or custom'.

Section 3 of the Customary Law and Primary Courts Act, 6 of 1981 conforms to this injunction by prescribing that customary law shall determine succession to the intestate estates of Africans. Julie Stewart (1987: 87–90) considers that it is not necessarily undesirable. The traditional pattern of customary succession provided maintenance for the deceased's dependants from the family landholding and did not apply to wage or other individual income characteristic of the modern economic order. Current agitation by women for radical amendments of the law of intestate succession results from dissatisfaction with an outmoded system and the failure to enforce customary law obligations.

Change is undoubtedly needed by those who choose to marry under the Marriage Act or those who adopt the household economy of the elementary family of parents and children. There are other people who are more concerned about the breakdown of the traditional extended family system and the failure of men to carry out its obligations, as in the common case of an heir who refuses to support a widow from property in the deceased's estate.

MAJORS AND MINORS

Zimbabwe used another device to emancipate women from what Colonel Walter Sanford, Chairman of the 1913 Senate Select Committee in the Cape Parliament, called the 'thraldom of native law and custom'. He approved a bill authorising magistrates to apply African customary law and claimed that the Cape's provision of majority status at 21 years for men and women of all races enabled African women to assert their rights as majors in areas where Christianity and European ideas had made headway (Simons, 1968: 46–7).

Zimbabwe's Legal Age of Majority Act, 15 of 1982, which granted majority status at 18 years to all persons, had a mixed reception. Welshman Nube, B.L., Staff Development Fellow in the Law Department, University of Zimbabwe, remarked (1983–4: 217–28) that few statutes in the history of the country had attracted as much debate and controversy as Act 15 of 1982. Critics complained that fathers lost control over daughters when they turned 18, and could no longer claim *lobolo* for them or damages for their seduction. Ms Teurai Ropa Nhongo, Minister of Community Development and Women's Affairs, told a gathering of delegates assembled to discuss women's rights in October 1984, that 'women feel certain aspects of customary law are simply obsolete and out of step with the situation in Zimbabwe today'.

The issue reached a climax in *Katekwe* v. *Muchabaiwa* which came to the Supreme Court on appeal from a District Court's decision that a father had a right to claim damages for the seduction of his daughter who had turned 18 before the seduction. Dumbutshena C.J. held in a judgment handed down on 7 September 1984 that an African father had no right to claim damages under customary law for the seduction of a major daughter. She could claim the damages under the general law of Zimbabwe which requires the woman to prove that there was sexual intercourse. Furthermore, a father of an African woman with majority status had no legal right to demand *lobolo*. The daughter was entitled to tell a suitor to negotiate with her father for the handing over of *lobolo*. If he refused, she was at liberty to reject, or even marry, her lover. In Ncxube's opinion, 'the institution of lobolo is inconsistent with the creation of equal status between men and women' (at p. 228).

ZAMBIAN CUSTOMARY LAW

The anthropological literature surveyed in chapter 2 of the present work contains the most valuable, and often the only reliable source of information about customary societies at an early stage in the colonial invasion. To account for this almost unique situation, we need to look at the early period of Northern Rhodesia's occupation by the British South Africa Company, whose Royal Charter authorised it to administer the Protectorates of Nyasaland and Northern Rhodesia. When they were transferred to the Crown in 1924, the African inhabitants had the status of 'British Protected Persons' and were excluded from the franchise which was confined to British subjects.

Professor Muna Ndulo, Dean of the School of Law at the University of Zambia, pointed out (1981: 67–73, in Armstrong, 1987) that the colonial regime recognised the customary law at the outset but tended to emphasise the superiority of the common law. A customary law wife and husband were not regarded as being lawfully married for the purpose of testifying in criminal cases against each other. Africans were not allowed, prior to 1963, to marry under the Marriage Act, and therefore could only contract customary marriages. Judges of the superior courts were largely ignorant and disinterested about the content of customary law. In the absence of published reports of cases decided in the local courts and without books on African customary law and practice, they had to be proved by expert witnesses, something that the received English law did not require. A local court justice was assumed to have the customary law 'in the breast', and needed no proof by a witness, but an increasing number of young people would run the courts in future and could not manage without the aid of systematic ascertainment and recording of the law.

Charles White, the local courts adviser from 1963 to 1969 when he retired, estimated (1975: 751–6) that local courts handled nearly 90 per cent of the civil litigation while 86 per cent of statutory crimes were tried in magistrates' courts. A digest of customary law cases showed that 12 per cent involved wives seeking a remedy against beatings by their husbands, and that a large number sued them in matrimonial disputes arising from their adulteries. Of 15 500 divorce petitions filed in 1968, in about 75 per cent divorce was granted.

In the absence of case records, information must be obtained in the field by collecting individual case histories. Dr Mphanza Mvunga collected data in this way for his PhD dissertation on 'Land Law and Policy in Zambia', which the University of London accepted in 1978. He selected patrilineal and matrilineal communities in different districts for intensive study by means of the panel technique, which consists of putting questions to groups of 'knowledgeable persons whose expertise derives from applying customary law both in the traditional context (such as chiefs and headmen) and in modern local courts, and those intimately affected and regulated by customary law in their day to day life' (Mvunga, 1982: 1–7, 48f).

INHERITANCE

Among patrilineal, polygynous Nguni 'the eldest adult sane male child is the automatic choice for an heir'. In the absence of sons, the eldest daughter inherits. The next in line is the eldest sister, then the father and next, failing other heirs, the widow. Her succession is not regarded as a departure from the principle of patrilineal descent because her persistent stay at the deceased husband's village means a willingness to belong to his paternal line.

The matrilineal Tonga entrust the selection of an heir to the *mukowa*, a group of persons who trace descent through the mother of the deceased. Good character is the primary consideration. When that is assured, nephews and brothers of the deceased have priority, males are preferred to females, but a woman of outstanding good character can be chosen in the absence of a suitable male candidate.

In all the areas studied, local courts agree that though a widow is not entitled to a share in the deceased husband's personal estate, her right to land is recognised and enforceable. She has a right to retain the crop fields and house she occupied during his lifetime, provided she remains in his village. If she remarries outside the deceased's family, she forfeits her rights in land left by him (p. 54).

DIVORCE

Although Zambian women have a limited capacity under customary law to acquire and own garden land and houses, they are denied any rights to family property or maintenance on dissolution of marriage. (Himonga, 1987: 56–84). Local courts have attempted to improve their position by adapting the law to changing conditions, but the High Court has ruled in cases heard on appeal that a wife has no right to maintenance by the former husband or a share of his property after divorce.

Zambian chiefdoms prior to the colonial invasion were made up of villages with self-sufficient extended families which provided food, shelter and clothing for their members. Divorced women and their children were taken back into their kinship group and absorbed in the joint family under the care of male kinsmen. They did not need support from husbands or access to their property after the dissolution of marriage by death or divorce.

Modernization has disrupted the self-sufficient economy and the traditional social order. In the words of Muna Ndulo (p. 60), 'The society is now highly individualistic, competitive and acquisitive.' Few urban dwellers can afford to maintain extended families in towns and support divorced women and their children. Women who earn wages and profit-making enterprises outside the home use their incomes to maintain their families and buy expensive durable goods like cars, fridges, cookers and television sets. To deny women rights to family property after the dissolution of marriage is unjust and causes great hardship. To assist, local courts may order men to pay compensation to divorced wives or share family property with them regardless of who was the plaintiff in the divorce proceedings. Magistrates' courts regularly overturn these decisions, on the ground that they are contrary to customary law.

Women married under the Marriage Act are likely to be better off. It applies English law which provides for property distribution and financial support in favour of spouses and children on divorce. Women married under the Act are often more secure than customary law wives and less likely to be left destitute upon the dissolution of marriage.

WIDOWS

Statutory marriages are strictly monogamous and largely confined to members of the well-educated, professional classes and upper-class couples who marry in church with pomp and ceremony. Most Zambians prefer a customary marriage. It is familiar, easily dissolved and enables a husband to marry more than one wife. It has the disadvantage of neglecting the interests of widows who, being Christians, object to the practice of inheritance by a member of the late husband's lineage group. If she rejects the man chosen for her, she may have to return to her village of origin with her children.

Dr Himonga describes the common practice of 'property grabbing' by the deceased's relatives (pp. 69–71). They

> seek to inherit the deceased's property and take it away without accepting the collateral customary law duty and responsibility associated with the deceased's role as husband and father. The relatives 'grab the property' from the widow and children who need it for their support. The term also signifies the disorderly and violent manner in which the relatives conduct themselves when taking away the property. This

practice has caused untold miseries and hardships to widows and their children.

Sara Longwe (1985: 22) conceded that the 'grabbing' was sanctioned in custom, but considered it to be a perversion derived from types of property unknown in pre-colonial times when private property was unknown other than clothes, pots and implements. In traditional society a widow kept this personal property and was looked after. Things did not 'belong' to the husband and the widow's claims to maintenance were recognised. The wage labour introduced gave rise to the idea that what the husband bought with his wages belonged to him. Since the wife's domestic labour had no recognised value, she was not allowed a share of the property to which, according to the deceased's relatives, she had made no contribution. The law should be changed so as to acknowledge that she is a part-owner by reason of her domestic labour, which enabled the husband to accumulate property.

Professor Ndulo, writing in the *Times of Zambia* (31 May 1986), remarked that the government had delayed the reform of inheritance laws for 20 years. He drew attention to other areas of legislation in which Zambia did less for women than Zimbabwe and Tanzania in succession legislation. In many ways the laws 'still regrettably buttress the picture of women portrayed by Shakespeare's Petruchio (*Taming of the Shrew*, III, ii): 'I will be master of what is mine own: she is my goods, my chattels: she is my house, my household stuff, my field, my barn, my horse, my ox, my ass, my any thing.'

The end result of customary law is that children and the wife who were most dependent on the deceased are ordinarily deprived of his assets. They suffer tremendous hardship and the family is split between the inheritors and the disinherited. Most women groups fail to realise that only legislation can get rid of some of these injustices. Women themselves are among the foremost property-grabbers. It is usually the aunts and sisters of the deceased who are most antagonistic to the widow.

Zambian women have failed to secure the badly needed changes in succession law that women in Kenya, Malawi and Tanzania achieved many years ago. Women are vital to the Zambian economy and ought to be recognised as a major economic force.

4 The Struggle For Equality

A THREEFOLD OPPRESSION

The leaders of South African women often complained of gender discrimination: a 'tripartite burden' which members of their sex have borne and yet must bear because they are women, workers and black. In other words, they suffer disabilities based on sex, class and race. The story of their oppression has been told in many books, papers, reports, declarations and, most significantly, in accounts of mass struggle. I intend to describe these experiences in order of time by following a trail which began in the early years of the twentieth century and continued into the present period of struggle for a democratic South Africa.

THE BANTU WOMEN'S LEAGUE

African women in the Orange Free State (OFS) went into battle in 1913 against municipalities which forced them to buy monthly permits allowing them to occupy houses in the segregated locations. In July, 600 women marched to Bloemfontein's municipal offices, delivered a bag of passes and said they would buy no more! The resistance spread. The protestors overcrowded prisons in the bigger centres and were transferred to neighbouring towns. Sol Plaatje, the Secretary of the African National Congress (ANC), reported on his visits to 34 women serving hard labour at Kroonstad; 52 women were imprisoned at Jagersfontein; and 800 marched, singing hymns, to Winburg's town hall. The ANC protested to the prime minister in Pretoria, General Louis Botha, that Free State women were in prison for refusing to carry passes which were not required of urban Africans in the Cape Province and were confined to men in Natal and the Transvaal.

The defiance campaign, which was suspended during the 1914–18 war, gave rise to the formation of the Bantu Women's League. Charlotte Maxeke (1874–1939), the League's president, led a deputation to Botha, who undertook to find a solution to the problem of passes for women. The permit system was done away with in 1920, and Charlotte found an honoured place in the history of the liberation movement. Born Charlotte Manye, at Ramakgopa in the northern Transvaal, she joined an African choir which toured Britain and the United States in the early 1890s. The choir broke up in Ohio State, and she went to a local college, Wilberforce University, run by the African Methodist Episcopal Church. She married a fellow South African student, Marshall Maxeke, returned to teach in the northern Transvaal around 1903, founded the Women's League and worked closely with the ANC (Walshe, 1970: 81, 84; Parsons, 1982: 236–7; Pampallis, 1991: 113).

Recent publications have given more information about the role of Charlotte Maxeke and the anti-pass campaign in Bloemfontein and locations in neighbouring towns. Miriam Basner, in her biographical account of former Senator Hyman Basner (1993), describes his relations with Charlotte Maxeke.

The chief magistrate of Johannesburg set up a bureau in a small hut in the prisoners' yard to interview Africans arrested under pass laws, deserters from mining compounds and Africans living in the municipal location without a permit, the person chosen for the job was Charlotte Maxeke who was ideal for this purpose and became known as the Prisoners' Friend.

Julia Wells (1992) reports that the crisis of women's passes followed the disturbances caused by the Anglo-Boer War of 1899–1902. Thousands of refugees fled from the rural areas to Bloemfontein.

The all-white town council made regulations which allowed black businesses to trade in the location only, and not in Bloemfontein itself, and forced African men and women to carry residential passes under the terms of section 2 of Law 8 of 1983.

Women in Waaihoek location refused to carry passes and marched in strength to the African police station where they tore up their passes stating that they preferred arrest and imprisonment to being compelled to carry passes.

On 29 May 1913 about 600 women marched to the Magistrates' Court carrying sticks and Union Jacks as emblems of liberty.

WITHOUT WOMEN

The African National Congress (ANC) saw the light of day on 8 January 1912, in Bloemfontein. Originally called The South

African Native National Congress, it was a wholly male organisation, a mirror image of the all-white male parliament established under the Act of Union which came into force on 31 May 1910.

Under the ANC's constitution, ratified in 1919, its membership was confined to men belonging to the 'aboriginal races of Africa', including Coloured, of whom one ancestor was assumed to be an indigenous African. There were three groups of full members: hereditary chiefs who belonged to an 'upper house'; men aged 18 years and over, who paid an annual subscription fee of 2s 6d; and honourary members, consisting of men who had rendered outstanding service to the African people.

Peter Walshe, the leading historian of the ANC in the period before 1953, reported, without comment, that 'auxiliary membership existed for the Bantu Women's National League. The women lacked the vote and were responsible for providing shelter and entertainment for delegates' (Walshe, 1970: 206). One reason for this drastic exclusion of women from the benefits of full membership, and the support they would provide for the ANC's cause, was the composition of Parliament and its franchise. Congress claimed that Africans had 'a constitutional right . . . to direct representation by members of their own race in all legislative bodies of the land, and refused to concede even the theoretical possibility of bargaining away the Cape common roll' (pp. 113–14). The ANC leaders wanted parity with whites in a parliament consisting of men only at a time when the presence of women in party ranks seemed to be irrelevant to the political struggle for power.

Africans, like Afrikaners, were patriarchs. In 1990, Nelson Mandela, then deputy president of the ANC, addressing a workshop on 'Gender Today and Tomorrow' (Mabandla et al., 1990: 6) said: 'South African society is profoundly patriarchal . . . We men, both black and white including many in the ANC, should accept our share of responsibility for the sexist stereotyping of women in our society and in our homes.' A woman's proper place was regarded as being in the home, producing and raising children, managing the household and catering for the man's needs of sex, food and labour.

This was the prevalent view also among white men. They excluded their wives and daughters from parliament and the franchise during 20 years of the Union's existence, until the suffragettes got their way after much agitation. Hertzog's government extended the vote in 1930 to all white women over 21 years of age and to all white men in 1931. The number of white voters rose from 410 728 in 1929 to 850 162 in 1931, whereas the number of Coloured, African and Indian voters fell from 41 744 to 38 991 and decreased relatively from 9.3 per cent to 4.4 per cent of the total electorate (Simons and Simons, 1969: 429-30, 661 note 31).

Discrimination on grounds of colour consequently became a feature of the Cape's franchise for the first time since the grant of representative government to the Colony in 1853. Having thus cleared the ground for his main objective, Hertzog published four interlinked racist bills in 1926, one of which would remove Africans from the Cape Electoral Roll. The bills failed to get beyond the first reading and were defeated in 1927, 1929 and 1930, because of inability to obtain the two-thirds majority of both Houses required by the Union constitution for the removal of Africans from the Common Electoral Roll.

The fusion in 1934 of the two main white supremacy parties into the United South African National Party enabled Hertzog to solve the problem. Parliament passed the Representation of Natives Act of 1936 which deprived Africans of the franchise and created a Native Representative Council consisting of six white officials, four nominated and twelve elected Africans, who received a stipend of £120 a year, discussed grievances and offered advice, which was usually ignored. 'We have been asked to co-operate with a toy telephone,' said Councillor Paul Mosaka in 1946, on the brink of the NRC's collapse. 'We have been speaking into an apparatus which cannot transmit sound and at the end of which there is nobody to receive the message' (Simons and Simons, 1969: 495).

UNDER XUMA'S RULE

Dr Alfred Bitini Xuma MD (1893–1962), practising physician and President-General of the ANC from 1940 to 1949, transformed Congress and 'Gradually, with patience and determination . . . built the attenuated and chaotic movement into an organisation able to mount the Defiance Campaign of 1952 and to generate a paid-up membership approaching 100 000' (Walshe, 1970: 258).

He was largely responsible for the drafting of a new constitution which the annual conference adopted in 1943. It set the aim of working for 'full participation of the African in the government of South Africa', eliminated the 'Auxiliary Women' section and admitted to membership anyone over the age of 17 who adhered to the aims of Congress and paid the annual subscription of 2s 6d. Women had full equality with men at branch level.

The Conference also directed the National Executive Committee to form Women's Leagues and Congress Youth Leagues (CYL). The African National Congress Women's League was accordingly introduced with Dr Xuma's American-born wife, Madie Hall, as the first president. She headed the Women's League from 1943 to 1948, founded the Zenzile self-help movement, was elected president of the National Council of the S.A. Young Women's Christian Association, then returned to the United States after Dr Xuma's death in 1962.

Though membership of the CYL under its 1944 constitution was 'open to all African men and women between the ages of 12 and 40', the only woman among the leaders was Vivienne Ncakeni, an outspoken member of the Transvaal African Teachers' Association, who participated at foundation meetings of the Youth League. Its leaders soon divided into separate ideological streams, the main ones being Africanists and Nationalists. Peter Walshe (1970: 355–8) listed the ANC members tentatively as Lembede, Sisulu, Mandela and Ramoroka, who put forward a modified version of the slogan 'Africa for Africans'; and the Nationalists, or African Nationalists, involving Ngubane, Mda, Mbobo, Tambo, Yengwa and Vivienne Ncakeni. (For biographical details, see Gerhart and Thomas, 1977.)

The factions joined forces in attacks on the Communist Party. They accused it of using a class analysis to limit the growth of African nationalism. In 1945 the Transvaal Congress accepted a motion proposed by Limbade, Mandela, Sisulu and Tambo rejecting dual membership. Members of political parties were to be expelled from Congress unless they resigned from these bodies. Another attempt was made in 1947 to clip communist wings, but 'This time the resolution was lost by thirty-two votes to thirty and communist witch-hunt was again avoided' (Walshe, 1970: 357).

UNDER APARTHEID

Africanists and communists found common ground at an ANC meeting held in 1946 where a large majority of the 500 delegates present voted for a motion introduced by Limbede and Moses Kotane urging Africans to struggle for full citizen rights and boycott elections to the Native Representative Council and Parliament. Two years later the National Party headed by Dr D.F. Malan came to power on a platform to totalitarian apartheid. In 1950 parliament passed the Suppression of Communism Act outlawing the Communist Party. James Moroka, President-General of the ANC from 1949 to 1952, summoned the ANC's National Executive Committee to an emergency meeting. It decided on a national day of protest, a stay-at-home of freedom lovers and a demonstration against the Unlawful Organisations Bill, the forerunner of the Suppression Act. Walter Max Ulyate Sisulu, a founding member of the ANC Youth League and secretary-general of the ANC from 1949 to 1954, pointed out that though appearing to be aimed against communists, the bill was designed to suppress the struggles of all oppressed peoples. The whites were determined to keep Africans in a state of permanent subordination, which the ANC would resist by all the means at its disposal. (Simons and Simons, 1969: 605f).

June 26 was declared a national day of protest and mourning. Dr Moroka called on Africans to put their eight million force behind the principles of democracy, in alliance with other freedom-loving people. Leaders of the Indian Congress, African Political Organization (APO) and Communist Party pledged their support. The Congress Alliance was taking shape.

Renamed Freedom Day, 26 June became a focal point for resistance in later years. It was on 26 June 1952 that the ANC launched a campaign for the defiance of unjust laws. It resulted in the imprisonment of more than 8000 defiers and the enactment of more repressive laws. The Public Safety Act of 1953 authorised the government to proclaim a state of emergency, which amounted to martial law, for twelve months at a time.

The Criminal Laws Amendment Act of 1953 imposed a maximum sentence of £300 fine, three years' imprisonment and ten lashes for breaking a law in the course of protesting against a law. Persons who incited others to commit such an offence were liable to a fine of £500, five years' imprisonment and 15 lashes.

The penalties were harsh enough to deter any defier other than the most hardy and committed. Professor Z.K. Matthews, President of the ANC in the Cape, suggested a way out of the choice between surrender and imprisonment. He proposed in a presidential address to the Cape Congress on 15 August 1953 that a National Convention be convened representing South African irrespective of race and colour. The delegates would meet in a Congress of the People to draw up a Freedom Charter for a future democratic South Africa (Matthews, 1983: 168–77).

Zachariah Keodirelang, 'Z.K.' Matthews (1901–68) was a member of the Natives' Representative Council from 1942 to 1950. He 'exercised a major guiding and moderating influence on African political history in its most crucial period, and was at the same time South Africa's, and perhaps the continent's, most distinguished African intellectual' (Karis and Carter, 1977, vol. 4: 79–81). While acting principal of Fort Hare University College he was joined by 155 other men and women accused of treason in a trial that began on 5 December 1956 and ended on 29 March 1961, when the remaining accused were found not guilty. Oswald Pirow, the chief prosecutor, a former Minister of Justice with pro-Nazi tendencies, made the Freedom Charter the focal point of the indictment, claiming that its aims of abolishing race discrimination and granting equal rights to all South Africans could be realised, if at all, only by violence amounting to insurrection.

THE FREEDOM CHARTER

The Congress of the People which adopted the Charter took place on 25–26 June 1955 at Kliptown, 15 miles from Johannesburg. It was attended by 2884 delegates, consisting of 2222 Africans, 320 Indians, 230 Coloured and 112 whites. Policemen and members of the Special Branch were also present, taking photographs of all white delegates and recording everything that was said. Towards the end of the second day, special branch detectives and police armed with sten guns and rifles invaded the delegates' enclosure, removed documents, cameras, rolls of film, monies collected from literature sales and huge quantities of literature. It was announced that treason was suspected (Karis and Carter, 1977, vol. 3: 61–3).

The Charter was partly a restatement of the aims contained in Dr Xuma's Bill of Rights 1943 which demanded full citizenship rights on a par with those enjoyed by whites, the right to vote and be elected to parliament, and the repeal of all laws and practices that discriminated against the African on the basis of race, creed or colour in South Africa. These demands were set out in a declaration entitled 'African Claims in South Africa'. It included 'The Atlantic Charter from the Standpoint of Africans within the Union of South Africa', and was drafted by a special committee whose finding were unanimously adopted by the annual conference of the ANC at Bloemfontein on 16 December 1943.

In addition to a restatement of aims taken from the Claims, the Freedom Charter called for the public ownership of mines, banks and industrial monopolies. Though far removed from the ANC's traditional economic policy of denouncing discrimination and demanding equal opportunities, the socialist tendency in the clause entitled 'The People shall share in the country's wealth' aroused less interest than the Preamble's declaration that 'South Africa belongs to all who live in it, black and white, and . . . no government can justly claim authority unless it is based on the authority of the people.' This, said Africanists, amounted to a betrayal of their claim that Africa belonged to Africans alone.

TREASON AND EQUALITY

> Treason doth never prosper: what's the reason?
> For if it prosper, none dare call it treason.
>   Sir John Harrington (1561–1612), 'Epigrams'

Oswald Pirow (who died in October 1959) had a strictly legal approach. 'Hostile intent', he said, 'was 'the essence of "high treason" and evident in the accused's demands for full equality.' They knew that to achieve the demands of the Freedom Charter 'in their lifetime' would 'necessarily involve the overthrow of the State by violence'. That aim was part of an international communist conspiracy to overthrow by violence all governments in countries where sections of the population did not have equal political and economic rights (Karis and Carter, 1977, vol. 3: 345–6).

The Freedom Charter recognised a link between capital and racial inequality, at least to the extent of calling for the return of South Africa's 'national wealth' to its citizens. This objective is compatible also with state ownership of public enterprises in a capitalist society, and falls far short of a mature socialism with centralised economic planning, public ownership of the means of production and workers' management. The founders of the ANC were radical liberals whose aims were, among other things, to 'unite all tribes and clans ... and by means of combined effort and united political organisation to defend their freedom, rights and privileges'. 'Furthermore, the ANC would agitate and advocate by just means for the removal of the "Colour Bar" in political education and industrial fields and for equitable representation of Blacks in Parliament or in those public bodies that are vested with legislative power or in those charged with the duty of administering matters affecting the Coloured races.'

The ANC has never been a workers' party with a socialist programme. It heads a liberation struggle open to members of all national groups and races. Its aim, in the words of Oliver Tambo (1917–1993), former President and National Chairman of the ANC, is to bring into being 'a united non-racial and democratic South Africa'.

'Equality' is the Charter's keynote. It is sounded in the Preamble's call for the building of a democratic state "without distinction of colour, race, sex of belief". An identical note is struck in the clauses on government, proclaiming equality of rights for all persons 'regardless of race, colour or sex'. The principle is extended to national groups. In the liberated South Africa[1] all people shall have equal rights to use their own language and to develop their own folk culture' (Simons, June 1985: 7).

The equality sought by Congress is formal, guaranteed by law and provides equal rights to all people. A formal, legal equality of rights is an essential element of a democracy. Another kind of equality is factual. It guarantees actual equality of power and opportunity by transferring the means of production to public ownership and distributing rewards under the rule: from each according to his ability, to each according to his needs. This is socialist equality which the Charter does not contemplate. The furthest that the ANC has gone in this direction is to declare its adherence to a 'mixed economy' of state ownership and private enterprise.

The wording of the Charter is not Marxist. In a survey made at the request of the defence in the Treason Trial of documents relied on by the prosecution, I pointed out that the Charter contained ideas and phrases drawn from the United Nations Charter of Human Rights, and has points of similarity with the People's Charter of the English Charter Movement of 1838. The Freedom Charter envisaged a bourgeois democracy based on natural rights doctrine and aimed at formal equality for individuals. It made no mention of the abolition of classes and the introduction of public ownership of the means of production, and contained no suggestion of a movement to a classless and socialist society (cited in Karis and Carter, 1977, vol. 3: 63–4).

The Freedom Charter left no doubt about the extent of women's oppression and their claims to equal treatment. 'Every man and woman shall have the right to vote for and stand as a candidate for all bodies which make laws'; 'Men and women of all races shall receive equal pay for equal work'; 'The rights of the people shall be the same regardless of race, colour or sex.' Biological differences and women's role in bearing and raising children are recognised as meriting special treatment in the form of maternity leave on full pay for all working mothers, 'with special care for mothers and young children'.

The presentation of claims and demands is an important stage in the struggle for women's rights, but it is only the first stage and unlikely to become a reality in the absence of favourable social conditions and organised pressure by women for emancipation. Christine Murray and Catherine O'Regan, joint authors of 'Putting Women into the Constitution' (in Bazilli, 1991: 35–6) draw attention to women's demands in the Charter and other manifestos for equal treatment with men. There are, they maintain, two contradictory approaches: one based on the idea of equality regardless of sex differences; the other claiming that women need protective legislation or special treatment.

> One can assert as a general proposition that although women bear the major responsibility in the home, running it and caring for children, the power to control finances, make choices and enforce decisions in generally the man's. . . . It is through the patriarchal structure of South African society that men are dominant. This structure determines women's lone domestic responsibility and the characterisation of domestic

work as women's work. It affirms that men are engaged in the
work that matters, work outside the home, and that in the
home, it is men who control while 'their' women labour.
(p. 43)

AGAINST PASSES

After the Defiance Campaign and adoption of the Freedom
Charter, the outstanding event in the women's resistance during
the 1950s was their campaign against the pass laws. The ANC's
National Executive Committee told the annual conference in
December 1954 that the Population Registration Act of 1950 and
the misnamed Natives (Abolition of Passes and Co-ordination of
Documents) Act of 1952 would compel all Africans over the age
of 16 to take out and produce on demand reference books
containing identity cards, record of employment, tax receipts and
fingerprints:

> By making the reference book producible on demand the Act
> in effect introduced a new pass which is applicable to women
> and to thousands of Africans, particularly in the Cape, who
> have hitherto not been required to carry documents demand-
> able on the spot. Subjecting women to powers of summary
> arrest is liable to grave abuse and will be strenuously opposed
> by Africans. (SAIRR, 1951–2: 30–1)

By 1956, when the issue of reference books began, numbers of
women were convinced that the pass was an instrument for the
control of their poorly paid labour and a badge of their inferior
status, humiliation and harassment. The awareness was given an
organised aim by the Federation of South African Women
(FEDSAW). Established in April 1954, it was conceived and
moulded in the combined forces of the trade unions, the ANC
and the S.A. Communist Party. Ray Alexander, the general
secretary of the Food and Canning Workers' Union (FCWU),
mobilised support from all three bodies and from the Women's
International Democratic Federation (WIDF) based in Berlin. In
recognition of the part she had played in shaping FEDSAW, she
was elected to the position of secretary of its national executive
committee. Its head office was in Cape Town, where she and her
family had their home.

A WOMAN'S CHARTER

FEDSAW's inaugural conference, held in Johannesburg on 17 April 1954, adopted a Woman's Charter: 'the first comprehensive statement of principles by the new women's movement and . . . a landmark in the evolution of an analysis of their position in society . . .' (Walker, 1991: 157 and Appendix, 279–82).

The Charter acknowledged that women and men form a single society. They share the same problems and efforts to remove social evils; but the emancipation of women from the disabilities imposed on their sex is a task that only they themselves can achieve. Lilian Ngoyi, one of the great leaders in the 1950s, rebuked husbands who preached democracy, but held their wives and daughters back from taking part in the struggle for equal rights.

These were set out in what amounted to a bill of rights, unequalled to the present time for its clarity and frankness. The aims included a universal franchise, equal conditions of employment, the removal of laws and customs which deny women equal rights in marriage, guardianship and family property, compulsory and free education, including pre-school care, the repeal of restrictions on free movement, association and participation in democratic organisations, the right to build women's section in national liberation movements and organise trade unions for women, and, finally, the right to 'strive for permanent peace throughout the world'.

Nothing less than the defeat of the apartheid regime could give effect to these aims. Lilian Ngoyi said as much when she told an ANC Women's League Conference in November 1955: 'We have decided to join battle with Verwoerd on this issue and we say without the slightest hesitation that we shall defeat the government.' Another popular saying during the anti-pass campaign in 1956 reflected what Cheryll Walker (1991: 189) called 'a mood of militant optimism'. It warned the government: 'You have tampered with the women, you have struck a rock!'

The first major protest took place on 27 October 1955, when FEDSAW assembled up to 2000 women in the grounds of the Union Buildings, Pretoria, the seat of the country's government. Most of the demonstrators were Africans, but Coloured, Indians and whites were there in sufficient numbers to make it a representative gathering. On being denied access to cabinet ministers responsible for the racist laws, four women representing the colour groups deposited bundles of signed protests outside the ministers' doors and joined the demonstrators resting on the terraces. Helen Joseph wrote a vivid account of the scene (1986: 12–13): 'Two thousand women were sitting where no black woman had sat before. It was a triumph. Their signed protests had all been handed to their leaders and now they could rest. "We have not come here to beg or plead but to ask for what is our right as mothers, as women and as citizens of our country . . .".'

The government hit back, choosing as its immediate target the Western Cape where, by 1957, the Cape Association to Abolish Passes for African Women had made the legal compulsion to take out reference books a dominant political issue. Iris Berger (1992: 207–9) explains that 'the extension of passes to the Cape formed an important aspect of the effort to expel the region's black population in order to create a "coloured labour preference area" '. This was the policy known as the 'Eiselen Line', imposed by Dr W. Eiselen, Secretary of the Native Affairs Department.

The registration of African women throughout the Western Cape began in earnest in 1954, and was accompanied by large-scale arrests, trials, imprisonment and deportations. Within two years, Berger reports, 2500 families had been 'endorsed out of the area and more than 2800 women living illegally in the Western Cape were ordered to leave.' The distribution of passes to women followed late in 1959, and within three months some 12 000 had been issued.

The pass tyranny spread from January 1956 onwards to rural areas, farms and villages with little resistance to the teams of officials who registered applicants for reference books. Large-scale opposition was encountered in Orange Free State towns, the home of the Bantu Women's League's resistance in 1913. The women of Winburg collected their pass books and set fire to them, an offence for which they were prosecuted. Women in other towns were inspired to follow their example.

The Federation of South African women decided on 11 March 1956, to stage another protest march on the Union Buildings to confront Prime Minister Johannes Strijdom. He agreed to meet African women only, but the Federation was non-racial and its petition included demands of all South African women. An estimated 20 000 assembled at the Union Buildings on 9 August

1956, and walked up the steps carrying copies of the petition. When these had been deposited, the women walked back to the bus terminus with babies on their backs and baskets on their heads. The Federation met in conference the next day, decided to move the headquarters from Cape Town to Johannesburg, and elected Lilian Ngoyi to the position of national president, with Helen Joseph as the secretary.

The petition presented to the prime minister described the sufferings of Africans under the pass laws. Homes were broken up when women were arrested under pass laws and lost their freedom of movement:

> In the name of women of South Africa, we say to you, each one of us, African, European, Indian, Coloured, that we are opposed to the pass system. We voters and voteless, call upon your Government not to issue passes to African women. We shall not rest until ALL pass laws and all forms of permits restricting our freedom have been abolished. We shall not rest until we have won for our children their fundamental rights of freedom, justice and security. (Karis and Carter, 1977, vol. 3: 250–51)

A COMMON SOCIETY

On 28 May 1957, Chief Albert Luthuli, President-General of the African National Congress, wrote his famous 'common society' letter to the prime minister. The Chief deplored the government's rumoured intention to ban the ANC and arrest 2000 more of its members. Such action would harm the country's true interests. Congress believed in the creation of a common society in which black and white citizens alike had the right to take part fully in the government and control of their future without domination by either group. No time should be lost in consulting organised African opinion with a view to consider the calling of a multi-racial convention to seek a solution to our pressing national problem (Karis and Carter, 1977, vol. 3: 396–403).

The only reply to these restrained and farsighted observations came from the prime minister's private secretary in a curt note acknowledging the receipt of Chief Luthuli's proposals. Strijdom died 15 months later, on 24 August 1958. His successor, the Dutch-born Hendrik F. Verwoerd, educated in Zimbabwe and

Stellenbosch University, and an ardent apostle of absolute apartheid, had a deep-seated faith in his mission. Chief Luthuli told the ANC's annual conference of 16–17 December 1954, that the 'Strydom–Verwoerd–Swart combination is possibly the greatest political misfortune that has ever befallen this unhappy land', but Verwoerd never doubted that his policy was correct. He listened with great misgiving to the 'Winds of Change' speech which Britain's prime minister, Harold Macmillan, delivered to the South African parliament on 3 February 1960. Macmillan said that it was Britain's aim in the modern Commonwealth to give people an opportunity to grow to their full stature in a society where individual merit was the only acceptable reason for advancement.

Verwoerd thanked the British premier but said, 'There must be justice also to the white man.' There were very great dangers in Britain's policies which might defeat the objects being aimed at. Later, on 23 March 1960, he told the Assembly that he saw black dictatorships developing in Africa, but 'We will see to it that we remain in power in this White South Africa.' The Bantu should be rooted in the areas inhabited by their forefathers.

PASSPORTS, BANNINGS AND BANISHMENT

To guarantee the continuation of white power, the government tightened its controls over the lives of its radical opponents. Proclamations No. 52 of 1958 and 138 of 1959 allowed the Minister of Bantu Administration and Development to restrict the movement of Africans in areas where unrest had taken place. Among the districts specified were Zeerust, Sekhukhuneland, Peddie and rural areas in Pietersburg and Potgietersrust districts.

In the years 1948–58 banishment orders for an unlimited period were served on 88 Africans. The Christian Council complained to the minister about the conditions of the orders: no reasons were given for them and no appeal was possible to the courts; the allowances paid to the banished men were totally inadequate; and though relatives were allowed to visit them, this facility had little practical value because of the long distances to be travelled.

François Erasmus, the Minister of Justice, told the Assembly on 29 January 1960 that in the last eight months he had prohibited

seven Africans, six whites and three Coloured from attending
gatherings, in each case for five years. The three Coloured were
officials of a committee responsible for organising protests against
the so-called Coloured Affairs Department (Anti-CAD); the
restricted Africans included Alfred Nzo, a member of the ANC's
national executive, and Peter Nthite, national secretary of the
ANC Youth League: and the whites were members of the
Congress of Democrats, including Vic Goldberg, his wife and
Miss Amy Rietstein (Mrs Amy Thornton), now Chairperson of
the ANC Veterans Association.

THE WHITE DICTATORSHIP

On 30 March 1960, the government took the repressive action
which Chief Luthuli had foreseen and warned against in his letter
of 28 May 1957 to Prime Minister Johannes Strijdom. The
opportunity to put theory into practice came in Sharpeville, an
African township in Vereeniging, 36 miles from Johannesburg.

My account of the subsequent events, in which I took part as
a participant observer, is concentrated on the declaration of a
state of emergency, the detention of people under emergency
regulations, the outlawing of the ANC and PAC, and the
consequences of violent imposition of dictatorial rule. My documentary sources are a splendid review by Muriel Horrell
(SAIRR, 1961: 52–87), an essay entitled 'The Nineteen Days' of
which my wife and I were the anonymous authors (in Segal,
1960) written on Miss Kathleen Murray's apple farm in Gra-
bouw, on the way to Onrus near Hermanus, where my family
had a seaside cottage; and the *Documentary History of African Politics
in South Africa* (Karis and Carter, 1977).

THE SHARPEVILLE MASSACRE

Robert Sobukwe, president of the PAC and lecturer in Bantu
languages at the University of the Witwatersrand, announced on
Saturday, 19 March 1960, that a campaign against the pass laws
would begin on Monday, 21 March. People should leave their
pass books at home and present themselves peacefully at police
stations to be arrested. No bail would be requested, no defence

offered and no fines paid. The campaign would be conducted in a spirit of absolute non-violence. It would be the first step in the African's bid for total independence and freedom by 1963.

On the morning of 21 March between 5000 and 7000 Africans marched to the municipal offices at the entrance to Sharpeville township. They came without sticks, other weapons and reference books, expecting to be arrested. When the crowd pressed against the fence surrounding the office, two white policemen opened fire, about 50 others followed, using service revolvers, rifles and sten guns. It was officially announced on 22 March that 67 had been killed and 186 wounded; of the latter, 40 were women and eight children. Firing continued after the demonstrators began to flee. According to the doctors who gave evidence at the subsequent inquiry, of the bullet wounds that could be classified, 30 shots entered the victims from the front and 155 from the back.

Verwoerd and other NP leaders tried to make light of the shooting. It was, they said, symptomatic of happenings on the African continent and could not be blamed on the pass laws or apartheid. Their bland reassurance failed to prevent waves of reaction in South Africa and abroad:

> In Cape Town and the Transvaal gun shops sold out their stocks within days to panicky whites, and inquiries about emigration inundated the offices of Canadian and Australian diplomatic representatives . . . protests against South Africa's policies poured in from every corner of the world. . . . Massive selling plagued the Johannesburg Stock Exchange, and speculation grew that the crisis would retard or halt the flow of foreign investment so vital to White South Africa's prosperity. (Karis and Carter, 1977, vol. 3: 335–6)

On 23 March, Chief Luthuli, the banned president of the ANC, called on Africans to observe Monday, 28 March as a day of mourning. This would take the place of the anti-pass law demonstration originally planned for 31, March and pre-empted by the PAC's action on the 21st. Serious rioting broke out in Johannesburg on the 28th, several hundred thousand Africans across the country obeyed the stay-at-home call; and many thousands of Africans crowded the Langa township in Cape Town to listen to PAC speakers' demands for the abolition of passes, minimum wages of £35 a month and no victimisation of strikers.

Verwoerd told the Assembly on 23 March of the ANC's plans for passive resistance and undertook to take immediate steps to meet the threats. On the following day, policemen raided homes and offices in the main towns. François Erasmus, a former Minister of Defence and then Minister of Justice, imposed a ban under the Riotous Act on the holding of public meetings in 24 magisterial districts. Luthuli responded by appealing to people of all races to stay at home on the day of mourning and attend church services. The stay-away, which the PAC supported, was largely ignored by the Coloured and had a lukewarm reception in Durban, but Africans in Cape Town, Port Elizabeth and Johannesburg responded in full force.

EMERGENCY REGULATIONS

Between 30 March and 2 April, the entire citizen and permanent force reserves, the reserve of officers and all commandos, were placed on stand-by in an amazing show of strength as though for an imminent civil war. It created a suitable atmosphere for the declaration of a State of Emergency on 30 March by Proclamation No. 90, issued in terms of the Public Safety Act, No. 39 of 1953 – a product of the Defiance Campaign of that year. The regulations were applied in 83 magisterial districts. A further 39 were added on 1 and 11 April, the total number covering all the large towns.

The essence of the regulations was an indemnity clause exempting from prosecution or civil law claims any state official or citizen force member who acted in good faith during the performance of his duties under the regulations. Section 4 of the regulations authorised the minister, a magistrate or commissioned officer to order the arrest without warrant and the detention of any person in the interest of the public order or of the person concerned.

South Africa's State of Emergency is a kind of martial law in which despotic decrees supersede the rule of law. One of its hallmarks is strict censorship. This was provided by the Publications and Entertainments Act, No. 26 of 1963 which set up a control board with power to ban the import of publications and films. The draft of the proposed measure was put before the Assembly on 5 March 1960. During the interval the government banned the left-wing journals *New Age* and *The Torch* for the duration of the State of Emergency, in continuation of a tradition that had begun under the Suppression of Communism Act 1950, which enabled the Minister of Interior to suppress the people's press by declaring that it was furthering the aims of communism. The first to be axed was the popular, well-informed and lively weekly, *The Guardian*, edited by an outstanding journalist Betty Radford, the wife of a leading surgeon, George Sachs. Her place was taken by Brian Bunting, the son of S.P. and Rebecca Bunting who were among the founders of the Communist Party of South Africa in 1921. It was banned in 1952 and replaced by a paper called *Advance*. When this in turn was banned, a periodical named *New Age* appeared. Then came *Spark* and *Fighting Talk*, edited by Ruth First, a fearless reporter and talented writer who was killed by a parcel bomb in Maputu, Mozambique. Political assassination of this kind left deep scars, but was less effective than the use of administrative measures to silence journals. Government Notice No. 296 of February 1963 prohibited listed communists and members of banned organisations from taking part in publishing or distributing any newspaper, pamphlet, book or other written material.

MARCHING TO PARLIAMENT

In Cape Town, where parliament was in session, white security seemed to be most directly threatened by the African revolt. On Sharpeville Day, 21 March, groups of Africans stayed away from work. Some gathered in Langa, a Cape Town township for hostel dwellers and family homes, to hear the PAC's spokesman Philip Kgosana, a young student at the University of Cape Town, discuss proposals for the surrender of their pass books to invite arrest. The local police used baton charges and firearms to disperse the crowd; the demonstrators stoned police vehicles and set fire to some public buildings. Three people were killed and 46 wounded. On Monday, 28 March, when the victims were buried, thousands of mourners assembled to hear PAC speakers repeat their conditions for a return to work. On the same day riots broke out in Johannesburg, and thousands of Africans across the country took heed of Luthuli's call to stay at home.

For more than a week after the day of mourning nearly all Africans employed in Cape Town's 'city bowl' stayed away from work. The local economy came to a standstill. The government declared a state of emergency on 30 March. Before dawn police began a nationwide swoop to arrest leaders and supporters of the extra-parliamentary opposition. They entered townships in Cape Town, and rounded up ANC and PAC leaders in Langa and Nyanga, and beat striking workers, but could not prevent the gathering of crowds as it became known that many leaders of trade unions and SACPO had been arrested under emergency regulations. Before noon more than 30 000 people marched in a column over 1 mile long on the 10-mile route from Langa to the city. Kgosana led the march. He intended to bring the demonstrators to parliament for an interview with the Minister of Justice, but the police persuaded him to divert them to the central police station in Caledon Square. He asked for the release of the arrested leaders, an interview with the minister and an assurance that the police would stop using force to break the stay-at-home:

> Kgosana was informed that his last two demands would be met if he would request the crowd to disperse. The gullible Kgosana, not realizing that his only bargaining power lay in his ability to keep the crowd behind him, took a police microphone and directed the people to return to Langa, telling them that the police had agreed to make concessions. The marchers returned home. That evening when Kgosana and several colleagues returned to the city for the promised 'interview', they were arrested and jailed under the terms of the new emergency regulations. A decisive historical moment had come and passed by, leaving whites shaken but still firmly in control. (Karis and Carter, 1977, vol. 3; Karis and Gerhart, 1977, vol. 4: 338)

A crowd of African women gathered outside the gates of parliament to protest and demand the release of Kgosana and his companions. A cordon of heavily armed police and soldiers surrounded the building and ordered protesters and onlookers to disperse, which they did after being threatened with a baton charge. Another group of women marched on the Langa police station. As they failed to obey an order to disperse, tear gas bombs were thrown.

During the night of 30 March heavily armed police, troops and sailors surrounded Langa and Nyanga and prevented people from entering or leaving the townships. Several thousand Africans, massed in Klipfontein Road, were halted and ordered back. Hundreds of Africans accused of inciting others to stay away from work were arrested. The cordons were withdrawn on 7–8 April when the inhabitants, now short of cash, returned on masse to work.

My dealings with Kgosana ended when I was released from detention and went back to my teaching post at the University of Cape Town. He asked me for advice on the conduct of his defence. I replied accordingly and reminded him of Sobukwe's slogan: 'No defence, no fine, no bail'. He must have had second thoughts, because he was granted bail, forfeited it and fled the country, probably for Algeria which welcomed refugees from apartheid.

DETENTIONS

Short of killing rebels, the most effective way of silencing them is to imprison them in varying degrees of discomfort and, in South Africa, according to race. From 2 o'clock in the morning of 30 March, the day on which the State of Emergency was declared, detectives and armed policemen raided sleeping households in white suburbs and African townships, and arrested, without warrant, wanted men and women. The statutory authority for this violent intrusion came on the next day in a government Gazette Extraordinary containing a proclamation which declared, in effect, that anyone could be arrested by policemen acting in the interests of public safety and order, and under the powers set out in section 4 of the regulations.

Many people of all races were arrested under section 4. Among them were the treason trial accused, members of ANC and PAC, leaders of the Congress of Democrats, Indian Congress and Liberal Party. More arrests were made in the following days and some people fled the country. On 16 May, Erasmus told the Assembly that 1907 persons were in detention, of whom 35 were women, all but two with children under the age of 16. An earlier count recorded 1451 Africans, 94 whites, 24 Coloured and Indians.

The Unlawful Organisation Act No. 34 of 1960, the draft of which was read in the Assembly on 28 March, authorised the Governor-General to declare by way of proclamation that the ANC and PAC were unlawful organisations. The ANC issued a defiant bulletin in April, refusing to submit to the ban and vowing to carry on fighting for the rights and freedom of the African people. 'We shall continue to work underground until the unjust and immoral ban suppressing the A.N.C. has been repealed!' The bulletin demanded the release of the detainees and included the first list of those imprisoned in Johannesburg, Pretoria, Durban, Port Elizabeth, Cape Town and country towns. They were 'crowded together under the most unhygienic, uncomfortable conditions', given dirty utensils to eat from and deprived of staple foods.

I was one of 12 white detainees held in Roeland Street jail in central Cape Town who asked for an immediate trial. Among the signatories were Brian Bunting, editor and journalist, Jack Barnett, a well-known architect, Harry Bloom, advocate and author, and Morley Turner, a foundation member of the Springbok Legion of ex-servicemen formed during the Second World War, who shared a cell with me in the modern jail at Worcester, 100 miles by rail from Cape Town (S. Bunting, 1960: 42–50).

Here we went on hunger strike in sympathy with the action taken by white women detained at Pretoria who refused food to draw attention to their grievances. The men joined and kept the strike going for ten days. It was broken when the women were divided into different groups, unable to communicate with one another, and doctors reported that some were in a critical condition.

Hannah Stanton, a British missionary in charge of Tumelong Mission in Lady Selborne, Pretoria, was arrested on 30 March at 3.15 am. She spent $7\frac{1}{2}$ weeks in Pretoria gaol, petitioned the Supreme Court which dismissed her application, and was deported on 19 May without having an opportunity to appeal. She concluded that the police were retaliating because she had regularly exposed their brutality in the township. She reported that the white detainees, both men and women, were kept in solitary confinement for three weeks. The prisoners were graded: whites had class I treatment, Coloured and Asians class II, and Africans class III, all under primitive conditions, regardless of differences in living standards and education.

On the sixth week of Stanton's detention, 20 white women were moved from Johannesburg to Pretoria. They started a fast on 13 May in protest against detention without being charged. During their hunger strike they learned from visitors that their children had been demonstrating on the steps of the Johannesburg Town Hall and had been arrested.

Alan Rake (1960: 15–20) identified three main groups of detainees: 'non-political' English-speaking whites, such as missionaries, newspaper correspondents and members of the Peace Council; former members of the Communist Party who had dropped out of political activity after it was banned in 1950; and the accused in the treason trial, then in its third year, members of the Liberal Party, ANC and PAC leaders, and lawyers who had defended African political prisoners.

Batches of detainees were released from time to time, often with severe restrictions on their freedom of movement and political activity. These conditions fell away and the remaining detainees were released when the State of Emergency came to an end on 31 August 1960. No detainee was charged with having committed an offence. The operation was clearly intended to silence protests against the banning of the ANC and PAC.

The ANC's emergency committee issued a statement on 1 April 1960 declaring that the State of Emergency was 'nothing but a naked police dictatorship'. Freedom of speech and organisation should be restored. Congress had adopted a policy of peaceful negotiations and struggle since its inception in 1912. In keeping with this spirit the ANC urged the holding of a national convention representing all South African which would lay the foundations of a multi-racial democracy.

OUTLAWED

On 8 April, 18 days after Sharpeville, the government banned the ANC and PAC, the main representatives of the resistance movement and the spokesmen for millions of voteless Africans. The bill authorising this grossly dictatorial measure was introduced by Erasmus, the Minister of Justice, on 28 March. In its final form the Unlawful Organizations Act, No. 14 of 1960, gave the Governor-General the power to declare the two proscribed bodies to be unlawful. The Act also trebled maximum penalties imposed under Act 8 of 1953 for protesting against any law.

Erasmus told the Assembly that the government had decided to call a halt to the 'reign of terror which the Pan-African Congress and the African National Congress have been conducting recently among the Bantu peoples of South Africa . . . and to the activities of the terrorists, White and Non-White, who act as instigators behind the scenes without taking an active part themselves'.

Only the three white members who represented Africans in parliament and the twelve Progressive Party members voted against the bill. Sir de Villiers Graaff, leader of the United Party, the official opposition, voted for the bill, in line with the policy of General Smuts, who regularly sacrificed principle in the interests of white supremacy and power politics. Few of the backbenchers who spoke were sufficiently well informed and courageous to draw attention to the difference between the PAC's refusal to acknowledge the validity of white interests and the ANC's willingness to negotiate.

The ban had far-reaching results. The legislators of 1960 were short-sighted and arrogant white supremacists, contemptuous yet afraid of Africans, and convinced that they could keep them in subjection by force of arms. They turned a deaf ear to the ANC's proposals for a negotiated settlement and ignored its warnings of continued resistance as in a statement issued on 1 April 1960. It declared that Congress

> refused to submit to the ban imposed on it by the Parliament of the Union of South Africa. We shall carry on our fight of the past half century for the rights and freedom of the African people. We shall continue our struggle for which we pledged ourselves to all the democratic demands of the Freedom Charter. We shall continue to work Underground until the unjust and immoral ban suppressing the A.N.C. has been repealed.

No big prophet was needed to see that a close alliance would arise between the Communist Party, banned in 1950, and the ANC, a newcomer to the shadowy life of the political underground. Political prospects for the PAC were less predictable. The ANC had a long record of attempts to negotiate with white supremacy governments, whereas the PAC made any avoidance of confrontation a damning condemnation. S.T. Ngendane, the secretary of the Transvaal PAC, wrote a letter on 2 November 1958 informing the ANC that the two organisations had come to the parting of their ways. The PAC had decided to distance itself from the ANC and on its own act as the caretaker of the policy pursued by the ANC from 1912 until the formation of the Congress Alliance.

POQO

The Xhosa word *poqo* means 'only, pure, standing alone', implying that people who called themselves by that name were Africanists seeking salvation for Africans. They came into prominence after disturbances at Paarl, 36 miles from Cape Town, where several hundred men armed with traditional weapons marched to the central police station in the early hours of 22 November 1962 with the intention of freeing some of the prisoners. The police intercepted them and opened fire, killing two men. The rest retreated and on the way attacked white homes, killing a man and woman who had come onto the street to find out what was going on, before reinforcements arrived at 5 in the morning.

Mr Justice Snyman, appointed to inquire into the Paarl incident, concluded that Poqo and PAC were the same thing, and put forward a far-fetched theory that Poqo planned to overthrow the government, create an African socialist democratic state and do away with tribes and chiefs. He also drew attention to the squalid shanties set aside for about 430 families and 2000 men living without wives and children who were excluded under influx controls. Added to these miseries were the corrupt practices of the municipal authorities who formed a petty dictatorship, imposed harsh penalties for trivial infringements of regulations and repeatedly raided the barracks at night to check on rent defaulters and illegal visitors.

Leballo claimed to be the leader of Poqo which, he said, had 150 000 members. Judge Snyman estimated that the actual figure was no more than several thousand concentrated in Langa and Nyanga in Cape town. On 29 March 1963 the local police arrested two young African women who had crossed the border into South Africa from Lesotho. Cynthia Lichaba, who had been

Leballo's book-keeper in Maseru, was in possession of 70 letters
written by Leballo to Poqo members in South Africa. Her
companion, Patricia Lethala, worked for a school principal who
was an associate of Leballo. She had been instructed to hand
various documents to a man in Ladybrand, in the Orange Free
State, the nearest South African town.

After the seizure of the documents, the General Law Amendment Act, No. 37 of 1963, which came into effect on 1 May 1963,
introduced the notorious 90-day detention provision and, on the
recommendation of the Snyman Commission, made it retrospec-
tive to 7 April 1960.

The Act authorised the Minister of Justice to order the further
imprisonment of persons sentenced for offences under security
laws – the Public Safety Act, Criminal Law Amendment Act of
1953, Riotous Assemblies Act, the sabotage clauses of the
General Law Amendment Act of 1962 and the new act No. 37
of 1963 – if he was satisfied that the prisoner after release was
likely to further the aims of statutory communism. Vorster added
that these powers were urgently needed because Sobukwe, the
PAC president, was about to complete his prison sentence and
'had undergone no change of heart'. His continued detention was
necessary for the security of the state. He remained in prison on
Robben Island until 13 May 1969, when he was taken to
Kimberley and served with a banning order placing him under
12-hour house arrest. His wife was allowed to join him in a house
in the African township. He refused the offer of a municipal post
and became articled to an African attorney (Muriel Horrell, Race
Relations Survey for 1969).

Verwoerd told parliament on 24 April 1963 that Leballo had
planned to launch attacks by Poqo throughout the country during
the weekend of 7 and 8 April, but prompt police action had
prevented serious trouble. Vorster claimed on 12 June that well
over 3000 Poqo had been arrested to date, of whom 124 were
guilty of murder. Muriel Horrell's list (Race Relations Survey for
1963: 52–3) showed that up to the beginning of December, 46
Africans had been sentenced to death, 6 to life imprisonment and
135 to imprisonment for periods ranging from 10 to 25 years.
The witch-hunt and the severity of the punishments assured
whites that they had no reason to fear for their safety. They
welcomed the '90-Day Act' which came into force on 1 May to
'break the back', said Vorster, of Poqo and Umkhonto (the

Spear). It 'was a landmark in the transformation of South Africa into a police state' (Karis and Gerhart, 1977: 672). All members of parliament approved the bill except Helen Suzman, the only one to vote against it at every stage.

UMKHONTO

The central committee of the S.A. Communist Party, in a statement published in *The African Communist*, of April–June 1963, accused Verwoerd and Vorster of 'steadily turning the country into an armed camp ruled by decree and martial law. They are heading for civil war.'

Brian Bunting, editor of *South African Communists Speak*, wrote an editorial (1981: 274) on the formation of Umkhonto we Sizwe (Spear of the Nation) in which he explained that the strike of 29–31 May 1961, decided upon as a protest against the inauguration of the Republic and organised by Nelson Mandela, was savagely repressed by the Verwoerd regime. Convinced that their call for a national convention to hammer out a new constitution would never be acceded to by the racist regime, the leaders of the liberation movement decided that more forceful methods of struggle were required. Umkhonto was formed in November 1961, with congressmen and communists among members of its high command. On 16 December, Umkhonto announced its existence with bomb explosions in various parts of the country. To meet the challenge, the government passed the Sabotage Act in 1962, and in 1963 introduced the 90-day law providing for detention without trial and opening the way to widespread torture.

RIVONIA

The High Command were given little time to plan and carry out a widespread revolt. On 11 July 1963 Special Branch policemen raided the house of Arthur Goldreich at Rivonia outside Johannesburg and arrested 17 men under the 90-day clause. Vorster said the tip-off had come from 90-day detainees. According to another version, the information came from a police agent, Gerard Ludi, who had worked his way into a group of left-wing university students.

Among the 17 men were Walter Sisulu, who was under house arrest for 24 hours and on bail awaiting the outcome of an appeal against a 6-year sentence for incitement and membership of a banned organisation; Ahmed Kathrada, a listed communist and full-time activist in the Transvaal Indian Congress who was under a 13-hour house arrest order; Lionel (Rusty) Bernstein, an architect and member of the Congress of Democrats who was under 12-hour house arrest; Dennis Goldberg, a Cape Town engineer and member of the Congress of Democrats; Govan Mbeki, a journalist and leading ANC member in the Eastern Cape; Raymond Mhlaba, ANC leader in Port Elizabeth; Harold Wolpe, a lawyer who had handled Communist Party money for the purchase of the Rivonia property; Elias Motsoaledi and Andrew Mlangeni, members of Umkhonto who had been arrested earlier; and a young lawyer, Robert Hepple.

Goldreich, Wolpe and two Indian detainees, Moosa Moolla and A. Jassat, bribed a young warder and escaped from jail on 11 August. They made their way by different routes to Tanzania.

Eleven men appeared in the Pretoria Supreme Court on 9 October 1963 before the Judge President, Justice Quantus de Wet. They were charged with plotting a violent revolution by means of sabotage, soliciting and receiving money from abroad, recruiting people and training them for Umkhonto. Justice de Wet said the case was actually one of treason. As this had not been charged, he would not impose the death sentence, but instead ordered them to be imprisoned for life.

Lionel (Rusty) Bernstein was found not guilty and discharged. Rearrested, he was placed under house arrest, escaped and fled the country. James Kantor, a legal colleague of Wolpe and his brother-in-law, who had not been involved in politics or Umkhonto, was discharged at the end of the prosecution's case. Bob Hepple, who indicated willingness to give evidence for the prosecution, was released. He and his wife promptly escaped and fled from South Africa.

Dennis Goldberg, the only white man to be convicted, was imprisoned in Pretoria's central prison. The rest – Mandela, Sisulu, Kathrada, Govan Mbeki, Mhlaba, Mlangeni and Motoaledi – were taken to Robben Island, at the entrance to Table Bay, about 7 miles from Cape Town. Used as a prison by the first white settlers, important chiefs captured in frontier wars were condemned to labour there in chains. In more recent time the

island was used as a leper colony until 1930–1, when the inmates
were moved to Pretoria.

Dennis Goldberg was released in 1985, Govan Mbeki in 1987,
Raymond Mhlaba, Ahmed Kathrada, Andrew Mangeni and
Elias Motsoaledi in October 1989, and Nelson Mandela on 11
February 1990, after spending 27 years in captivity.

THE FISCHER TRIAL

Three weeks after the conclusion of the Rivonia trial Advocate
Abram Fischer, QC, who headed the defence team, appeared
with 13 white men and women on 16 November 1964 before
magistrate S.C. Allen in the Johannesburg Regional Court.
Abram Fischer went into hiding in January 1965 to continue the
struggle from underground. The 13 were described in the charge
sheet as 'former members of the Congress of Democrats', which
had been banned in September 1962. They were Lewis Baker, a
Benoni attorney and secretary of the local SACP branch before
the party was outlawed in 1950; Hymie Barsel, former secretary
of the Society for Peace and Friendship with the Soviet Union;
Mrs Molly Doyle; Miss Florence Duncan, physiotherapist; Dr
Costa Gazides; Norman Levy, teacher; Jean Middleton, teacher;
Ann Nicholson, art student; Sylvia Neame, teacher; Paul Trew-
hela, journalist; and Eli Weinberg, a banned trade union organiser of more than 30 years standing.

Hymie Barsel was found not guilty; Schermbrucker and Weinberg were sentenced to five years; Ester Barsel, Lewis Baker,
Norman Levy and Joan Middleton to three years; Molly Doyle,
Florence Duncan, Sylvia Neame, Ann Nicholson and Paul Trew-
hela to two years; Costa Gazides to 12 months. They were
convicted only of membership of the banned Communist Party;
but not of having committed or even planned acts of violence.
Most of the accused were held for long periods under the 90-day
detention law and tortured for many hours by the security police
(Nkosi, 1965: 46–55).

Abram Fischer was released on bail to enable him to appear
before the Privy Council in London in a case involving patent law
rights. He won the case, and returned to South Africa, but on 25
January 1965 went into hiding, concealing his identity. He had
been struck off the roll of advocates on 2 November. Nine days

later the police arrested him. He appeared in the Johannesburg Regional Court on 26 January 1966 for a preparatory examination. Mrs Lesley Schermbrucker, his alleged co-conspirator, refused to testify and was sentenced to 300 days' imprisonment under provisions of the Criminal Procedure Act relating to recalcitrant witnesses. Other people who had been detained under the 180-day clause gave evidence for the state, among them Hlapane, Ishmail Dinath, M. Naidoo and Doreen Tucker.

He was charged with offences under the Suppression of Communism Act and other offences arising from steps taken to conceal his identity while in hiding. During his trial in the Pretoria Supreme Court, he admitted much of the evidence given by state witnesses, including Hlapane, Byleveld and the secret agent, Gerald Ludi. Fischer was found guilty on the main charges and some of the others. The judge said that the prosecution had established beyond a reasonable doubt that the accused, being a member of the Communist Party and chairman of its Central Committee, had conspired with the ANC and Umkhonto to procure acts of sabotage. He was, the judge said, a very serious threat to the safety of the state and was sentenced to life imprisonment in Pretoria's central prison.

DEATH OF A HERO

Abram Fischer (1908–75) had the stuff that heroes are made of. He came from an Afrikaner patrician family in the Orange Free State. His grandfather was a former prime minister of the OFS, his father its judge president. Abram was a Rhodes scholar, Oxford graduate, distinguished lawyer and Queen's Counsel. He joined the Communist Party in the late 1930s.

> With his qualification and background, he could have attained any height in South Africa's legal or political structure, but he was a man of principle and courage and never wavered, not only in his resistance to the injustices of apartheid, but also in his support for the basic principles of Marxism and the programme of the Communist Party which he believed held out the best promise for the achievement of a just society in South Africa. (Bunting, 1981: 345)

While in London for the case before the Privy Council he impressed friends and leading politicians. They urged him to remain in Britain, but, he said, 'I gave my word to return.' When Byleveld, at one time a chairman of the Congress of Democrats and a close associate of Bram's, testified against him and was questioned about his attitude to his former leader, 'Fischer', he replied, 'was well known as a champion of the oppressed . . . a man widely respected in all parts of the community.'

In 1964, the night after he had concluded the defence in the Rivonia trial, he and his wife Molly left for Cape Town. On the way he swerved when crossing a bridge to avoid a cow and crashed into the stream. Molly, trapped in the car drowned (Benson, 1990: 160–8). He stood trial after his capture by the police on 11 November 1965 with this tragedy hanging over him; and made a statement from the dock, explaining that he was on trial for his political beliefs and membership of the Communist Party. In his final statement he quoted a translation of the Afrikaans inscription on the base of Paul Kruger's statue in Church Square in Pretoria: 'In confidence we lay our cause before the whole world. Whether we conquer or whether we die, freedom will rise in Africa like the sun from the morning clouds.'

Helen Joseph (1986: 176) was allowed to visit him twice in gaol and found him 'so natural, so much like himself, the same friendly loving Bram', but distressing news came from the gaol before the end of 1974. Bram had terminal cancer and was rapidly growing weaker. Only then was he released to the care of his brother Paul in Bloemfontein. Placed under house arrest and allowed no contact with the outside world except for his immediate family, he died in his sleep on the morning of 8 May 1975. The ANC said in an obituary statement, 'He died as he lived – fighting and sacrificing his all for the liberation of the oppressed people in racist South Africa. He sacrificed wealth, fame, comfort, high position, a privileged life in an already privileged white society for the hazardous role of working with our cadres in the underground movement.'

THE END OF FEDSAW

The Federation of South African Women (FEDSAW) was plunged into confusion during the upheavals following the state of emergency imposed after the Sharpeville massacre. Leading members were detained, went into hiding or left the country. Lilian Ngoyi was banned in October 1961, listed as a communist and confined to Orlando township in Soweto where she died in 1980. Florence Matemola, a founding member and stalwart of FEDSAW in the Eastern Cape was sentenced in 1963 to five years' imprisonment for furthering the aims of the ANC. She died in June 1969 soon after her release. Florence and Frances Baard were 'the outstanding leaders of women in the Eastern Cape, a formidable pair of fearless women. They endured years of political persecution, bans, detentions, solitary confinement, but nothing could break the spirit' (Joseph, 1986: 162–3).

All members of the Federation's national executive and some members of regional executives were banned. Among them were Amina Cachilia, Bertha Mashaba, Mary Moodley, Albertina Sisulu and Violet Weinberg. Helen Joseph, banned in 1957 and again in 1962, was the first person to be house-arrested. For ten years she was forbidden to leave her home at night and during weekends, or have visitors at her home.

The Federation itself was not banned, but its membership dwindled until only a handful of activists remained:

> There is no single date which marks the collapse of the FSAW. It was a cumulative process rather than a sudden event. Perhaps 1st February 1963, the day on which it became compulsory for all African women to carry reference books, can be taken as a symbolic date for the ending of the FSAW. . . its members did not have the resources or the numbers to resist taking out reference books any longer. Grimly, reluctantly, it instructed those women who were still without books to submit.

Frances Baard, tall, massive, dignified and reserved, a woman of authority, stubbornly refused. In 1969, after having served a five-year jail sentence under the suppression of Communism Act, she was still without a pass book. She was arrested soon after her release because of this and sent back to jail for a further 14 days. Only later did she bow to the pressure and accept the 'terrible document – under protest' (Walker, 1991: 274–5).

Women were prosecuted for treason, terrorism, sabotage, membership of banned organisation, helping people to escape, recruiting guerrillas. Women of all colours, ages and religions served jail sentences, detention, trial, discharge and rearrest. Of more than 200 put on trial, 123 were acquitted or received suspended sentences and 83 served prison sentences with hard labour for period ranging from three months to 15 years (Bernstein, 1975).

BANS AND HOUSE ARRESTS

On 31 July 1962, the Minister of Justice, J.B Vorster, released a list of 102 names of persons currently banned from attending gatherings – 52 whites, 35 Africans, 9 Coloured and 6 Indians. Another 130 names were added up to the beginning of December 1963. Most of the leading members of the resistance movement of all colour groups were included. Of the 232 prohibited persons, all were forbidden to attend political gatherings; 66 to attend also social gatherings; 65 were ordered to report daily or weekly to a police station; all were prohibited from taking part in the publishing of printed material; 26 were forbidden to give lectures at education institutions (SRRSA, 1963: 41–4).

Twenty-five people were subjected to house arrest for periods ranging from 12 to 24 hours. The 24-hour ban was imposed on Sonia Bunting, Michael Harmel, Jack Hodgson, Moses Kotane, Alex la Guma, I.D. Maseko, Joe Morolong, Thomas Nkobe, Duma Nkowe, Alfred Nzo, Walter Sisulu, Jack Tarshish and C.G. Williams. The rest were told to stay at home for 12–13 hours a day. This group consisted of Rusty Bernstein, Brian Bunting, Mitta Goeieman, Rica Hodgson, N.I. Honono, Helen Joseph, A.M. Kathrada, M. Lekoto, Douglas Manquina and J.B. Marks. All were ordered to remain at home during weekends and on public holidays.

THE MINISTER

Balthazer John Vorster, the tough, authoritarian minister directly responsible for the dictatorial atrocities, became Minister of Justice, Police and Prisons in August 1961. Soon afterwards he put Hendrik van den Bergh in charge of the security police. The two men had been members of the Ossewabrandwag (OB), the Oxwagon Sentinel, a pro-Nazi organisation which opposed

South Africa's participation in the Second World War on the side of the Allies against Hitler's Germany. They were detained in the internment camp near Koffiefontein in the Orange Free State together with other followers of the OB's leader Commandant-General Van Rensburg who had engaged in sabotage, conspiracy, corruption and occasional political assassination, according to Prime Minister D.F. Malan (Walker, 1962: 715).

Though no less committed than Verwoerd to the vision of totalitarian apartheid, Vorster tended to concentrate on smelling out and hunting down members of the resistance movement, which he blamed on communists and 'white agitators'. In an attempt to crush them he used powers of detention, imprisonment without trial, house arrest and bans on movement and residence contained in a battery of security laws, notably the General Law Amendment Acts No. 37 of 1963 and No. 80 of 1964. These measures, enforced by hundreds of security police in all big population centres, aroused less international censure, said Verwoerd, than the state of emergency imposed after the Sharpeville shooting of 1960.

PROFILE OF A RESISTER

Elijah Loza (1918–77) was the third child in a family of four. His father was a devout Christian and ward headman in the district of Alice, 88 miles from East London, and famous because it contained the Lovedale Mission School and the University of Fore Hare.

Elijah left home at the age of 16 for Cape Town, where he found work at Bauman's Biscuit Company. Attracted to trade unionism, he attended political classes and joined the South African Congress of Trade Unions (SACTU), formed in March 1955 in opposition to the white-dominated centre, the Trade Union Council which admitted only registered trade unions and therefore excluded African unions (Luckhardt and Wall, 1980: 90–9, 20).

Appointed co-ordinator of an organising campaign in the Western Cape, he became the Secretary of the African Commercial and Distributive Workers' Union. Like many SACTU members he was detained on 10 May 1963. Released 90 days later on 8 August, he was promptly rearrested. His wife, Girlie, filed a habeas corpus writ for his release, but the Cape Supreme Court and Appellate Division turned it down. On 7 November, Sir de Villiers Graaff urged the minister to attend to the case of Loza, the first man to be held for a third term running, and was told that the police could not do otherwise to a detainee who refused to give the required information.

A few days later Loza was charged under the Suppression of Communism Act and sent to Robben Island. International trade union pressure helped to secure his release under strict conditions, forbidding him to attend gatherings or work outside his home. He had to report daily to the nearest police station. In 1966 the Wynberg magistrate gave him permission to take a labouring job with a building firm in order to support his family and keep his children at school, on condition that he had no conversations with fellow workers and returned home immediately after working hours. He managed with financial aid from abroad to keep four of his children at school.

Lydia Kazi, a close friend of the family, said that Elijah personified the conflict between an undying national spirit and granitic apartheid, a clash that gave rise to savage strife and a tragic waste of life. He joined the political underground, was arrested in May 1977 under the Terrorism Act, 83 of 1967, and held in the jail at Worcester, where he was beaten and given electrical shocks, applied to his genital organs. He collapsed and was taken to Tygerberg Hospital in July where he died. While in the hospital his wife and daughter Funeka were allowed to visit him for the first time since his detention. Up to that time, they said in a public statement, he had been in good health. Their request to have him examined by their family doctor was refused. The district surgeon's certificate attributed the death to a stroke suffered three weeks previously and which was not reported to the family.

The Terrorism Act operated retrospectively, coming into effect as from 27 June 1962. This, said Vorster, was the time when the terrorists began their training. The security police were allowed a free hand, without intervention by judges, magistrates and district surgeons, to keep political prisoners in solitary confinement for months on end and interrogate them continuously for hours. The methods used were described at length by Barney Desai and Cardiff Marney (1978: 129–42) in their account of the death of Hadji Abdulla Haron, who was detained on 28 May at

Caledon Square police headquarters in Cape Town and died on 27 September 1969. In addition to holding political prisoners in solitary confinement for periods of 90 days at a time, the police systematically assaulted them, beating them with batons, hose-pipes and fists, and kicking them as they lay on the floor. They were made to strip and stand naked for hours, taunted, humil-iated and beaten. Some victims became deranged and were committed to a mental institution, some hanged themselves in their cells, some gave the information required and turned state witness for the prosecution. Only the most hardy and resolute refused and suffered the fate of Elijah Loza and the Imam Abdullah Haron.

EXECUTIONS

In a year of great turbulence, sometimes verging on sedition and treason, seven men were hanged for politically motivated mur-ders. One was Frederick John Harris, a 27-year-old school teacher and the chairman of the South African Non-Racial Olympics Committee (SANOC), from which he was banned. This petty-minded and needless action by the security officials must have upset him to such an extent that he placed a time-bomb in the main hall of the white section of the Johannes-burg railway station on 24 July 1964. It exploded, causing damage, injuring a number of people and killing an elderly woman. He explained to a magistrate that he 'had intended a spectacular demonstration as a means of bringing about a change of government'. Mr Justice Ludorf found him guilty of murder and sentenced him to death, the only white South African executed for a political murder since the 1922 Rand Revolt. He went to the gallows singing, 'We shall overcome', the American civil rights song. At his funeral a young schoolboy read an oration on behalf of his parents, who had been banned. He was Peter Hain, who, in later years, played a leading role in halting South African sports tours abroad and was elected to parliament in Britain.

Three leading members of the South African Congress of Trade Unions (SACTU) in Port Elizabeth in 1963 were arrested and charged with sabotage and complicity in the killing of a police informer in January. The leader was Vuyisile Mini, an executive member of the local committee of SACTU. His fellow conspirators were Wilson Khayinga and Zinakile Mkaba, also members of the committee.

Mini, a talented actor, songwriter and poet, was the driving spirit in the local committee. After being held in solitary confinement under the 90-day law, and finally sentenced in March 1964 to hang for complicity in the murder, they were executed in Pretoria's central prison on 6 November, in spite of world-wide appeals for clemency. They walked defiantly to the gallows, singing one of Mini's freedom songs. 'Their execution set a precedent in South African legal history as three other men were hanged for the *actual* murder' (Luckhardt and Wall, 1980: 20, 177–8).

TOWARDS TRANSKEIAN SELF-RULE

Verwoerd told the Assembly on 5 February 1965 that peace would come to South Africa only through a maximum degree of separation, not territorial or physical segregation. Africans must seek their political future apart from the whites. This concept envisaged a vertical division into two separate and self-contained communities, each with its own political institutions.

He put theory into practice by introducing the Transkei Constitution Act of 1963. It created a Legislative Assembly of 64 'chiefs', the former district headmen and 45 members. They elected Chief Kaizer Matanzima to the position of Chief Minister by 54 votes to 49, while a majority of the elected members supported Chief Victor Poto, founder of the Democratic Party, who stood for democracy and non-racialism for Transkei and all South Africa.

Lord Hailey, Britain's leading authority on colonial rule, referred to Verwoerd's concept of total segregation and its relation to the future of the High Commission Territories, Lesotho, Botswana and Swaziland, whose governments strongly resisted South African attempts to incorporate them in accordance with an implied undertaking in the Act of Union of 1910. Hailey (1963: 124–5) questioned the assumptions about population growth, the continued presence of a large African population within the 'white' area, and the likelihood that it will tend to invade the political field of the white community. The scheme of satellite states – the Bantustans – is unlikely to prove as durable as anticipated by the Nationalist Party.

VORSTER AND THE ARM

Vorster told the assembly on 10 June 1964 that communists and their associates were regrouping in an organisation called the African Revolutionary Movement. It was distributing leaflets and carrying out acts of sabotage. The security chief, Hendrik van den Bergh, said that its aims and membership had been identified. Launched in October 1961 under the name of the National Committee of Liberation, the ARM had about 50 members, most of whom were so-called white intellectuals. On 27 September he said that the founder of the organisation was D.E. Montague Berman, who had gone to London to raise money and whip up support for the movement.

Verwoerd issued a proclamation on 25 September declaring the ARM – also known as the African Freedom Movement and the Socialist League – to be an unlawful organisation which carried on some of the ANC's activities.

Before leaving the country, Berman called on me and asked for my support of his revolutionary enterprise. I refused, saying I was opposed in principle to the use of violence and would not ask others to do what I would not do myself. Perhaps it was this restraint that made my department of Comparative African Government and Law in the University of Cape Town's School of African Studies something of a haven for left-wing radicals wanting to show that Mandela's militiamen were not the only people prepared to use violence to stop apartheid despotism.

Muriel Horrell (SAIR, 1964: 71, 93) noted that many alleged members of the ARM left South Africa before the arrests. Those who stood trial were young and well educated. The median age of the twelve, who were charged by 4 November 1964, was 26. Apart from E. Daniel, a Coloured man, they were whites. Among them were three junior lecturers, two university students, three newspapermen, two photographers, a teacher and physiotherapist.

Much of the evidence in the cases came from alleged co-conspirators who had been held under the 90-day detention law for considerable period from early July until the hearings began.

Five ARM trialists were junior lecturers and students in my department: Neville Rubin, a former president of NUSAS (the National Union of Students) and son of Senator Rubin, Alan Brooks, who grew up in Zimbabwe, Adrian Leftwich, John Laredo and Robert Watson.

Rubin and Watson left South Africa before 4 November. Watson was cited as a co-conspirator with Randolph Vigne, E. Daniel, N. Rubin, A. Leftwich and others from Cape Town, in a trial on 20 October of five alleged ARM members: Baruch M. Hirson, Hugh F. Lewin, Raymond Eisenstein, Frederick Prager and G. Cox, who was subsequently released. According to the indictment they had founded 'The National Committee for Liberation' prior to May 1962 in collusion with representatives of the Socialist League, the African Freedom Movement and other bodies. Hirson, Eisenstein, Prager and Lewin were accused of blowing up power pylons, traction masts and railway signals with the aim of showing their opposition to the government's repressive policies.

THE SENTENCES

At the conclusion of the trial in Pretoria, Frederick Prager was found not guilty. The three other accused, who pleaded guilty to some of the charges, were sentenced: Hirson to 9 years' imprisonment, Lewin and Eisenstein to 7 years' imprisonment each, John Laredo and D. Evans appeared in a Pietermaritzburg court on 12 October on two charges of sabotage. They were accused of numerous acts of sabotage in Durban, but were found guilty only of possessing explosives, and were each sentenced to five years' imprisonment.

Edward J. Daniel and David G. de Keller were charged on 6 October with causing damage to pylons and railway installations. Adrian Leftwich and Miss L. van der Riet, who had been under house arrest, gave evidence as state witnesses. On 5 November the two accused pleaded guilty to sabotage, their purpose being to encourage changes in the attitudes held by the electorate and government. They were found guilty of sabotage. Daniel was sentenced to 15 years' and De Keller to 10 years' imprisonment.

Alan Brooks, Antony Trew and Stephanie Kemp, for whom a separate trial was ordered, were found guilty of belonging to an unlawful organisation. The judge said that though they played minor roles in the ARM, they must have known that it planned acts of sabotage. The two men were each sentenced to four years' imprisonment, of which two were suspended; and Miss Kemp to five years' imprisonment, three being suspended.

Kemp and Brooks were released from gaol in 1966 before their sentences had expired. They claimed damages from the Minister of Justice and two members of the security branch for assaults while they were under 90-day detention. Kemp claimed R2000 and accepted R1000 with costs in full settlement, without admitting liability and to put an end to the litigation. She left South Africa on an exit permit.

Brooks demanded R4000 and settled the case out of court. While in gaol he was called as a witness at Fred Carneson's trial. Brooks, a British subject, was released on condition that he left South Africa immediately.

Carneson, a 180-day detainee, appeared at a magistrates' court in Cape Town during January 1966, on charges of sabotage and Communist Party activities. He was committed for summary trial which began in March. One of the principal witnesses for the prosecution was Alan Brooks, then serving a sentence for having been a member of the Communist Party, taking an active part in its activities and being in possession of banned literature.

Many people were detained in December and January under the 180-day clause as potential state witnesses against Carneson. They included Alfred Aronstam, Mrs Caroline de Crespigny, Simon Egert, Eric Flegg, Barnard Gosschalk, Bernard Huna, Gillian Jewel, Alexander la Guma, Zolly Malindi, Amy Rietstein and Albie Sachs. Since Carneson pleaded guilty to some of the charges against him, most of the detainees were not called upon to give evidence. They were released from detention at the end of April. Zolly Malindi and Bernard Huna were immediately arrested on charges of belonging to the banned ANC and furthering its aims.

Carneson and Malindi had been banned under the Suppression of Communism Act. They appeared in the Cape Town Regional Court on three charges of having met each other. Carneson was acquitted on technical grounds; Malindi was sentenced to three months' imprisonment. Banning orders were reimposed after their release on Egert, Flegg and Gosschalk. Mrs de Crespigny, a

British citizen, returned home; Egert, Gosschalk, la Guma and Sachs left South Africa on exit permits.

EXILED

Vorster announced on 4 September 1964 that from the beginning of 1965 listed communists would be forbidden to lecture or teach in any state-aided university, technical college, school or other education institution. He added that he possessed all the powers he needed for the ban under the suppression of Communism Act of 1950, and that of the listed persons who were still in South Africa at least three were university lecturers.

My wife and I read this announcement with dismay, but agreed to continue our normal family life and occupations as best we could until the contents of the banning order were made known to us. It was served by two Special Branch policemen during December at our beach cottage in Onrus near Hermanus. Professor Edward Roux of the University of the Witwatersrand received a similar order at the same time. It prohibited us from teaching or being on university premises for five years. We were forbidden to write for publication, attend gatherings or law courts, communicate with other banned persons or move more than 3 miles away from our home. After much discussion and consultation, my wife and I decided, in January 1965, to join the stream of banned people and refugees who had gone into exile. We obtained exit permits and left South Africa to settle in Zambia, where we hoped to find employment and continue the struggle for liberation and against apartheid.

The third university lecturer referred to by Vorster on 4 September 1964 was Dr Margaret Kalk of Witwatersrand University. Detained during the 1960 state of emergency she was released on Republican Day, 31 May 1960. When banned from the university in September 1964 she was in Australia on a scholarship from the International Association of University Women and went to Australia to study the use of electron microscopy as a research tool. While there, Vorster issued the order banning her from teaching. The Principal's Committee terminated her appointment but prevailed on the government to withdraw the ban. She was warned to keep out of South Africa and found employment in the newly established University of

Malawi, where she directed a multidisciplinary research project on Lake Chiiwa, and its people, Malawi (personal communication, dated 25 November 1992).

THE REPUBLIC

Verwoerd announced on 20 January 1960 that the government would hold a referendum on the republican issued, the decision to be by a majority, no matter how small. In fact, the result of the referendum of 5 October was clearly in favour of a republican constitution, with 52 per cent of the voters, all of whom were white, being in favour and 48 per cent preferring to remain under the monarchy.

Armed with this result, Verwoerd attended the London conference of Commonwealth premiers in March 1961, with a mandate to inform it of the change in South Africa's constitution while remaining within the Commonwealth. He received a severe rebuff from the African and Asian delegates, who condemned his racial policies, and withdrew the application for membership. The Republic of South Africa came into being on 31 May 1961 with much the same constitution as that of the Union. The changes were largely formal. The office of Governor-General became that of president, the holder, C.R. Swart, remaining the head of state, while the prime minister, Dr Verwoerd, continued to control the government.

The declaration of the Republic of South Africa (RSA) was hailed by most whites as a great triumph of Afrikaner nationalism. Dr B.J. Liebenberg, a history professor at the University of South Africa, wrote (in Muller, 1980: 437–9) that the transition to the Republic was a victory over the old enemy, British imperialism. 'Whereas the Afrikaner had previously been dominated by British imperialism, since 1948 he has not only succeeded in freeing himself completely from its toils, but also has mastered his opponent. Afrikanerdom has now disposed of all signs of its past degradation.' Verwoerd realised the one dream of many South Africans that had been unfulfilled.

Dr Yusuf Dadoo, representative of the United Front in London, wrote a message under the heading 'Verwoerd's end is near' which appeared in *New Age* on 23 March 1961 (Bunting, 1981: 267–8). He described South Africa's enforced withdrawal from the Commonwealth as 'a resounding victory for the people' and 'a stunning defeat for Verwoerd'. It was also a 'dismal failure for Macmillan in his frantic attempt to retain Dr Verwoerd's Government within the Commonwealth'. The world, he wrote, was 'solidly against Verwoerd's racial policies' and concluded with the prediction that 'Verwoerd's end is near'.

Dadoo's condemnation was far removed from the opinions of the white electorate, who went to the polls in a general election on 30 March 1966. The Nationalists won 126 seats, reduced the United Party's share to 39 and demolished the Progressive Party, leaving it with only the one seat held by Mrs Helen Suzman, the member for Houghton, a wealthy, upper-class constituency in Johannesburg.

This was the second largest majority in South Africa's political history, being exceeded only by the United Party's victory in 1938 elections when the Nationalists won 27 seats in a House of 153. This was an 'all-time low', said Senator Jan de Klerk, the father of President F.W. de Klerk, in 1956. 'In the political sphere the Nationalist Party was practically paralysed, and we had this wild flow of Communism engulfing the workers on the Rand.' Afrikaner churches and organisations combined to rescue Afrikaner workers from communism, liberalism and non-racial trade unions (Simons and Simons, 1969: 524–5).

ASSASSINATION

On 6 September 1966, less than six months after his electoral victory, Verwoerd was stabbed to death in the Assembly, minutes before he was to have made his first big speech in parliament since the general election. The assassin, Dimitrio Tsafendas, who stabbed him four times, was born in Maputo in about 1920. The son of a Mozambican woman and a Greek, he was widely travelled and a remarkable linguist. He was hired as a parliamentary messenger less than a month before the assassination. This was the work of a lone killer, said Vorster, and added that there was no sign of an assassination plot.

Tsafendas appeared in the Cape Town Supreme Court on 17 October 1966. The Judge President presided, flanked by two assessors, one being a psychiatrist. Before the accused was asked to plead to a charge of murder, expert evidence was heard on his mental state. The judge declared him to be insane and unfit to stand trial, and committed him to a mental institution for life or until cured. At the time of writing this account, he was said to be still in detention.

After much lobbying the Nationalist parliamentary caucus which was held to elect a new leader decided on Vorster by a unanimous vote. He became the new president, and retained control for the time being of the Police Department. In a national broadcast on 14 September 1966 he reaffirmed his faith in separate development of white and black South Africans.

5 The Apartheid Years

NAME CALLING

Languages in multi-racial societies are rich in words that describe the skin colours of people and their alleged spiritual, moral, material and physical qualities. The naming system – its nomenclature – reflects their ranking order and interrelations. They were mentioned in earlier chapters and are repeated briefly for the sake of continuity.

Like other African languages, those of the Xhosa and Zulu, grouped together under the name of Nguni, have different words for kinds of cattle and humans. Dark-skinned peoples are called *abantu abuntsundu* in Xhosa, a white person is *umlungu* or *umphlope*, a coloured man in *umnumtu webala* or, more grossly, *ibahastile*, a bastard! The Xhosa word for Afrikaner is *umbhulu* (Boer), a word which also describes a policeman, otherwise known as *ipolisa*.

Colonial conquest and settlement added another quota to the glossary of ethnic terms. Western Europe's era of colonial expansion began in the early sixteenth century. Spain and Portugal took the lead, followed closely by England, Holland and France. Two Portuguese explorers were the first Europeans to sail around the cape of Good Hope: Bartholomew Diaz in 1486 and Vasco de Gama in 1498. The Dutch East India Company took the first step towards the annexation of the Cape in 1652 when it built a fort at the foot of Table Mountain and founded a small settlement commanded by Jan van Riebeeck, whose period of office at the Cape lasted until 1662.

The settlers seized the grazing land, water-holes and cattle of the original inhabitants whom they called 'Hottentot', a name possible related to a word *hautitou* which recurred as a refrain in songs that accompanied dances welcoming travellers and recorded by European explorers in 1620. This is mere supposition. What we do know is that the herders were widely spread over Southern Africa, had a similar culture and called themselves Khoikhoi, meaning 'men of men'.

Like other victims of colonial conquest – the Caribs of the West Indians, the Red Indians of the Americas and the aborigines of

Australia – the Khoikhoi were vilified, humiliated and oppressed. The conflict arose from competing claims to land and water. The Khoi fought back as best they could with simple customary weapons in a sustained guerrilla war. The conflict ended with a smallpox epidemic of 1713 during which an estimated nine out of ten Khoikhoi died. They never recovered to form an economically viable society (Smith and Pheiffer, 1993: 17). Their descendants were absorbed in an expanding Coloured population, the third largest group, estimated as 3.4 million in South Africa's total population of 40 million in 1992.

Closely related to the Khoikhoi are the San, hunters and food gatherers. Professor Inskeep (1978: 9, 21), a leading archaeologist who taught and researched at the University of Cape Town, suggested that the first South Africans were the hunters who immigrated from East Africa just under 2 million years ago. Called Bushmen by the Dutch, they were named San by the Khoikhoi and now also by anthropologists.

W.H. Bleek, the great German philologist, coined the word Khoisan to reflect the affinity between the two parent stocks; and also introduce the word 'Bantu', meaning 'people', to describe one of the four main language clusters in Africa.

The San stubbornly defended their hunting grounds and water-holes against the trekboers who travelled into the interior during the eighteenth century. Hunted and slain like wild game, the San were forced to retreat into semi-arid regions and mountain ranges to escape from Boer firearms. Those who survived adapted their lifestyles to the culture and environment of the settlers.

Colonists, sailors and travellers on their way to and from the Indies had sexual intercourse with slave and Khoisan women. The offspring of 'mixed descent' added a new strain to the local community. Called 'kleurling' by the Dutch and 'Coloured' by the English, they made an important contribution to the emergence and spread of Afrikaans, practised the same religious beliefs, usually in separate churches, and formed a sub-group of Afrikaner culture.

Martin West (1988: 100–4) explains that South Africa's system of population classification is not based on physical qualities alone. With the exception of Africans, officially known as 'blacks', people are grouped according to a number of criteria, including descent, language, appearance, acceptance by their community and lifestyles. Seven sub-groups were created for the Coloured population and elaborate procedures, involving much personal suffering, was provided for the transfer of persons from one category to another.

Ethnicity conceptualises the division of the population into separate folk-communities, each with its own distinct language, territory and loyalties to an emerging nationhood. 'Afrikaner nationalism represents a prime example of the ethnic nationalist vision. The ethnic nationalist argument is, moreover, the ideological link between Afrikaner nationalism's vision of itself and the apartheid vision in South Africa' (Sharp, 1988: 83). It spawned ethnic nationalism among the Coloured, such as the Griqua who are descended from white and Khoisan ancestors, and Muslims, formerly known as Malays, the descendants of political exiles and enslaved men and women transported from Java to the Cape in the days of Jan van Riebeeck. In recent times they acquired many converts, drawn from Coloured and Africans, who were attracted by the rebirth of a militant Islamic nationalism which took the place of earlier attempts to upgrade status by applying for reclassification from 'Malay' to Coloured, Indian or white.

THE GREAT MAJORITY

South Africa's estimated population in 1992 was 40 million of whom 30 million were Africans. About 17 million lived in the Bantu homelands together with less than 1 per cent of the Coloured, Indian and white population. There are ten homelands. They comprise 14 per cent of the country's surface area and contain 44 per cent of its population. The 22 million people who lived outside the homelands in 1992 included in round figures 13 million Africans, 5 million whites, 3 million Coloured and 1 million Indians (SAIRR, 1992/3: 253–4).

Some 50 years ago the estimated population was 11 million, consisting of 7.75 million Natives, 2.33 million Europeans, 0.9 million Coloured and 0.25 million Asiatics. Shepherd and Paver, who cited these estimates (1947: 3–7), remarked that Bantu was the accepted name for those Natives who were neither 'Bushmen nor Hottentots' (p. 8). When General Smuts told a Cape Town audience that South Africa's population was not 2 million but 10 million, it was a revolutionary notion: 'White and Black together constitute the population. Their destiny is inextricably bound up one with the other.'

The official idioms for blacks were Bantu, Natives and Bushmen. Whites called themselves Europeans and lumped other people together under the blanket term non-European. In Afrikaans 'blanke' was the approved word for South African whites. Dark- skinned people were called 'nie-blanke' or 'kleurling'. The S.A. Institute of Race Relations labelled its Joint Councils in 1931 as European-Bantu, Indo-European and Eur-African.

African was seldom used because it had no acceptable equivalent in Afrikaans, the dictionary term Afrikaan (-kane) being too close for comfort to Afrikaner (-s). I was appointed in 1937 to lecture in Native Law and Administration at the University of Cape Town in the School of African Studies and agitated for the replacement of Native and Bantu by the word African. It took far more time to change the title of my department to Comparative African Government and Law (CAGL).

Steve Biko's Black Consciousness Movement which rejected non- white and replaced it with black was a boon to Afrikaners who gladly adopted 'swartmense' (black people) in exchange for the familiar terms nie-blank, naturel and Bantu.

UNIVERSITY APARTHEID

In 1958 the 'open' universities which admitted students of all races had a combined enrolment of 11 694 whited, 441 Coloured, 458 Asians and 298 Africans. Afrikaans universities and the University of Rhodes (which operated together with the prestigious University College of Fort Hare) had 14 309 white students and no blacks. Fort Hare had 320 African, 59 Coloured and 50 Asian students.

Because of segregation, black students were taught through the medium of English – the language of free thinkers and social reformers – by lecturers, many of whom were critical of apartheid and race discrimination. In contrast, Afrikaans universities, encapsulated in an exclusive brand of racist nationalism, had little contact with the future leaders of Africans, Coloured and Indians, and could not counteract what they regarded as harmful and a potential source of revolt against white authority.

The Eiselen Commission on Native Education, appointed in January 1949, recommended the introduction of a separate system of education for Africans and the establishment of university colleges for racial and ethnic groups. In spite of long and determined opposition, the proposals were put into effect in terms of the Extension of University Education Act, 45 of 1959. The enrolment of Africans at the universities of Cape Town and the Witwatersrand dropped to a mere seven by 1968. The one medical school open to blacks was situated in Durban. It began in 1951 with 34 students; by 1968 it had enroled 209 Indians, 130 Africans and 31 Coloured (Horrell, 1968: 8, 14–19).

In 1960 – the year of the Sharpeville massacre and declaration of a country-wide state of emergency – separate university colleges were opened: one for Coloured at the University of the Western Cape (UWC) in Belville, another for Zulu and Swazi at Ngoya in KwaZulu, and a third for Sotho, Tswana, Venda and Ndebele in the University of the North at Turfloop near Pietersburg in the Northern Transvaal. The Minister of Bantu Education appointed the all-white councils and senates and their non-white advisory counterparts, decided the ethnic composition of students at the various colleges and enforced the general rule prohibiting them from admitting white students.

FORT HARE

The College of Fort Hare, originally known as the South African Native College, was deprived of its unique status by the University College of Fort Hare Transfer Act, 64 of 1959. It prohibited, as from 1 January 1960, the new registrations of whites, Coloured and Indian students and gave the minister full control of the staff; served notice that the principal, Professor H.R. Burrows, would be dismissed and replaced by Professor J.J. Ross from the University of the Orange Free State; dismissed two other senior staff members and superannuated six with full pension rights.

Five professors and senior lecturers resigned in protest, forfeiting their pension rights. One of them was the vice-principal, Professor Z.K. Matthews (1901–68), the head of African Studies, a distinguished educationist, member of the ANC and the dissolved Native Representative Council, Treason Trialist and leading freedom fighter. Born in Kimberley in 1901, the son of a

Tswana miner who later opened a tearoom, he exercised a
major guiding influence on African political history in a crucial
period. His father was a Cape voter, his cousin, Sol Plaatje, a
founder of the ANC, and Tshekedi Khama, a fellow student at
Lovedale.

He entered Fort Hare, and in 1923 became the first African to
obtain a South African BA. In 1925 he was appointed head of
the high school at Adams College in Natal where Chief Albert
Lutuli was his colleague on the staff. His students included Anton
Lembede and Jordan Ngubane. He married Frieda, a daughter
of John Knox Bokwe, in 1928; became the first African to obtain
the LLB in South Africa and was then admitted to the Transvaal
division of the supreme court. He completed an MA at Yale
University in 1933, and spent the following year at the London
School of Economics studying social anthropology under Bronislaw Malinowski, where I was a fellow student. After resigning
from Fort Hare, he joined the World Council of Churches in
Geneva and later became Botswana's ambassador to the United
States and the United Nations.

The South African Native College was opened in 1915 with the
backing of missionaries, African leaders and the Union government. Alexander Kerr, the first principal, guided its development
for 33 years, raising it from modest beginnings to the level of a
recognised university of high quality greatly appreciated for its
multi-racial composition and the presence of students from
Zambia and neighbouring states. Its friends and its student body
resented Verwoerd's arrogant assault on a venerated institution
which had spread the light of western, Christian culture for half
a century (Kerr, 1968; Matthews, 1988: 168–99; Karis and
Carter, 1977, vol. 4: 79–81).

STUDENT UNREST

Eleven Fort Hare students were refused readmission in 1960. The
Minister of Bantu Education told the Assembly in March that
their presence was not in the best interests of the College. The
SRC was ordered to disaffiliate from the multi-racial National
Union of South African Students (Nusas). Its president and
president- elect visited Fort Hare and addressed the students in
Alice, away from the college premises. On the next day the

students demonstrated in the dining halls and decided to dissolve their SRC pending the adoption of a new constitution.

A set of revised regulations, gazetted in September, obliged students to apply every year for registration, with certificates of good conduct signed by church ministers, or magistrates and native commissioners. The Minister of Bantu Affairs could refuse to register any student whom he considered unworthy; the rector could expel a student found guilty of misconduct by a disciplinary committee of which he was the chairman. The regulations authorised the rector to appoint the members of hostel committees, nominated their officers and arranged their elections.

Dissatisfaction continued. In 1968, for the eighth year in succession, the students decided that SRC was not wanted. Its members would become government stooges or be labelled as such. Students who spoke out freely would be questioned by policemen and victimised. Academic freedom did not exist.

A sustained offensive was launched against Nusas. The SRC's of the new tribal colleges and the UWC were forbidden to affiliate to it, but it flourished and continued to speak up strongly against racism and apartheid. In September 1963, the Minister of Justice B.J. Vorster urged students to resign from Nusas, which he accused of being a mouthpiece of leftists and liberals who had been tainted for many years with communism.

Vorster continued to take charge of the Justice Department after becoming prime minister in succession to Verwoerd, who was assassinated in September 1968. He carried on with the vendetta against Nusas, deported its officials, refusing to issue them with passports or, as in the case of Dr Raymond Hoffenberg, imposed a banning order. Hoffenberg a highly esteemed lecturer, researcher and physician at the University of Cape Town's medical school, had offended by acting as chairman of the banned Defence and Aid Fund, and by serving on the advisory panel of Nusas. The five years' banning order, served in 1967, prohibited him from teaching, writing for publications, attending gatherings, taking part in student activities, or entering any non-white area. The minister rejected the representations of a university deputation, whereupon Hoffenberg left the country with an exit permit, rising to great heights in his profession abroad.

The resistance of students to apartheid measures spread in 1968 throughout the English universities. Many issues were involved – SRC constitutions, attempts to censor student newspapers, affiliations to Nusas, the opposition to its policies by conservatives on the campus, the formation of the University Christian Movement (UCM) and the appointment of Archie Mafeje, a Transkeian Xhosa to the post of senior lecturer at UCT's department of social anthropology, to which the Minister of National Education objected, saying that it flouted traditional outlooks. If his views were ignored, he would use other means to uphold traditions. The Council accordingly cancelled the appointment, but issued a statement protesting against the government's intervention in university affairs. Angry students decided to hold a sit-in protest outside the administrative block where more than a thousand gathered from time to time until, after nine days, the sit-in was threatened by a crowd of Stellenbosch students backed by UCT conservatives. The police were summoned. They ordered the visitors to go home but said they could not provide protection if the demonstrations continued.

Students at other English-language universities took supportive action. Witwatersrand university students planned a protest march through the city but Vorster intervened to stop them. He issued a warning that if order had not been restored by 11 am the police would move in. He received delegations of students from Cape Town and the Witwatersrand, told them that sit-ins, picketing and protect marches were provocative and 'un- South African'. If they failed to recognise 'racially exclusive organizations' legislation would be introduced in 1969 to make these compulsory.

He had in mind students from the all-white, newly formed Rand Afrikaans University and Teachers Training College who, with the support of conservative Witwatersrand university students, had attacked the anti-apartheid demonstrators with whitewash, paint, eggs and fruit while the police stood by passively or took down the names of the demonstrators and confiscated their placards.

ENLIGHTENED CHRISTIANS

Verwoerd, Vorster and their fellow racists blamed communists for the promotion of unity between races and colour groups, but were no more tolerant of Christians like Roman Catholics and nonconformist sects – Seventh-Day Adventists, the Apostolic Church, Jehovah's Witnesses and the like – who opened their doors to people of all races and had a following among poor whites.

The ecumenical University Christian Movement (UCM) was regarded as falling in this category of die-hard 'liberalist- humanists'. Formed in December 1966 it was consolidated at a conference held in Grahamstown in July 1967 by members of the Anglican, Congregational, Presbyterian and Roman Catholic Churches. More than half the delegates were Africans, Asians and Coloured. It was reported to have enrolled more than 3000 members within its first year of existence.

Vorster said in August that he was busy 'looking at' the UCM and threatened to take steps against it. This was a signal for the kind of repressive action taken against Nusas: the interrogation by security police of office-bearers; the withdrawal of a passport issued to the Rev. Basil Moore, the president of UCM, who intended to take up a research scholarship in the United States; raids on the home of his successor, the Rev. James Moulder and the removal of documents. African university colleges thereupon banned the UCM from entering their grounds.

Father Colin Collins, the general secretary, reported in May 1969 that the police were conducting a campaign against UCM members. In the following month ten white students from Johannesburg were arrested while attending a church service near Turfloop, the University College of the North. Charged with being on Bantu trust land without a permit, they paid admission of guilt fines and went back to their homes, dismayed at the display of ill-will towards Christians by a government pledged to uphold Christianity.

Its repressive policies seemed to have achieved the aim of driving a wedge between African students and whites of racially mixed groups. Both the UCM and Nusas, while continuing to assert adherence to the principle of a race-free social order, acknowledged that black students had a right to stand on their own feet and manage their affairs independently of whites. It was apartheid, they said, which had imposed the doctrine of racial exclusiveness and caused it to spread like a plague to all parts of the social structure.

SASO AND BPC

The African Students' Association (ASA) and the African Student's Union (ASU) were formed in 1961–2 as student wings of national resistance movements. They collapsed after the authorities of the new universities established for blacks prohibited their students' representative councils from having dealings with Nusas. The message was loud and clear: association with anti-apartheid whites was dangerous. At the 1968 UCM conference about 40 blacks from the tribal colleges decided to investigate the possibilities of forming a racially distinct organisation.

The South African Students' Organisation (SASO) was established in December 1968. Its constitution affirmed the principle of one national students' organisation for all races in South Africa but declared that for reasons beyond their control, blacks were unable to take part in any kind of plural system. In the 1970 conference attitudes that had been carefully hidden came to the surface. SASO withdrew its recognition of Nusas as a national union, because 'in its principles and make-up, the black students can never find expression for aspirations foremost in their minds'. The emancipation of black peoples depended on the role they themselves were prepared to play. A SASO pamphlet issued in 1972 claimed that black students were rapidly consolidating their positions within the black community in a great surge towards the attainment of their aspirations. Black consciousness was their philosophy and correct approach (Van der Merwe et al., 1978: 279–84).

Writing in the same volume (pp. 355–63) D.A. Kotze, Professor of African Politics at the University of South Africa (UNISA) explained that SASO and BPC (Black People's Convention) came into being as a result of the increasing momentum of the Black Consciousness idea in South Africa. While SASO grew out of the now defunct multi-racial University Christian Movement and as a reaction during 1969–70 against the white domination of the National Union of South African Students, the BPC was the result of prolonged consultations among representatives of a number of African voluntary associations in the fields of welfare, religion, sport and education. The BPC was formally established in July 1972 after further study and recommendations by an ad hoc committee. The BPC, SASO and Black Community Programmes were crippled through a series of restrictive orders

served on employers and officials by the South African government during 1972 and 1973. The organisations as such were not
affected.

Cutting off the head of a chicken might not immediately
extinguish all signs of life, but death is bound to follow. Black
people's organisations were duly banned in course of time, as was
foreseen by the Transkeian Manasseh Tebatso Moerane, former
editor of *The World*, teacher, school principal in Natal and
member of the ANC before it was outlawed. He chaired a
conference in Soweto during December 1971 which decided to
form a political body for black people of all groups. An ad hoc
committee, convened by a trade unionist, Drake K. Koka,
arranged a three-day congress at the Lay Ecumenical Centre in
Edendale, Pietermaritzburg in July 1972. It was attended by
more than 100 African, Indian and Coloured delegates who
adopted a convention drafted by the ad hoc committee. It stated
that there was great need for blacks to reassert their pride, dignity
and identity, achieve solidarity through a political movement
which would express their needs, make religion relevant to their
aims and encourage black communalism – the philosophy of
equal sharing. Membership would be open to blacks only, the
term used to include Africans, Indians and Coloured (SAIRR,
1972: 27–9).

The conference condemned foreign investments in the country
because they supported the white economy and the exploitation
of black workers. The executive was told to write to firms, asking
them to withdraw their investments and not to take part in the
development of Bantu homelands and their border regions.

This appeal coincided with a decision taken in March 1972 by
the World Council of Churches (WCC) to withdraw its funds
from companies investing in or trading with South Africa and
other white-dominated states in Southern Africa. The 250 member churches of the WCC were urged to influence corporations
to follow suit. The WCC also decided to open a fund to combat
racism and provide grants for the welfare, education and medical
needs of freedom fighters.

Dr J.D. Vorster, the moderator of the Dutch Reformed Church
general synod, brother of the prime minister and, like him, an
ardent supporter of Hitler's Nazi Party in the Second World War,
said that the WCC was 'the most powerful leftist organisation in
the world'.

The disinvestment campaign touched a raw nerve in the body politic of apartheid. Banning orders signed by the Minister of Justice on 26 February 1973 were served on office-bearers and some other members of the BPC prohibiting them from attending gatherings, meeting more than one person at a time, visiting factories, printing and publishing works, entering black residential areas other than the township where the banned person lived, and taking part in SASO and BPC activities. The banned people included Chris Madibeng Mokoditoa, BPC's vice-president, Sathasivan (Saths) Cooper, the public relations officer, Sipho Buthelezi, the secretary-general, Mrs S. Moodley, Mathew Diseko, Drake Kgalushi Koka, a trade union organiser and Mosebudi Mangena, the BPC's national organiser, who was jailed for five years under the Terrorism Act. The trial judge, Acting Justice de Wet, sitting with two white assessors, chose to believe the perjured evidence of two African police witnesses and refused leave to appeal.

Drake Koka, in a circular dated 8 March 1973 setting out the terms of his ban, praised the Lord for having been allowed to carry on with his union's administration, though prohibited from visiting factories and addressing workers. He trusted the government to allow banned people to do their own thing if they avoided confrontation, which 'we cannot afford to do at this stage'. He appealed for funds to cover the union's estimated expenditure in 1973–4, amounting to R11 840 of which R6140 were required to pay his and the organiser's salaries of R2400 each per annum and the typist's salary of R1340 a year.

ISOLATIONISM

Escape from the white-dominated society was not possible or even desired. Blacks studied in schools with white administrators and often principals, lived by working in mines, factories, workshop and other enterprises owned and controlled by whites, were converted to Christianity by missionaries who taught the three Rs and the elements of western culture, all of which were necessary for the intelligentsia who formed the core of the Black Consciousness Movement.

The withdrawal for which they longed was limited to the minute sector of their lives resulting, ironically, from the attempts of secular missionaries attached to open-ended, multi-racial bodies such as Nusas to befriend them in a spirit of equality, fellowship and goodwill. Persecution by their common enemies made life difficult for the would-be benefactors and penalised black students who dared to associate with them. The desired independence from whites was for the most part a mental construct. John Cell (1982: 15) noted that in racially segregated societies,

> the subordinate caste must have two faces, two manners, to some extent two personalities, which are hard to keep completely separate. Outward accommodation becomes inward self-depreciation. From W.E.B. Du Bois to Steve Biko, the foremost freedom fighters have always stressed that the first and most crucial stage in the struggle must therefore be the liberation of the victims from the oppression that exists within their own minds and souls.

Like Esau, who sold his birthright for a pot of lentils, Drake Koka compromised his principles for an illusory security. Other Black Consciousness leaders were made of sterner stuff. Stephen Bantu Biko, the founder of BCM and SASO's first president, who was to die in police custody of brain injury, explained in court that students decided to drop the term 'non-white' because they saw in it a negation of their being. They set out to replace it with the term 'black' which was in keeping with the build-up of their dignity and self-confidence. 'All in all', he wrote,

> the black man has become a shell, a shadow of man, completely defeated, drowning in his own misery, a slave, an ox bearing the yoke of oppression with sheepish timidity . . . The first step is therefore to make the black man come to himself, to pump back life into his empty shell, to infuse him with pride and dignity, to remind him of his complicity in the crime of allowing himself to be misused and therefore letting evil reign supreme in the country of his birth. (Biko, 1978: 29)

Nyameko Barney Pityana, Biko's successor to the office of president of SASO (and currently director of the World Council of Churches' Programme to Combat Racism) said in 1971 that blacks must stand on their own feet, build themselves to a position of non-dependence on whites, and work towards a deeper realisation of their potential as self-respecting people. 'This was not the same as separate development, which dictates to us what we should have. We envisage a situation where we ourselves can make demands.' There was no close parallel with the Black Power Movement in the United States where blacks were aiming at the implementation of guaranteed rights. In South Africa racism was an established way of life. There was nothing the system to which blacks could aspire. They had to start doing things for themselves (SAIRR, 1971: 42).

GOING IT ALONE

Black consciousness was a highly refined and developed version of Poqo, the approach favoured by Robert Sobukwe and the Pan African Congress (PAC) as the ideal solution of the black people's burden. They too rejected fellowship with whites, condemned the African National Congress for practising reconciliation with resistance in a common society, but made no visible attempt to address the problem of coping with the evil and despotic techniques of the white bureaucracy and the approval it received from the five million whites who supported the dictatorship.

Defiance was necessary to sustain belief in the justice of the black people's cause but it exposed the resisters to the arsenal of repressive measures available to a totalitarian state controlled by political police supervising the activities of citizens in an undeclared civil war.

The ban imposed on the ANC and PAC in 1960 failed to deter obstinate militants from continuing the struggle in the political underground, but it was a dangerous undertaking to which Black Consciousness seemed to provide an alternative. The government's first approach was favourable. It regarded SASO as a convert to separate development and approved the use of 'black' instead of non-European, Native, Bantu or African. The administration allowed the new 'bush' college to give SASO official recognition, but the honeymoon soon came to an end. SASO's conference in July 1972 instructed the executive to have nothing to do with white racist institutions which held out false promises to the oppressed black people, and taught a biased version of history and social sciences. The conference appointed a commission to investigate the possibility of introducing a 'free Black university'. This simple-minded assumption of being able to compete with the government's structures was never put to the test. It was rudely disrupted by a revolt of students of the University of the North, earmarked for Sotho-Tswana people, at Turfloop near Pietersburg.

TURFLOOP

In 1972 Onkopotse R. Tiro, president of the SRC, was elected the students' spokesman at a graduation ceremony in April. He used the occasion to criticise Bantu education, white control of black universities and general discrimination against blacks. An all- white disciplinary committee expelled Tiro, a former mine-worker, and rejected a petition for his reinstatement. A number of students started a sit-in, whereupon the administration suspended the SRC, banned all campus meetings, and after waiting eight hours announced that the entire body of students, numbering 1146, would be required to leave the college by 6 May. This they did, protesting loudly, under the escort of policemen armed with riot sticks and dogs.

Petitions and appeals on behalf of Tiro and the expelled students came from SASO branches, Soweto residents, black parents in Pretoria and students who demonstrated solidarity throughout the country. The rector, Professor J.C. Boshoff, refused to re-admit the 22 SRC members when students returned to Turfloop. By June student leaders from seven black colleges demanded freedom for their organisation and the introduction of black councils and senates. The agitation spread to the University of Durban- Westville where a new constitution imposed by the council on the SRC banned it from affiliating to SASO and Nusas. The rector, Professor S.R. Oliver, told a graduation ceremony that Marxists and Maoists were to blame for disruption of South African universities. At Fort Hare the security police arrested 'Satch' Lekalake, the chairman of the local SASO branch, whereupon the SRC issued a statement on 7 June claiming that 'all Black institutions of higher learning are founded upon an unjust political ideology of a White racist regime bent on annihilating all intellectual maturity of Black people in South Africa' (SAIRR, 1972: 391).

UWC

On 13 May students at the University of the Western Cape (UWC) began a boycott of lectures in support of Turfloop students and later in the month refused to eat the hostel's food. After six had been expelled, the student body demanded the appointment of a black rector, an African, Coloured or Asian, in the place of Rector Silberhagen, and the installation of an all-black university council (*Cape Argus*, 10 June 1972). Four UWC lecturers criticised the administration for collaborating with the police. G. 'Jakes' Gerwel, a lecturer in Afrikaans and Nederlands – and today the rector and vice-chancellor – was visited by the police, who also interrogated members of the SRC after the student body had refused to comply with the rector's ban on SASO.

Student representation was the biggest cause of friction, mainly because the rector, Dr Nicholas Silberhagen, refused to allow the SRC to affiliate to the National Union of South African Students (Nusas), It took two years for a new SRC to resume activities, but within a month of taking office it defied the administration, invited Tem Sono, president of SASO, to address them and expressed solidarity with the Black Power movement.

Tom Swartz, chairman of the executive of the Coloured Representative Council, made a statement to the press (cited in Venter, 1974: 345–7) stating that 'Black Power' does not exist: the power in force is 'White Power'. Students would have to reconcile themselves to it or take the consequences. He had reminded the prime minister, John Vorster, that when the UWC was established the government promised to give Coloured students and lecturers all the privileges and opportunities available to them elsewhere. After 12 years had gone by, the university's staff of 75 included only seven Coloured, of whom two held permanent appointments.

STATE AND CHURCH

The government blamed 'liberalists', leftists and neo-communists for the student unrest, but was no less censorious of Christian churches which condemned apartheid and leaned towards an expanding black theology. The Christian Institute of Southern Africa, headed by the Rev. C.F. Beyers Naudé, reported in May

1972 that the state authority had taken repressive action in the past five years against at least 80 churchmen, mostly in 1971. The main denominations attacked were Anglicans, Lutherans, Catholics and Methodists, but Baptists, Moravians and Presbyterians had also been victims of punitive measures which included deportations, the withdrawal of residence permits, refusal of passports or visas, police raids and bannings.

This was more than most South African churches could stomach. Objections came from the S.A. Council of Churches – 85 of whose member churches were black – the Anglican Synod, United Evangelical Lutheran Church and the Presbyterian Church, whose commission decided by 11 votes to 10 to withdraw from the WCC.

SCHLEBUSCH

In 1972 the prime minister, B.J. Vorster, appointed a commission chaired by A.L. Schlebusch, a National Party member of parliament, to report on the affairs of the Christian Institute of South Africa, the University Christian Movement (UCM), Nusas and the S.A. Institute of Race Relations.

The UCM dissolved itself. Schlebusch reported in June 1975 that its main aim was to divide black and white people into separate and conflicting groups. This was quite contrary to the UCM's declared purpose of promoting common ground in a multi- racial organisation, but Schlebusch arrived at its questionable verdict without calling witnesses.

It met with direct resistance from the Christian Institute of Southern Africa whose Director, Dr C.F. Beyers Naudé, complained that the Commission was not fit for a country claiming to be Christian and democratic. His long experience of conflict with racist theologians in Dutch Reformed churches had qualified him with authority to make judgements on both counts. The Institute had been formed in August 1963 with a multi-racial and inter-church management board to unite Christians and revitalise their beliefs. It published a monthly journal called *Pro Veritate*, which Naudé edited, for the discussion of church and community problems in the light of the Bible and to foster unity in fellowship.

The Transvaal synods refused Naudé's application to accept the post of Director while remaining a minister of the church. He appealed against the rejection, saying that a choice had to be made between God and man. Sustained attacks on the Institute and Beyers Naudé followed. Professor A.D. Pont of Pretoria University told a student audience that the Institute and *Pro Veritate* were channels for the spread of communism into the churches. At his suggestion a congress was held in April 1964 on the theme 'Christendom against Communism'. Nearly half the 2400 people present were clergy or office-bearers of the Dutch Reformed churches. No blacks were present and only 15–20 per cent of the audience were English-speaking. Abusive letters distributed by an anonymous group made false allegations about the Institute and its officials; security police searched the office and home of the Director and removed documents.

Members of the Christian Institute were in a defiant mood when subpoenaed to appear before the Schlebusch Committee in September 1973. Of at least ten people ordered to testify, nine refused to give evidence. Six were ministers of religion: the Director Beyers Naudé and the Reverends Brian Brown, Theo Kotze, Roelf Meyer, James Moulder and Danie van Zyl; the lay members were Mrs D. Clemenshaw, Horst Kleinschmidt and Peter Randall. On 13 November Beyers Naudé, Brian Brown and Roelf Meyer appeared in the Pretoria regional court on charges of refusing to take the oath or testify. Dr Naudé was found guilty and fined R50 or one month's imprisonment and a three months' suspended prison sentence. The trials of other accused members of the Christian Institute were postponed until 1974. After much wrangling among judges of the Pretoria Supreme Court, and a decision by the Appellate Division, Mr Justice Heimstra rejected Naudé's appeal on 9 October 1976. He presented himself at the magistrates' court in Pretoria, saying that he would rather go to prison than pay the R50 fine imposed on him in 1974. He was taken into custody and released the following day because the fine was paid without his knowledge by the rector of the Reformed church where he worshipped. He stated that he would gladly have spent the 30 days in prison to demonstrate his belief that the Schlebusch Commission was unworthy to sit in judgment.

Apartheid South Africa was as far removed from the teachings of Christ as from any standard definition of democracy. In March 1973 the Christian Institute said that the government applied repressive measures while pretending to observe democratic procedures. In June 1974 Naudé supported a motion adopted by the S.A. Council of Churches on the contentious issue of national military service, which was compulsory and for whites only. Both Catholic and Protestant theologians considered that the taking up of arms was justified only to fight a 'just' war. South Africa's society was both unjust and unfair. Race discrimination was the primary cause of the state's violence which provoked counter-violence by 'terrorists' who were actually freedom fighters. Vorster told the Nationalist press that the resolution was meant to bring about confrontation between the state and church. He warned those who played with fire to take careful thought before burning their fingers beyond the hope of repair.

SCHLEBUSCH AND THE INSTITUTE OF RACE RELATIONS

The Commission's fifth interim report, issued in 1974, continued an investigation begun in 1973 with subpoenas served on eleven people, including the Institute's Director, Mr F.J. van Wyk and the previous Director, Dr Quintin Whyte. Four who refused to testify were Mrs I. Kleinschmidt, Peter Randall, Clive Nettleton and Dudley Horner. Mrs Kleinschmidt was sentenced by the Pretoria regional court on 19 September to a fine of R50 or 25 days in jail. Her appeal to the Supreme Court was turned down and she chose to go to jail, but an unidentified person paid the fine.

Schlebusch found that the Institute's financial accounts were in order and that the Ford Foundation was satisfied with the management of its grants for research and publications. The Commission also noted that the Institute had started with notions of liberal humanism and then moved to the promotion of social change by peaceful means, quite unlike the radical upheavals that leftists had in mind. It was not a place of study and teaching but an organisation for the collection of facts objectively and with care to ensure their accuracy.

The Commission criticised the Institute's youth programme and accused Nusas and other radicals of trying to take over the management and shape its policies. The Institute retorted that the Commission was unsuited to perform what was actually a judicial function and that it attacked young people in an attempt to justify its probe.

As was to be expected, Schlebusch grossly underrated the value of the Institute's publications. Its annual surveys, admirably compiled and edited by Muriel Horrell and colleagues, first appeared in 1928 and provided an unbroken record, increasing in bulk and price, of events in all parts of social life, from sport, art, welfare, health, education, economy, religion, population growth to constitutional and political affairs.

NUSAS

The National Union of South African Students was founded in 1924 by Leo Marquard, a rare Afrikaner with liberal leanings. Born and educated in the Orange Free State, he studied in Oxford with the aid of a Rhodes Scholarship and returned in 1922 to the OFS where he taught for 17 years until the outbreak of war. His book, *The Black Man's Burden*, which he wrote under the pseudonym of John Burger, was published by Victor Gollancz in 1943. The reference to Nusas and its counterpart the 'Afrikaanse Studentbond' (ASB) appears in his historical survey *The Peoples and Policies of South Africa* (1952: 200–1).

All university centres were membes of Nusas when it was established. By 1932 it had split and the main body of Afrikaans students had broken away to form ASB. 'The split was political and cultural. Nusas was felt to be too liberal and unnationalistic and, as it had shed the more conservative Afrikaner element, Nusas became increasingly leftist in its political tendencies.'

Nusas and ASB tried to find common basis for intervarsity co-operation, but all attempts failed because of differences on the question of non-European students. Nusas admits them, while ASB refuses to go further than to have conferences with them provided they come from separate universities and are not represented by white students. There are also cultural differences in the matter of Christian National Education and language. 'As with the single medium schools, so the single medium universities have tended to perpetuate divisions between the two European groups in South Africa.'

Paul Pretorius, the president of Nusas in 1972, told a national seminar in April that from its foundation in 1924 the Union had attempted to unite English-and Afrikaans-speaking students. Factors external to their affairs had caused this policy to fail. Most

Afrikaans students left the Union well before the Second World War. After more than 30 years Nusas opened its door to black students in an attempt to provide a basis for its existence. The rise of SASO between 1968 and 1970 had made the breakaway of black students also a matter of history.

Nusas's difficulties did not arise from failure to represent the aspirations of black students, but from the white society. White liberals, including some churches, the English press, Nusas itself, the S.A. Institute of Race Relations and Black Sash, were an integral part of the white power structure and offered little serious challenge to the state authority. While condemning the inhuman practices of the Nationalist government, they would not use their power in a concerted struggle to end them. Nusas would have to reject many white liberal policies and institutions if it were to cease obstructing black development (SAIRR, 1972: 392–4).

Nusas launched a 'free education' campaign on 22 May, with the Turfloop upheaval as its main theme. Students in English-speaking universities held meetings and demonstrations which were broken up by policemen using batons, dogs and tear-gas. Many people were arrested and hundreds were charged for holding unlawful meetings. The courts acquitted most of those accused, but leading cabinet ministers called them terrorists and said that all student demonstration should be stopped. Prime Minister Vorster told a Stellenbosch audience that the student demonstrations were part of a softening-up process aimed at taking over the government. Legislation would be introduced to deal with the problem (*The Argus*, 10 June 1972).

SCHLEBUSCH VS NUSAS

The Schlebusch Commission released its final report on 12 August 1973. It ran to 641 pages and dealt mainly with Nusas. The Commission recommended that no action be taken against it as a body, and pointed a finger at eight persons who were said to endanger internal security. They were highly political, did not support any existing political party, but tried to change the existing social order including its capitalist system and forms of authority. They rejected 'even liberalism' and forecast confrontation between white and black people. In order to obtain financial aid from overseas sources, they boosted Nusas's own image while presenting the country's official institutions in the worst possible light.

As yet, Nusas had remained within the law, but its congress, held towards the end of 1972, adopted a resolution indicating a determination to take a stand in the event of the government removing its fundamental and lawful right to meet, discuss and decide on issues. The congress expressed the hope that this right would remain in force and added that any action taken by students would be peaceful.

When Vorster tabled this report on 27 February 1973 he said that the Minister of Justice had decided to impose restrictions under the Suppression of Communism Act on the eight people named, even though the Commission had failed to find evidence of their being motivated by any intention of furthering the aims of communism.

Nusas denied the allegations, claiming that its policies were determined, not by a 'clique', but by majority vote at annual meetings of student representatives. Far from being alienated, at least nine of its executive and national council members had been employed by the Progressive Party or its associates. The protest was of no avail. Schlebusch presided over a political and not judicial inquiry. It was an instrument of the government, which was determined to break the back of student resistance to its repressive policies.

The eight members named by Schlebusch as being dangerous were Paul Pretorius, the Nusas president, Neville Curtis, a former president, Miss Paula Ensor and Phillipe le Roux, the two vice-presidents, Miss Sheila Lapinsky, the general secretary, and committee members, Clive Keegan, Richard Turner and Christopher Wood. They were banned from being Nusas office-bearers, attending educational institutions and therefore from continuing their studies in South Africa. The distinction of being named was conferred on them because the happened to be the executive when Schlebusch reported, and were no more or less of a 'threat' to the social order than Nusas executives before and after!

Four principals of English-medium universities met Vorster on 21 March 1973 to discuss the effect of the bans on the long-term careers of the eight students. He said that the bannings were preventive, not punitive, and complained of 'weak discipline' at some universities. The Minister of Justice told the Assembly in

September 1974 that the government would review the affected organisation declaration if Nusas became a purely student body which did not concern itself with radical politics of change.

AFFECTED AND TAINTED

One way of punishing dissident churchmen and rebellious students is to cut them off from their supplies of money. This operation was carried out by the Affected Organizations Act, No. 31 of 1974. It authorised the state president to declare an organisation to be 'affected' if, in his opinion, it took part in politics with the aid of foreigners or under their influence.

An affected organisation committed an offence by asking for or receiving foreign money. The Prohibition of Political Interference Act of 1968 had applied the same kind of constraint to political parties. The 1974 statute extended the scope of the repression to extra-parliamentary social groups. The prime minister, B.J. Vorster, speaking during the debate on the bill, said that it dealt with evils exemplified by Nusas and other organisations which served as a front for overseas communists and leftists seeking the downfall of South Africa.

Nusas and its subsidiaries were branded as affected organisations in proclamations published on 13 September 1974. Karel Tip, the president elect, said that about 70 per cent of the annual budget of R100 000 came from overseas. Nusas issued a press statement announcing that a fund-raising campaign would be launched within South Africa and accusing the government of attacking the right of students to discuss the wrongs in their society and the possibilities for a better future.

THE IMPORTANCE OF BEING BLACK

The S.A. Institute of Race Relations decided in 1972 to use the word 'black' when referring collectively to South Africans other than whites. Its own preference was to specify Africans, Coloured and Asians, but the collective term was useful for the sake of brevity. Though not all Coloured and Asians, and indeed not all Africans, approved of being labelled black, they preferred it to 'non-white'. To be described as the negative of the dominant white group was humiliating. Black became the chosen word in the English press editorial columns and news coverage. *Swart*, the Afrikaans word for black, gradually took the place of *nie-blank* (non-white), *naturel* (Native) and Bantu (people). The black peril in Afrikaans was *die swart gevaar*. From 1982 onwards legislation applying specifically to Africans was restyled 'black' instead of 'Native' or 'Bantu', as in the Black Administration Act of 1927, the Blacks (Urban Areas) Consolidation Act of 1945 and the Black Development Trust and Land Act of 1945.

A survey in 1972 of opinions among Soweto matriculation students found that 96.5 per cent of a random sample of 200 respondents were proud of being called black, but out of every 100 questioned about their name preferences, 64 wanted to be called African, 13 chose black, 7.5 Native and 7 Bantu. Mr M.L. Edelstain, chief welfare officer of Johannesburg's municipal non-European Department, who supervised the survey with a team of trained African social workers, reported that 88.5 per cent of those questioned wanted their children to be educated through the medium of English, 9.5 per cent chose their home language and 2 per cent Afrikaans. In reply to other questions, 90 per cent wanted more social contact with whites, 88 per cent thought that Africans should form one nation and Soweto should not be divided into tribal zones (SAIRR, 1971: 38–42).

Well-informed observers, among them the Mayor of Johannesburg, the director the Race Relations Institute, and Chief Gatcha Buthelezi, spoke of feelings of frustration and despair in Soweto, explosive discontent among urban Africans and a growing antagonism among them which the government did not recognise or preferred to ignore.

BLACK STUDENTS REVOLT

A rash of students' clubs and societies spread to the main urban centres in 1972. Their origins, aims, setbacks and gains were recorded in *Black Review*, published in Durban by Black Community Programmes between 1972 and 1976. Ben A. Khopapa, who edited the first number and wrote an account of its objectives, was placed under a banning order in October 1973.

The *Review* set out to inform readers of what was taking place in all areas of the public life of blacks: politics, culture, religion, the spread of black consciousness; trade unions and government institutions, bantustans, Coloured and Indian councils. Political trials, detentions and bans were a central feature of the *Reviews*. In what follows material is gleaned from the issues of the *Review*. Its last number, the victim of severe repression and overshadowed by the shooting of Soweto students on 16 June 1976, tended to avoid critical comment of political action by the state.

Bans were imposed in March 1973 on eight youth leaders, of whom two, Bantu Stephen Biko and Bokwe Mafuna, were fieldworkers with the Black Community Programmes. Some were officials of the Black Peoples' Convention. Included in this group were the vice- president, Chris Masdibeng Mokoditoa, the secretary-general, Sipho Buthelezi, the public relations officer, Sathasivan 'Saths' Cooper, and the national organiser, Mosebudi Mangena. Harry Nengwekhulu, Saso's permanent organiser, was arrested at his office and charged under the Urban Areas Act for being an 'idle and undesirable Bantu'. Jerry Modisane, newly elected Saso president, was arrested in Cape Town in September and charged with trespassing at the University of the Western Cape. The Publications Board banned two designs for Saso T-shirts. Nyameko Barney Pityana, Saso's secretary-general, Strini Moodley, its administrative assistant and Rubin Phillip, the immediate past president, were refused passports. Saso's October newsletter stated: 'The whole intimidation campaign being conducted by white South Africans comes at a time when Saso and the Black Consciousness Movement are sweeping the country ... black people are coming out of their trance and the philosophy of blackness cannot be intimidated.'

POLITICAL TRIALS

Imprisonment was a sure way of removing resisters from the battlegrounds in their communities. The first trial reported in the *Review* took place in 1971–2 in Pietermaritzburg. The accused were members of the African Peoples' Democratic Union of S.A. (Apdusa), an offshoot of the non-European Movement (NEUM), founded in 1943 in Cape Town to oppose the Smuts government's policy of segregating Coloured in a separate department.

Isaac Bangani Tabata, founder and leading theoretician of the NEUM, was born in Queenstown in the Cape in 1909. Educated at Lovedale he attended Fort Hare for some time and left in 1931 to seek work in Cape Town. He became a truck driver, joined the Cape African Voters' Association and in 1935 attended the founding conference of the All African Convention. Author of the AAC pamphlet, 'The Awakening of a People', he was one of the founders of the Anti-Coloured Affairs Department (Anti-CAD) group.

A strong opponent of the ANC and the Communist Party, he favoured a peasant-based liberation movement and political education rather than immediate action campaigns. He was banned in 1956 for five years. On the expiration of his ban in 1961 he helped to found Apdusa and became its president. He fled South Africa in May 1963 and took refuge in Zambia with his wife, Janet Gool, Wycliffe Tsotsi, Nathanial Honono and Dr Ismael Limbada, a medical practitioner in Pietermaritzburg. Tabata and his wife managed a printing and publishing firm in Lusaka. Dr Limbada opened a surgery and supervised a flourishing farm.

The prosecution in the Apdusa trial alleged that Tabata and his colleagues sent secret agents into South Africa to recruit people for military training abroad. Thirteen men were charged under the Terrorism Act and found guilty by Justice James, Judge President of Natal, in April 1972 of plotting to overthrow the government by force of arms, recruiting people for military training and assisting known terrorists. By the time that their trial came to an end, they had been in custody, with long periods of solitary confinement, for more than 12 months and in some cases for 16 months. All the accused were found guilty on two or more of the charges and sentenced to effective imprisonment for periods ranging from five to eight years.

COMMUNISTS ON TRIAL

Mrs Amina Desai, Mohamed Salim Essop, Indrehasen Moodley and Yusuf Hassem Esack stood trial in the Pretoria Supreme Court in June 1972 on charges under the Terrorism Act and alternatively under the Suppression of Communism Act. Arrested in October 1971, they were kept in solitary confinement until brought before Mr Justice Snyman to answer the charge of having conspired with one another, the Communist Party, Ahmed Timol and other persons to promote the cause and policies of the banned CP and ANC. The prosecution alleged that they had distributed leaflets by means of explosive devices and broadcast messages threatening Vorster, the prime minister, in August 1970 and August 1971.

Justice Snyman found them guilty and sentenced them to an effective five years' imprisonment, the least on the scale of compulsory punishments prescribed by the Terrorism Act. He said that they had probably been trapped into the conspiracy by Ahmed Timol, who had died on 27 October 1971 while in police custody. The police said he had committed suicide by jumping through a window on the tenth floor of their headquarters at John Vorster Square in Johannesburg. At about the same time Mohamed Essop, a medical student aged 21, also died in police custody. The two alleged suicides sparked a widespread protest against the Terrorism Act and the power of the security police. Several lawyers 'bar' councils and a number of churches called for a judicial inquiry. On 9 November 1971 the General Assembly of the United Nations adopted a resolution condemning the maltreatment and torture of opponents of apartheid.

The security police, aided by undercover agents and turncoats, searched far and wide for persons who left South Africa to undergo training in guerilla warfare, revolutionary strategies, communist theory, propaganda and espionage. This was the substance of the indictment in the case against Fana Cletus Mazimela, who appeared before Judge Henning in the Pietermaritzburg Supreme Court on 20 November 1972. Mazimela pleaded guilty and was sentenced to 15 years' imprisonment. The trial attracted much attention because of the evidence given by Leonard Nkosi, a special branch undercover agent who had trained in Moscow and deserted his platoon, after its skirmishes with security police in Rhodesia. An unnamed witness testified to having left the PAC to join the ANC in 1963 in Tanzania, from where he went with a party of trainees led by Joe Modise, commander-in-chief of ANC's armed forces, to Odessa where he met Mazimela. On his return to Tanzania in 1964 he took an oath of allegiance to the ANC administered by Oliver Tambo, the president of the ANC in exile. I witnessed oath-taking ceremonies of this kind in 1977–8 when teaching political sociology to MK recruits in Angola; and heard Joe Modise tell MK trainees that a punitive squad had shot dead another such a turncoat while in bed with his wife.

The 1972 *Black Review* reported that trial on 24 November 1972 of six men charged under the Terrorism Act. Arrested in June 1971 and detained during police investigations, the accused were Alexander Moumbaris, an Australian of French extraction, John William Hosey, a citizen of Northern Ireland, Justice Mpanza and Petrus Tembo from Natal, Gardener Sejaka and Theophilus Cholo from Transkei. Moumbaris and his wife had been arrested on the Botswana border on 19 July 1972. She was pregnant and deported to France to join her parents. The men appeared in the Pretoria Supreme Court. They were charged on 19 counts of conspiring with one another and with Oliver Tambo, Joe Slovo and Dr Yusuf Dadoo. Judge Boshoff found them guilty of one or more of the charges, sentenced Moumbaris to 12 years' imprisonment, Hosey to 5 years and the four Africans to 15 years each for activities which the judge said were close to treason.

THE MATSAU CASE

Judges were no less sensitive to signs of Black Consciousness than to the growing strength of the military wing of the resistance movement. Their apprehension came to the surface in the treatment of Nkutsoeu Matsau, the organising secretary of the Sharpville Youth Club in Vereeniging and member of the Black People's Convention. He was arrested on 5 October 1973 with six club members. They were detained under the Terrorism Act until the end of November, when all except Matsau were released.

After several appearances in court he was found guilty on 26 April of two acts of participation in terrorist activities with the intention of endangering law and order. Justice Cillie, the judge president of the Transvaal Supreme Court, sentenced him to five years' imprisonment for publishing a poem and newsletter which, in the judge's opinion, were likely to incite feelings of hostility between whites and blacks. He added that Matsau had evidently devoted his life to spreading the doctrines of Black Consciousness, Black Solidarity and Black Communism.

A GENERAL ELECTION

Most voters showed a preference for the prime minister's assurance of a firm, determined policy which he had promised during the run-up to the general election held on 24 April 1974 for the all-white parliament and provincial councils. The National Party won 123 seats, increasing its majority in the Assembly by five as compared with the 118 seats it obtained in the last previous election of 1970. The United Party emerged with 41 seats, losing two to the NP and six to the Progressive Party which won seven seats, six more than it had in 1970. The NP obtained 43 seats in the newly elected senate of 45 elected and 10 nominated members.

The jubilant National Party emphasised its strict apartheid aims in response to post-election surveys by Progressive Party leaders Colin Eglin and van Zyl Slabbert, Bantustan spokesmen, Coloured and Indian politicians. In what follows, observations will be made on statements by members of each colour group, commencing with the Coloured.

The estimated Coloured population in 1974 was 2.3 million, more than half the size of the white population of 4.16 million, and divided into seven groups by the Population Registration Act of 1950: Cape Coloured, Cape Malay, Griqua, Chinese, Indians, other Asians and other Coloured. A government-appointed board dealt with applications for reclassification – from African to Coloured, from Coloured to White, and from White to Coloured. The Coloured were aggrieved by the board's humiliating procedures and the bans on marriage and sex between white and all shades of black South Africans.

Connie Mulder, the Minister of Internal Affairs, told the Assembly on 8 August 1974 that Coloured would be allowed to develop along parallel lines – which of course never meet! Integration with whites in a multi-racial parliament was ruled out for ever. Vorster issued a press statement on 19 August saying that Mulder had correctly expressed government policy on the political future of Coloured. They were deeply offended by this exclusion – which Mulder said would, 'continue into infinity' – from a position they had occupied for more than a century, from 1835 under representative government to 1951–6, when the apartheid government removed them from the common voters' roll after a long political and juridical battle.

In the aftermath of the general white election, their resentment came to a head in the Coloured Representative Council (CRC), a toothless body with a chequered career going back to the abortive Persons Representative Council Acts of 1964 and 1968. In the Council's 1974 session a majority of members voted for a resolution moved by Sonny Leon, leader of the Labour Party, stating that they had no confidence in the policy of separate institutions and wanted direct representation of Coloured, voting on a common roll, in parliament and other national councils as a prelude to the enfranchisement of all South Africans. The motion was carried by 29 votes to 25.

Vorster, in an opening speech to the CRC in November 1974, again rejected Coloured representation in the white parliament. He was willing to raise the Council's executive to cabinet status and give it responsibility for departments of Coloured Affairs, but the white parliament would continue to be sovereign.

Ten years later President P.W. Botha, the first important reformer of apartheid laws and policies, piloted the adoption of the Republic of South Africa Constitution Act, No. 110 of 1983, which provided for a white House of Assembly of 178 members, a Coloured House of Representatives with 85 members, and an Indian House of Delegates of 145 members.

The Indian Council of South Africa was reconstituted in September 1974 so as to consist of 30 members, half of whom were nominated by the government and half elected by local authorities and committees. Of the elected members, ten came from Natal, four from the Transvaal and one from the Cape. The Orange Free State was unrepresented because Indians were not allowed to settle in the province.

The Council's chairman, Mr H.E. Joosub, said that the community was not satisfied with these limited powers and the failure to register voters on a roll. They would eventually have to be given a vital say in the running of the country. The management committee of Lanasia, a segregated Indian settlement in Johannesburg, decided to boycott elections to the Council, which it regarded as an affront to the dignity and citizenship rights of Indians. Members of all racial groups, it claimed, were inherently capable of contributing to the growth of a multi- racial society.

Vorster met homeland leaders in Pretoria on 6 March 1974 and 22 January 1975. In a report of the talks, Chief Mangosuthu Gatcha Buthelezi said that the leaders had raised many issues –

the consolidation of the reserves, race discrimination, wage gaps, black businessmen, the phasing out of passes, the medium of instruction in schools and the issue of independence for bantustans. Vorster gave customary assurances of looking into grievances but no promises of reform. As for the question of independence, people were free to ask for it, but only within the limits of the Native Land Laws, these being the Act of 1913 and the Land and Trust Act of 1936 which, as Buthelezi pointed out, meant that Africans would 'end up with nothing more than 13 per cent of the whole area of South Africa, when they constitute 80 percent of the population' (van der Merwe et al., 1976: 569–70).

BLACK NATIONALISM

Vorster and his fellow racists were blind and deaf to the symptoms of a national spirit underlying the rejection by Coloured, Indians and Africans of spurious promises of separate and parallel development or illusory assurances of independence. Blacks wanted to take part in the creation of a multi-racial, non-discriminatory social order, but the self-centred, arrogant spokesmen for white supremacy rejected any proposal to share power with their darker-skinned fellow countrymen.

Manasseh Tebatso Moerane, former ANC member and editor of *The World* newspaper, told University of Cape Town audience on 16 February 1973 that the motivation of black nationalism was to struggle and organise people until they were strong enough to assert rights and bring justice to their land. He showed more caution at a National Organisation Conference held in Johannesburg on 18 December 1971, the third in a series of successive consultations. In his opening address he spoke eloquently of the rise of new forces of men and women which would gain momentum till blacks had forged the way to victory in a struggle to regain their own; but when the conference decided to form a Black People's Convention (BPC) he with some others withdrew, being more in favour of a non-political service organisation.

The BPC's constitution, drafted by a congress at Edenvale, Pietermaritzburg, in July 1972 urged blacks 'to re-assert their pride, human dignity and solidarity through a political movement if their needs, aspirations, ideals and goals were to be realised'. The convention would operate outside government structures and not seek election into them. Membership would be open only to blacks, defined as meaning Africans, Indians and Coloured.

On 16 December the BPC held a conference at Hammanskraal in the Transvaal and consolidated its programmes on many fronts – foreign investments, trade unions, women, youth, education, health, churches and culture. B.A. Khoapa, the Director of BPC and editor of its publications, compiled its first major book which was published in 1973 with the title *Black Review* for 1972. He was banned by the government before the book appeared in print. Banning orders were served at the same time on office-bearers and leading members of the BPC: Steve Biko and Bokwe Mafuna, both fieldworkers with the Black Community Programmes, Chris Madibeng Mokoditoa, vice-president, Sipho Buthelezi, secretary-general, Sathasivan 'Saths' Cooper, public relations officer and members, including Drake Koka, Mrs S. Moodley, Mathew Diseko, a young poet, Mosebudi Mangena, national organiser and others of the office staff who escaped from South Africa with Bokwe Mafuna.

Though Saso and BPC did little to organise workers or engage in direct political action, the moral impact of the Black Consciousness Movement was an important link in the chain that led to the Soweto student revolt which surfaced in June 1976.

BANS

During the debate in the Assembly on 18 May 1976 of the draft Internal Security Amendment Act 79 of 1976, Jimmy Kruger, the Minister of Justice, said that the legislation was aimed at people other than communists, at young Black Power leaders who allowed themselves to be misled by the Christian Institute, at people who in spirit were trying to besmirch South Africa, and the Nusas Wages Commissions which were trying to organise African trade unions for revolution.

He would continue to flush out communists. They were being restricted in terms of the Suppression of Communism Act of 1950. Records kept by Muriell Horrell (SAIRR, 1974: 67–8) showed that from 1951, when the Act came into effect, to the end of April 1974, the number of persons banned under it was 1240, of whom 913 were Africans, 139 Whites, 104 Asians and 64

Coloured. Some bans had lapsed, some were withdrawn, leaving 206 people on the banned list at the end of April.

The restrictions were standardised, with variations to fit individual circumstances. The ban imposed on me, for instance, which Vorster signed on 3 December 1964, prohibited me for five years, ending 30 November 1969, from leaving the Cape magisterial district, entering any court of law except to interview the magistrate or attend legal proceedings to which I was a party. I was forbidden to enter or be in any 'Native' place of residence or areas set aside for Coloured and Asians; or be in any harbour, factory, printing shop and other premises used for preparing or publishing publications; be in any place of learning or give educational instruction to anyone other than my children, or communicate with any listed communist 'except your wife Rachel'.

The loss of basic rights – freedom of movement, residence, speech, social contact and expression – was depressing, the more so because of constant surveillance by special branch security police waiting to pounce for any infringement of the banning order.

Among the people banned in 1974 were Halton Cheadle, David Hemson and David Davis, members of the Students' Wages Commission at Natal University and organisers of African trade unions. They were banned for five years and placed under house arrest. Davis left the country on a valid passport and was given asylum in Britain. Neville Curtis, one of the banned Nusas leaders, escaped to Australia. Two members of Saso and the Black Consciousness Movement, B.A. Khoapa and Theo Moatshe, fled to join exiles in Botswana. Several people were banned for a third consecutive period of five years, including Mohamed Bhana, former member of the S.A. Indian Congress and Mrs Albertina Sisulu, wife of Walter Sisulu, serving a life sentence on Robben Island. Abraham Tiro, one of the exiles, was killed by a parcel bomb posted in Geneva, which exploded at his place of refuge near Gaberone. The Office of the President in Botswana issued a strongly worded statement denouncing 'the inhuman and dastardly manner' in which Tiro, an outspoken critic of apartheid, had been killed.

MEETINGS BANNED

In 1974 the government prohibited gatherings organised by Saso to commemorate Sharpeville Heroes Day, and meetings called in

support of Frelimo's victory in Mozambique. The prohibition
included meetings held anywhere in South Africa on behalf of
Saso or the BPC. In spite of the ban, a large crowd gathered at
Curries Fountain in Durban. Using dogs and batons, the police
broke up the meeting and made several arrests; after which they
searched the offices and homes of Saso and BPC members at
various centres, making more arrests and detaining some of those
arrested under the Terrorism Act 1967, which set no limit to the
period of detentions.

A meeting of students in support of Frelimo was held at
Turfloop on 25 September in defiance of the ban. The police
warned them that the meeting, which took place in a university
hall, was in breach of the Riotous Act and ordered them to
disperse. This they did, but after leaving the hall they were
attacked by police with batons and tear-gas. The rector, Professor
Boshoff, decided to close the university and told the press that the
students came to Turfloop with anti-white sentiments, which
some members of the black academic staff encouraged.

Gessler Nkondo, a senior African lecturer, explained that white
and black staff members lived in separate areas, and did not mix
socially. The students, he pointed out, were isolated at Turfloop
from the country's main streams of thought and activity. The
Frelimo victory had given them hope that change was possible in
their lifetime.

During a university recess the police detained the SRC president, Gilbert Sedibe, and the newly elected president of Saso, P.
Nefolovhodwe. On their return the students held a mass meeting
at which a majority decided to boycott classes and stage a sit-in
until the detainees had been released. A third student, Cyril
Ramaphosa, chairman on the local committee of Saso (and
current General Secretary of the African National Congress
[ANC]), was also arrested and detained.

BLACK CONSCIOUSNESS TRIAL

Twelve members of Saso and BPC appeared in a Pretoria
magistrates' court on 31 January 1975, four months after most of
them had been detained. The trial got under way on 7 August
before Judge Boshoff in the Pretoria Supreme Court when nine
men were charged with conspiring to transform the state by

unlawful, revolutionary and violent means. The indictment, which ran to 105 pages, alleged that they published subversive and anti-white statements while discouraging investments in the country's economy. It was left to the defence to explain that a spirit of nationalism filled the hearts and minds of people who, defeated but defiant, had been humiliated and treated as outcasts for centuries by settlers and imperialists.

The *Black Review* for 1975–6 (pp. 82–3) remarked that as the trial reached its first anniversary on 4 August 1976, it had become known as the 'Trial of Black Consciousness'. It gave rise to widespread concern. Meetings, demonstrations, church vigils and prayer services were held in Durban, Johannesburg and Cape Town's Cathedral. Protests came from the Black Women's Federation, Black Sash and Race Relations Institute. Mrs Helen Suzman, spokesman on justice for the Progressive Reform Party, accused the government of using the Durban rally as an excuse for trying to smash the black consciousness movement.

Justice Boshoff, the presiding judge, pointed out that the 1967 Terrorism Act put the onus on the accused to prove their innocence. They had to show, among other things, that their actions were not likely to harm the dignity or self-respect of the state, cause disruption, disturbance and disorder, inflict substantial financial loss on any person or the state, and hamper anyone from assisting in the maintenance of law and order.

The nine Saso-BPC officials who appeared before Judge Boshoff on 7 August 1976 were Sathasivan 'Saths' Cooper, 24, former public relations officer of the BPC, and banned under the Suppression of Communism Act; Justice Edmund Lindane Myeza, 24, former president of Saso and its present general secretary; Mosiuoa Gerald Lekota, 28, permanent organiser of Saso since 1973; Maitshewe Nchaupe Aubrey Mokoape, 30, founder member of BPC and Saso, banned under the Suppression of Communism Act; Nkwenkwe Vincent Nkomo, 24, national organiser of BPC; Pandelani Jeremiah Nofolovhodwe, 25, national president of Saso and final year BSc at the University of the North; Gilbert Kaborane Sedibe, 24, president of the SRC at the University of the North; Strinivasa Rajoo Moodley, 28, banned under the Suppression of Communism Act, former director of Saso publications and editor of its newsletter; and Absalom Zithulele Cindi, 25, secretary general of BPC.

Alternative counts brought against some accused alleged attempts to provoke the police in using violence and spreading reports about the value of armed struggle to promote change in South Africa.

THE TRIAL

Months of solitary confinement and interrogation did not quench the faith of the accused in their cause. They appeared in court on 7 February 1975 singing from the cells, up the stairs until they entered the courtroom, that arrests would not deter them; their burden was heavy but they were determined to unite for liberation. They repeated the demonstration on 12 March and 7 August when entering the crowded Supreme Court, singing loudly, their arms raised high with clenched fists in the black solidarity salute. 'When they turned to face the public gallery, the people stood up and joined the singing with clenched fists raised' (*Black Review*, 1974–5: 84–5).

The prosecution closed its case on 19 December after calling 59 witnesses. Council for the defence took over on 29 March 1976. The accused spoke for themselves. Saths Cooper, who was cross-examined for six days, spoke for all, explaining Black Consciousness's aims, concepts and methods. A formidable body of experts took the stand. Among them were Adam Small, poet, essayist and former lecturer in philosophy at the University of the Western Cape, Dr Rick Turner, banned former political science lecturer in Natal, the Rev. Farisani, a former president of the BPC, who explained that its objective was to express black people's needs with a view to relieving their depression. Steve Biko, the founding president of Saso, spoke at length on the origin and aims of Black Consciousness.

The trial ended in December 1976. Judge Boshoff found the accused guilty and read them a homily on South Africa's democracy. Freedom of speech and assembly were important elements of the country's party system, which was based on opposing views and ideas, but this did not mean that everyone was free to address a group of people in any public place and at any time. He was well aware that blacks had no effective voice or vote and could only protest against their grievances. Though Saso and BPC had none of the features of a revolutionary conspiracy,

Black Consciousness, when building group solidarity, encouraged hostility between blacks and whites. For this reason he convicted the nine accused of being 'terrorists', and sentenced six of them to six years' imprisonment and three to five years. (Bernstein, 1978, 1987: 16–17).

WHITE SECURITY

The search of voters and government for total security was never ending. Early in the century, the Riotous Assemblies Act of 1912 was introduced by General Smuts to quell white workers' strikes. In later years security laws were wholly concerned with rebellious blacks and their white sympathisers. The Internal Security Amendment Act, 79 of 1976, was one in a long series of such laws. Originating in recommendations by the Schlebusch Commission in 1973, its keywords were 'the security of the state' and 'the maintenance of public order'. They recurred, like the end of a stanza, in every clause authorising the government to declare an organisation unlawful, prohibit the printing, publication or distribution of journals, prohibit people from attending gatherings or being within or leaving defined areas. The minister could order the imprisonment of any person engaging in activities 'which endanger or are calculated to endanger the security of the State of the maintenance of public order'.

The legal system tolerated such violations of the United Nations' Charter of Human Rights as detention without trial, solitary confinement for months on end, ill-treatment, often amounting to torture with the aim of extracting confessions and information for use in political trials. State security measures, introduced to cope with emergencies, tended to become permanent features of the system. The turbulence which the government gave as the reason for the severity of its repressive policy developed from an initial subdued, low-profile protest into armed revolt.

White voters, kept in ignorance of the underlying causes by strict censorship, right-wing racist propaganda and the government's control of the media, persistently voted the National Party into office with policies agreeable to the dominant Afrikaans-speaking majority in the white population.

The judiciary, for the most part, was as establishment-minded as the executive, willing to adopt an interpretation that would favour its aims rather than defend the liberty of the subject by upholding the rule of law. In August 1968 the International Commission of Jurists observed that because of South Africa's unjust and discriminatory social order, its legal system was 'so eroded and perverted as to become itself an adjunct of tyranny based on racial discrimination'. In September 1969 the Jurists stated that racial discrimination in South Africa had become worse. 'Recent legislation, increased security measures, incidents of brutality, and continued disregard for the rule of law, indicated that the regime in the Republic was tightening its hold.' On 13 December 1967 the United Nations General Assembly ratified a resolution by 89 votes to 2 (South Africa and Portugal) condemning the policies of apartheid as a crime against humanity and a threat to international peace.

International disapproval and threats of sanctions intensified the white group's collective feeling of guilt and insecurity; weakened the self-esteem they derived from belonging to the prestigious western democracies to which they were linked by descent, culture, language, religion, sport and the arts; and exposed them to the danger of becoming outcasts in the countries of their ancestors where they were acceptable only to fellow racists, neo-Nazis and rebellious Sinn Feiners. South African whites were walking on thin ice when the Soweto students' revolt of 1976 challenged their ability to maintain an endless domination over the black majority.

SOWETO

The immediate cause of the revolt was the introduction by the Minister of Bantu Education of Afrikaans as the medium of instruction in mathematics, social studies, geography and history. English would be the medium for general science, home economics, needlework and woodwork; African languages the medium for religion, music and physical exercise. The ranking order was evident. Afrikaans was to have pride of place, used to teach mathematics, the queen of sciences, and the subjects of indoctrination: history, geography and social science.

Teachers and pupils in African schools throughout the country resented the imposition for which they were unprepared and which added another burden to an overloaded teaching programme. Soweto's senior students gave vent to their indignation on the early morning of 16 June 1976 by chanting slogans, singing freedom songs and carrying placards abusing Bantu education and the Afrikaans language on their way to an agreed assembly point. They were fired on by policemen using live ammunition and tear-gas canisters. Between June and December more than 1000 people were shot dead by police and more than 5000 were injured in clashes spreading from townships in the Transvaal to Coloured and African residential areas in the Western Cape. The violence resulted from the Soweto revolt and the killing of unarmed school children (Brooks and Brickhill, 1980: 8–9, 256).

The imposition of Afrikaans was a legitimate grievance, but it was only one dimension of a political struggle. Africans had no inherent objection to learning Afrikaans. It was an official state language, useful to men and women who aspired to rise above the ranks of less skilled wage workers. Afrikaans was the home language of some six million speakers, who included a sizeable number of Africans (Wilson, 1991: 93–4; Jenkins, in Race Relations Survey, 1992/3: 256).

Given effective pressure from opponents of the policy, the decision to impose Afrikaans was open to discussion as M.C. Botha, the Minister of Bantu Education, showed. Following student boycotts and strikes, he announced on 5 July 1976 that the imposition would be dropped for the time being.

The strategy that led to the pressure was the work of high school Soweto students belonging to the S.A. Students Movement (SASM). Formed in March 1972, it set out to co-ordinate student activities and promote information programmes concerning social injustices and the Black Consciousness Movement (*Black Review*, 1972: 182). SASM provided much of the leadership of the schools that took part in the revolt, called the demonstrations held on 16 June and created the Soweto Students Representative Council from which leaders of the revolt were drawn (Hirson, 1979: 102–3).

LAW AND ORDER

On 17 June, the day after the Soweto massacre, James Kruger, the Minister of Justice and Police, told parliament that Mr Justice

Cillié, the Transvaal Judge President, had been appointed to investigate the 'disturbances'. Two months later, on 23 August, it was announced that the Commission's brief had been extended to include troublespots among students throughout the country. The assignment was no exception to the rule that investigations of this kind serve the purpose of clamping down on protests against wrong policies, blunders, repression of liberties and demands for the dismissal of ministers who are to blame.

The Commission presented its report on 21 January 1980, three and a half years after the event, when the noise and fury of the riots had died down and a new prime minister was in office. Justice Cillié found that officials and police in Soweto had failed to recognise the symptoms and foresee the upheaval. They were unprepared in all respects for the demonstration, and consequently had no control over the rioters. Once the disturbances had taken place, it was the duty of the police to restore law and order, and this they did very well.

EXODUS

The riots and their effects brought to a head differences between members of the Black Consciousness Movement (BCM) as well as within the Black People's Convention (BPC). They lost cohesion and broke up into groups that moved in different directions. Towards the end of 1976, Steve Biko and his close associates had talks with leaders of banned bodies in exile – the ANC, PAC, APDUSA and AZAPO. The results were disappointing. He then tried to form a united front of BPC and BCM members to negotiate with those in exile. The detentions of BPC members in 1976 and the murder on 12 September of Biko by security police wrecked these plans. BPC members and their allies came to a parting of their ways in 1978–9. Some chose to work in the political underground or join the Azanian People's Organisation (AZAPO) in South Africa (No Sizwe (pseud.), 1979: 172–81). A majority went into exile. An estimated 60 per cent joined the ANC and its armed wing, Mkhonto we Sizwe (Mokoape et al., in Pityane et al., 1991: 137–42).

The BCM people who attached themselves to the ANC after the Soweto rising included Curtis Nkondo, AZAPO's first president who was banned and left AZAPO; Jackie Selebe, who went into exile and was elected to the NEC of the Congress in 1988; Zwelakhe Sisulu, who declared his full support for the Freedom Charter; Steve Tshwete, member of the Communist Party who, after his release, was made ANC's chief of security in Botswana and later in Lusaka. Saths Cooper and others refused to join the ANC and drifted into the ranks of the PAC.

The ANC's long record of armed struggle, superior organisation and good relations with neighbouring states enabled it to satisfy the demand of most students who left South Africa to continue their studies or receive military training. Before the end of 1976, about 4000 men and women had left. Some went to school in Nigeria and later to the Solomon Mahlangu College (SOMAFCO) in Tanzania. The most important training centre was in Angola where political commissars, MK instructors and Cuban reservists developed the political understanding of recruits and taught them how to handle weapons in a guerrilla bush war. Novo Katenga in Banguela Province, was the largest camp, which the ANC shared with Cuban reservists guarding the Benguela railroad. By 1987 the ANC managed a training school for engineers in Luanda and more camps in the north at Viana, Quibaxe, Panga and Quatro, the latter a detention centre for dissidents (Ellis and Tsepo, 1992: 84).

I was a non-combatant instructor, teaching political sociology at Nova Katenga (known as the 'University of the South') in 1977–9. On 14 March 1979 three SADF planes destroyed the camp, razing the barracks to the ground. Warned by Cuban officers that an attack was imminent, the camp commander ordered me and some others to leave before the bombing raid took place. I returned to my home in Lusaka; and from there went to Somafco, a large comprehensive school in Morogoro district, named after Solomon Kalushi Mahlangu, who was hanged on 6 April 1979 at the age of 21 in circumstances to be described later.

DETENTIONS

The apartheid regime panicked. Having failed to stop the exodus, it launched a country-wide assault on leaders of the resistance movement and of the students who belonged to SASM, BCM, BPC and SASO. This leadership was largely eliminated during the second half of 1976 through the wave of detentions imposed under the Internal Security Act Amendment Act 79 of 1976. It authorised the Minister of Justice to order the detention for a specified period of any person who in his opinion was a danger to the security of the state of the maintenance of public order. At the end of November, 434 persons were being held in detentions (SAIRR, 1976: 113).

They included the past and present office-bearers of the South African Students' Movement, Soweto's SASM; leaders of the South African Students' Organisation (SASO); members of the Student Representative Councils at English-medium universities and outstanding activists in the Black Consciousness Movement. Among them were B. Barney Pityana, a founder of SASO, banned since 1972 and released with his wife Dimza, only to be sent back to prison in August. Steve Biko, first president of SASO, was detained on 17 August under the General Law Amendment Act and later under the Terrorism Act. Detention orders were served in July on Kenneth Rachidi, president of the Black People's Convention, and its vice-president, Nxolisi Mvovo; Zweli Sizani, organising secretary of SASM together with other Black Consciousness activists.

Also at risk were organisations entitled 'black'. The word had the approval of bureaucrats, who used it in their officialese, but regarded it with suspicion when blacks used it in their own organisations, such as the Black Parents Association, formed early in 1976 by Mrs Winnie Mandela and Dr Nthato Motlana to find answers to community problems in Soweto. They were detained, as were seven members of the Black Women's Federation, all prominent in black communities. Four were executive members: Dr Fatima Meer, renowned sociologist and professor at the University of Natal; Mrs Winnie Mandela; Mrs Jeannie Noel, assistant secretary; and Mrs Sally Motlana, president of the African Housewives League, vice-president of the S.A. Council of Churches and Conference of Churches.

Mrs Vesta Smith, executive member of the Black Studies Institute, Bobby Mari and Govin Reddy of the Institute for Black Research were detained in August. In the same month Dr Mamphela Ramphele, the superintendent of Zanempilo Clinic ('the one bringing health'), her colleagues Dr Solembela and Dr Masauli were detained. The clinic, formed by the Black People's Convention, and Black Consciousness Movement near King Williamstown (where Steve Biko was confined) flourished and planned to spread its wings, but 'With the 1977 bannings of all BCM organisation, the intended expansion nationwide from the initial focus in the Eastern Cape never came about' (Ramphele, 1991: 169).

BANNINGS

The bans imposed on dissidents, real or imaginary, took the place of the repression that followed the Sharpeville massacre of 1960, when the Verwoerd government declared a state of emergency on 21 March and ordered the detention of thousands of people who were set free, without being prosecuted, when the emergency was brought to an end on 31 August. Alan Brooks and Jeremy Brickhill (1990: 39f) examined at some length the 'paradox' between the government's policies in the two situations, but a simple explanation might be enough for present purposes. Vorster wanted to avoid the international and domestic repercussions of a State of Emergency and preferred the more individualised and low-profile approach involved in detentions and bans.

The bans put the onus of compliance on dissidents, over whom the security police keep a close watch. In this section, the names of the banned will be listed in much the same order as they appear in the main source of information (SAIRR, 1976: 102–5).

Restriction orders issued under the suppression of Communism Act numbered 128 at the end of 1975. Those banned under this Act were subjected to the provisions of the Internal Security Amendment Act, 79 of 1976. The names of 95 blacks and 18 whites appeared on a list of banned people published in July 1976. Some were long-term political prisoners who were banned soon after they had served their sentences.

Phillip Matthews, released at the end of December 1975 after 12 years' imprisonment, was immediately restricted to Johannesburg. Andrew Masondo, a former mathematics lecturer at Fore Hare, was released in April after serving 13 years' imprisonment and restricted to Umlazi district in Natal. He escaped and joined the MK cadets in Angola, where he was appointed political commissar in Novo Katenga.

M.H. Soci, H. Ntibixelwa and H. Jinta were banned upon their release from Robben Island in July 1976. Marius Schoon and Michael Ngubeni were released on 17 September after serving

10-year sentences and served with 5-year banning orders. W. Hamilton, Johnny Ramrock and Christopher Wymers, detained under the Terrorism Act and set free in May, were banned in June from attending meetings for five years. They fled the country and found political asylum in Botswana. Eli Weinberg (68), an accused in the Abram Fischer case, trade unionist and celebrated photographer, spent five years in Pretoria jail for offences under the Suppression of Communism Act. On being released he fled via Swaziland to Tanzania. His daughter Sheila, secretary of the Human Rights Committee in Johannesburg, was banned on 30 November.

Jeannette Curtis, archivist at the Institute of Race Relations and formerly attached to the Industrial Aid Society, was banned on 18 November. Banning orders were served on the same day on Durban trade unionists: Miss Pat Horn, John Copelyn, Mr and Mrs Murphy, Chris Albertyn, Alpheus Mthetwa and Mfundisa Ndlovu.

The banning orders on several people were lifted or allowed to lapse in 1976. Among them were Clive Keegan, the Rev. Stephen Hayes, Halton Cheadle and Mrs Phyllis Naidoo, whose banning was allowed to lapse after 10 years' house arrest.

Banning orders were served in Cape Town during 1976 on Graeme Block, member of the university's SRC and president of the Students for Social Democracy. The students' wages and economic commission at UCT was badly hit by restrictions placed on its leading members: Miss Debbie Budlender, Willie Hofmeyer, Jeremy Baskin and Gideon Cohen. Among the trade union workers banned were Miss Wilma van Blerk, of the Food and Allied Canning Union and Miss Judy Favish, a literacy worker with the Western Province Workers' Advice Bureau, Elija Loza, who died of injuries suffered during detention. Other people banned were John Frankish, a UCT medical student, Eric Abraham, a local correspondent for overseas newspapers and Jack Lewis, now teaching at the University of the Western Cape. Mary Simons, a UCT lecturer, and her sister Tanya, a librarian at UCT, the daughters of exiled Ray and Jack Simons, were prohibited from working or being at the university for five years.

Not surprisingly, some people who had been banned and some who had reason to expect being banned chose to leave South Africa illegally for more hospitable surroundings. The refugees included Jerome Modisane, the banned former leader of SASO,

Drake Koka, a banned Soweto trade unionist, Tsietse Mashinini (19), reputed to have been chairman of the Soweto Students Council and two fellow students who fled to England via Botswana in September after the police offered a reward of R500 for information about their whereabouts. The Rev. Maurice Nkakane, a national executive member of the SA Council of Churches fled with his wife and three children to Botswana in September. Mrs Paula Petersen (née Ensor) and her husband Robert Petersen fled in May to Botswana.

By 12 November 500 students from South Africa were officially estimated to be in Botswana with 200–300 adults. Most of the political refugees were in transit, waiting for UN travel documents, which would enable them to settle elsewhere. In 1978 large numbers of banned Black Consciousness youth went to Lesotho, which had a strong ANC presence. In 1979 a former president, permanent organiser and general secretary of SASO, as well as former regional SASO leaders, were in Lesotho.

The banned people who fled into exile sacrificed much. They left their home and children, family and friends, place of work and source of livelihood to venture into a new world and build their lives afresh. The late Dr Francis Meli (1989: 176) observed that 'Banning means a life full of restrictions and tensions and required constant alertness by the banned person to avoid further police action against him or her.' They had reason to fear the consequences of failing to comply with the conditions laid down in the banning order. In the reign of terror imposed by the apartheid state non-compliance, however trivial, might lead to prosecution or detention under the Internal Security Act or Terrorism Act, which provided for indeterminate imprisonment, and possible interrogation by security police. They inflicted violent pain to extract information, by using measures which are briefly described in a number of case histories set out below.

TERRORISM

South Africa's Terrorism Act, 83 of 1967, which applied retrospectively to acts done from 27 June 1962, created the new offence of participation in terrorism activities, defined as acts endangering law and order, including the training of people for such acts. B.J. Vorster, the Minister of Justice, when introducing the second reading of the draft measure, said that the stage of an ideological struggle under the Suppression of Communism Act 1950 had passed. The government was dealing with red arms and no longer with red ideology.

The Act authorised any police officer of or above the rank of Lt.-Colonel to order the arrest without warrant and the detention for interrogation of any person whom he believed to be a terrorist or who withheld from the police information relating to terrorists or to offences under the Act. No one was allowed to have access to a detained person except the minister or an officer of the state acting in his official capacity. Detainees could be held without trial for an unlimited period and had to prove their innocence. The maximum penalty for 'terrorism' was death.

What the apartheid state called 'terrorism' was a form of political violence resorted to by its opponents in a 'people's war', a strategy adopted by the African National Congress in 1985 at its conference in Kabwe, Zambia. Jacklyn Cock (1989: 1–5) points out that political violence was a feature of both state repression and resistance in contemporary South Africa. An estimated 3574 people died in incidents of political violence in 1984–8. Some people called it terrorism or black on black violence, the result of a genetic factor or inter-tribal enmities.

The ANC claimed that it was fighting a guerrilla war of liberation against apartheid and colonialism of a special type. A race war was contrary to the traditions and composition of Congress, which opened its ranks to all races at the 1985 Kabwe Conference. Oliver Tambo, president of the ANC, set a precedent in guerrilla warfare by signing the Geneva Convention binding the signatories to refrain from attacks on civilians and to pursue a humanitarian conduct of the war.

Spokesmen for the regime reject these contentions. Cock quotes Brigadier Hermanus Stadler as saying in a treason trial that the government was facing a revolutionary onslaught (*The Star*, 2 August 1988). In another treason trial he said that South Africa was at war in Angola, but only acts of terror took place in South Africa.

Against this background of contention, an attempt is made to assess the violence inflicted on political activists while in detention.

DEATHS IN DETENTION

Seventy-three black men died while in police detention between 1 September 1963 and 19 August 1985 (Meli, 1988: 177–9). The names of the prisoners, the dates of their death and the official reasons given of the causes of death are tabulated by Meli (1988).

Suicide by hanging were said to have accounted for 24 deaths, 12 to have died from 'natural causes', eight from 'undisclosed' causes, seven from falling out of a window or tumbling down a flight of stairs. Gunshot wounds killed four detainees, four died of head injuries, three were tortured to death, one was 'suffocated', another 'strangled' himself, one was beaten to death, one died of heart failure, another from thrombosis, and so forth.

Most of the official explanations, presumably entered on death certificates or arrived at by inquests, are unsatisfactory. Any competent and vigilant district surgeon or coroner is unlikely to be satisfied with so vague a description as 'natural causes'. When the cause of death is said to be 'undisclosed', one assumes that no death certificate was made out or made public. How were men in solitary confinement under intensive police supervision able to hang themselves? How did prisoners manage to dodge their guards and succeed in jumping through windows or falling down stairs?

These and other questions were put by critics of apartheid, human rights organisation and overseas observers. Among the cases discussed at length in civil rights circles were the deaths of Imam Abdullah Haron, reported to have died on 27 September 1969 by 'falling' down a flight of stairs; Ahmed Timol who on 27 October 1971 'fell' out of a tenth floor window in police headquarters in John Vorster Square, Johannesburg; Elijah Loza who died in hospital on 1 August 1977 while still in police custody, allegedly after suffering a stroke three weeks previously.

Some of the deaths listed by Dr Francis Meli justify closer scrutiny. They were included in a group of 19 persons who died in 1976–7 while in detention under security laws. The circumstances of each death are described in the *Survey of Race Relations* (SAIRR, 1976: 122–6; 1977: 150–67). Biographical notes of selected cases are set out in what follows.

Joseph Mdluli (50) was detained in Pietermaritzburg, Natal on 18 March 1976 and died in his cell the following night because of the 'application of force to his neck'. He was one of a group of ANC members charged with conspiring to recruit men for military training abroad. Justice Howard sentenced Harry Gwala (today still a firebrand in Natal) and four other accused to life imprisonment and five to terms ranging from 7 to 18 years. In a comment on Mdluli's death the judge said there was a reasonable possibility that the police had assaulted him but no positive finding could be made.

Four policemen were charged on 25 October with culpable homicide arising from the death. They were said to have subdued him when he tried to escape during the interrogation. He fell, with his neck or chest hitting the back of a chair. On 28 October Justice James acquitted the policemen, though he acknowledged to having grave doubts about the evidence of police witnesses who gave evidence for the state. James Kruger, Minister of Police, told a press conference in February 1977 that policemen had grappled with Mdluli when he made a suicide attempt. C. Reese, the attorney-general of Natal, said on 25 February that no further action would be taken in connection with the death. No inquest was held because of the decision to charge the four policemen with culpable homicide.

Luke Mazwembe (32) was detained in Cape Town on 2 September 1976 and died the same day. He was a member of the Western Province Workers' Advice Bureau, which together with other concerned organisations called for a full inquest; this began on 11 November. The police claimed that Mazwembe had not been interrogated and had hung himself with a noose made of strips of blanket cut with a razor blade and tied with twine. They were uncertain about how he had obtained the razor and twine, or how injuries on his body had been inflicted. Advocate Farlam for the family accused the police of having inflicted the injuries; but the magistrate who conducted the inquest found that death was by suicide consistent with hanging and that he was unable to infer homicide by the police.

Mapetla Mohapi (25), a former SASO and BPC official, was detained on 15 July 1976 in Kei Road jail near East London in terms of the Terrorism Act. He died the same day. According to the police he had been found hanging from the cell bars by his denim jeans. Dr Hawkes, who conducted a post-mortem the day after the death, in the presence of Dr Mamphela Ramphele and

Dr Msauli, Mrs Mohapi's physicians, and her attorney G. Mxenge, attributed it to force applied to his neck. Mohapi's funeral on 15 August was attended by more than 1500 mourners; memorial services were held in Johannesburg and Cape Town, Drs Ramphele and Msauli were detained in terms of the Internal Security Act, making it difficult to received information from them.

Acting on instructions from the Attorney-General, the King Williams Town magistracy opened an inquest on 17 January 1977. The police produced a suicide note alleged to have been written by Mohapi and testified that Capt. Schoeman and Sgt. Nicholson had interrogated Mohapi during his detention. Dr Cooper, speaking for the Mohapi family, said all the evidence suggested homicide. The magistrate found that the death was due to hanging and not by any living person, but he did not deliver a formal verdict of suicide.

George Botha (30), a Coloured high school teacher in Port Elizabeth, was detained on 10 December 1976 and reported to have died on 15 December after falling down the stairs from the sixth floor to the ground floor of Sanlam Building where the security police had their offices. Major Snyman, Capt. Slebert and Sgt. Prinsloo had interrogated him. They testified at the inquest into his death on 3 May 1977 that as they left the lift, Botha broke loose, jumped over the railing around the stairwell and fell to the ground. Dr B. Tucker, the pathologist who conducted the postmortem examination, found many injuries on parts of the body which were on the deceased probably 2–6 hours before he plunged to his death. Dr Cooper, for the Botha family, said that only the interrogators could explain how he received the injuries. The magistrate, J. Coetzee, said he could not decide how the injuries were sustained. The police witnesses, who denied inflicting any form of violence on Botha, had made a good impression and the court accepted their evidence in full. It found that Botha had died of a head injury sustained when he fell, and this was not due to any offence committed by a person.

IN BRIEF

Dr Naobath Ntshuntsha, a Soweto naturopath, detained on 14 December 1976, was reported on 11 January 1977 to have died in a police cell on 9 January in Leslie Springs in the Eastern Transvaal. Col. C. Coetzee said he hanged himself with a vest torn into strips. An inquest into the death began on 15 September. Mr E. Wentzel, speaking for the family, said that the detainee was willing to talk to the police and had no reason to hang himself. The inquest magistrate returned a verdict of death by hanging, probably suicide, and said no living person could be held responsible.

Elmon Malele (51) was detained in Soweto on 7 January 1977 in terms of the Terrorism Act after explosions in a Klipspruit house. He underwent two brain operations in a Johannesburg nursing home on 20 January. The police testified at a post- mortem on 21 January that Malele had fainted while being interrogated and hit his head against a desk. A neurosurgeon and a government pathologist reported punctures and abrasions on the head which could have been older than a week. The magistrate found that Malele had died of hypertension and spontaneous bleeding of the brain for which no one was to blame.

Phakamile Mabija (27) was detained on 27 June 1977 in the vicinity of stone-throwing in Kimberley. He worked for the Anglican church at the time of his detention and was due to appear in court on charges under the Riotous Assemblies Act. He fell to his death from the 6th floor of the Kimberley police station on 7 July. At the inquest on 1 August, police witnesses alleged that he had jumped through a window – the only one in the building without protective screens and left unlocked and open. The police said they let in fresh air because of bad smells in the room!

Hoosen Haffejee (26), a dentist at a Durban hospital, was taken into custody on 2 August 1977 and held on charges pending under the Terrorism Act. He was found hanging in a police cell the following morning. An inquest was held on 27 February 1978 in the Durban magistrates' court. Police witnesses testified that Dr Haffejee's body had been found hanging with his trousers tied around his neck and attached to the bars of the cell door. Family members took colour photographs of the body, showing some 25 injuries, while Professor Gordon, the senior state pathologist, reported that there 40 to 50 widely distributed injuries. Lieutenant Taylor of the security police said the deceased had resisted getting into the car taking him to the prison and was forced to take a seat. Dr Cooper, for the family, pointed out that the injuries, which had been inflicted up to 12 hours before death, must have resulted from third degree methods used during the interrogation. Mr Blunden, the magistrate, giving his judgment on 15 March 1978, ruled that the death was caused by hanging and no living person was to blame. The reason for the injuries were irrelevant in terms of the Inquests Act, which dealt only the cause of death.

Lungile Tabalaza (29) died on 10 July 1978 at the Sanlam Building, the headquarters of the security police in Port Elizabeth. He was not a political prisoner. He and a 17-year-old youth were arrested on charges of arson and robbery and held under the Criminal Procedure Act, which requires an accused to appear in court within 48 hours after the arrest. They were handed to the security police for interrogation. Tabalaza was alleged to have committed suicide by jumping from the fifth floor of the building. The inquest was held on 15 August in the Port Elizabeth Regional Court. Witnesses testified that shortly before he died at 2.00 pm, Tabalaza had told magistrate W. de Waal Lubbe that he made a statement to Sgt. Nel, his only interrogator, who told him to repeat it to a magistrate. He did so, unwillingly, and only because of being afraid that Nel would beat him up if he refused. On hearing this Lubbe decided against taking a statement and gave his report on the interview to Major de Jongh. Nel told the court that he had neither assaulted nor threatened Tabalaza. Col. van der Merwe, who had investigated the circumstances of the death, said he accepted Nel's account. Many allegations had been made against him, but all were found to be untrue.

Dr Cooper, who appeared for the defence on the criminal charges, told the court that de Jongh and Nel were criminally and morally responsible for Tabalaza's death, but J.A. Coetzee, who conducted the inquest, found on 3 October that it was impossible to determine reasons for the jump and that no person had committed a criminal offence related to the death. He accepted the evidence given by de Jongh and Nel as being honest and concluded that there were no signs of an assault prior to the death.

Tabalaza's funeral on 22 July 1978 was attended by 5000 people and a squad of policemen in anti-riot uniforms who kept a low profile. The charges against Tabalaza were dropped in the third week of July, when staff changes were announced. Colonel Goosen, head of security police in the Eastern Cape, was transferred to another post in another area. Major de Jongh and Sgt. Nel were transferred to the CID. General Geldenhuys said that the changes were made because of failure to carry out instructions regarding the safety of detainees (SAIRR, 1978: 117–19).

BANTU STEPHEN BIKO (1946–77)

Born on 18 December 1946 in Tarkasatd, 40 miles from Queenstown, Biko matriculated at the end of 1965 at the Roman Catholic school at Marianhill in Natal. He joined Nusas but soon left it to form the South African Students Organisation (SASO). Elected its first president in July 1969, he warned students against falling into the trap of accepting a division along colour lines which would seem to be a form of apartheid and be subjected to much scrutiny. Organisations of this kind would have little chance of surviving (Wilson, 1991: 17–25, 68–71).

He was detained in Grahamstown on 18 August while travelling with Peter Jones, a BPC organiser, who was also detained. They were taken the next morning to Port Elizabeth and imprisoned in terms of the Terrorism Act in the police headquarters. Jones was held without trial for 533 days and released in February 1979. On his release he wrote down all he could remember of what happened to him during the first 25 days before Biko died on 12 September.

The security police who interrogated him were Major H. Snyman, Captain Siebert, Warrant Officers Ruben Marx and Beneke, and Detective Sergeant Nieuwoudt. The same team interrogated Biko from 6 September until he died, using the same kind of violence but with different results. 'Peter Jones lived to tell his tale, Bantu Stephen Biko did not' (Wilson, at p. 71). The violence was cruel and out of all proportion to any offence they committed by defying the conditions of their banning orders. They had no weapons or explosives, were not accused of committing acts of violence and did no more than preach the doctrine of Black Consciousness and self-reliance. The tormentors, insisting that they were plotting treason, used the modern equivalents of the medieval rack to extract confession that would justify the use of horrendous torture.

Jones was made to stand, carrying heavy steel chairs, on small bricks for hours while being questioned. The treatment was repeated, interspersed with blows to the head and lumbar region by loaded hosepipes, open hands and fists, until the policemen were out of breath. 'My mouth was very cut and swollen and I could just nod a reply' (Wilson, at p. 70).

The Biko Inquest

Biko died of a brain injury on 12 September 1977. A post-mortem inquiry, headed by Professor Loubser, the state's chief pathologist, began on 14 September and lasted 15 days. Policemen testified that Biko was held from the date of his detention until 5 September in the Walmer Street police cells, kept naked to prevent him hanging himself, and denied outdoor exercise, contrary to prison regulations, on instructions from the security police. A visiting magistrate testified that Biko had complained of being kept naked and given only bread to eat. He was chained in leg irons and handcuffs during the interview in the office of the security police.

He was transferred to the offices of the security police on the 6th floor of the Port Elizabeth Sanlam buildings. Major Snyman led the five-man team that began questioning him on 6 September. A night squad led by Lt. Wilkins guarded him while he was chained in the office. Wilkins noticed a mark on his forehead, denied interrogating him, but said that Biko had undertaken to give a statement and then fell asleep before doing so.

Major Snyman testified that Biko had become aggressive on the morning of 7 September after being questioned about his involvement in drafting and distributing a 'Black Power' pamphlet and had to be subdued by the entire team. In the scuffle Biko hit his head against a wall. Mr S. Kentridge, S.C., representing the Biko family, pointed out that none of 28 affidavits made by doctors and policemen had mentioned the incident, but Snyman claimed to have noted it on 8 September in the police station occurrence book. He called Col. Goosen, divisional commander of the security police to see Steve Biko. Goosen said he saw a swelling on Biko's lip. He had a wild expression and refused to talk. Dr Lang, the district surgeon, was called to see him. He signed a certificate at Goosen's request stating that he found 'no evidence of abnormal pathology'. He admitted under cross-examination that the certificate was wrong because Biko had refused water and food, was weak in all his limbs, had a cut on his lip, a bruise on his rib, swollen feet, ankles and hands, slurred speech, and could not walk properly. Goosen suggested that Biko was shamming.

On the following day, 8 September, Dr Lang with Dr Tucker, the chief district surgeon, examined Biko. He was still in leg irons, lying on a mat in the office with blankets wet with urine. They recommended that he be removed to the prison hospital for examination by a specialist. Dr Hersch, a physician, who examined him, conducted a lumbar puncture and consulted Mr Keeley, a neurosurgeon. He said that Biko should be sent to the Livingstone Hospital for observation. Goosen refused and ordered Biko to be sent back to his prison cell on the 11th.

The spinal fluid from the lumbar puncture was sent under a false name to the S.A. Institute for Medical Research. The test showed that there were red blood cells in the sample, an indication of abnormality. Hersch could not say who had put a false name on the sample and why he had signed a letter saying that the test showed the liquid to be 'clear'.

Dr Tucker was called to see Biko on the 11th after his return to the police cell. Goosen told him that Biko was lying on the floor in an 'apathetic condition'. Dr Tucker said he should be admitted to hospital. Goosen ordered him to be sent to Pretoria for treatment in a prison hospital. He was in a coma when placed naked with blankets over him and a bottle of water in a police Landrover for the journey of hundreds of miles from Port Elizabeth to Pretoria. On arrival he was carried into a police cell. Dr A. van Zyl examined him at 3.00 pm on 12 September without having received his medical history or report that the case was urgent. He found him comatose, lying on mats on the cell floor, and ordered him to be given an intravenous drip and a vitamin injection. He died during the night of the 12th.

Advocate Kentridge, in his closing remarks, accused the police of giving false evidence to conceal their assault on Biko. Goosen misled the doctors by telling them that Biko was shamming, and tried to persuade the Pretoria police to swallow the same story, but the subservience of the doctors in Port Elizabeth to Goosen came close to collusion which might have contributed to the death (SAIRR, 1977: 159–64).

The inquest magistrate, Marthinus Prins, in a three-minute verdict, declared that on the available evidence the death could not be attributed to a criminal offence on the part of anyone, but he sent the post-mortem record to the South African Medical and Dental Council. A preliminary committee of the Council decided in April 1980 that there was no obvious evidence of improper conduct by the practitioners. The full Council, meeting in private, ratified the decision without making their reasons public.

The Medical Association of South Africa (MASA), a voluntary body without statutory powers, but strongly represented in the SAMDC, reviewed in September 1980 the treatment of Biko by Drs Long and Tucker, who were members of MASA. While supporting the SAMDC's decision, they urged it to consider whether Biko's life would have been saved if he had received intensive medical and nursing care. The boards of the medical faculties of the Witwatersrand and Cape Town universities disassociated themselves from the Council's decision; and Professor Stuart Saunders, principal designate of the University of Cape Town, resigned from the Association over its findings and called on it to conduct a full and open inquiry.

Barney Pityana (1991: 7–8), in a comment on medical ethics, security laws and Biko's death, argued that doctors feel they have a duty to support the police in their treatment of political prisoners. Clinical independence is sacrificed in the process. A similar attitude is taken by the Medical and Dental Council, a statutory body formed to look after the interests of the profession and ensure a high moral standard among practitioners. The Council's behaviour in the Biko case resulted from political pressures rather than an attempt to uphold ethical values. It is customary bias which occurs in all criminal trials. Judges are part of the state apparatus and habitually prefer to take the word of police witnesses while tending to belittle evidence given by accused persons and their defence. The court proceedings arising from the death of Steve Biko and Neil Aggett demonstrated the dominant role of the security police.

NEIL AGGETT

Neil (28) was a medical doctor and the Transvaal organiser of the Food and Canning Workers Union (FCWU), which had agreed in September 1979 at a national conference in Paarl to invite him to work for the union. In September 1980 he was one of seven delegates who negotiated an agreement with the management of Fatti and Moni, a large manufacturer of food products in Cape Town. The FCWU was a militant union organised by Ray Alexander-Simons, whose struggle to form a multi-racial union open to all colour groups exposed it to much intimidation and harassment by the Labour Ministry and security police.

For reasons that were never fully explained, Aggett was detained on 26 November 1981 in the John Vorster Square police station in Johannesburg under the Internal Security Act, and later under the Terrorism Act which allowed indeterminate detention. He died in his cell on 5 February 1982. His funeral was attended by about 11 000 people of all colour groups. An inquest into his death began on 3 March and lasted for 44 days. The official explanation was that he had hanged himself.

Widespread condemnation followed. Protest meetings were held in the big towns and cities. Speakers called for the repeal of detention laws and the release of all detainees. Among the protesting organisations were trade unions, student organisations, academic staff at English-speaking universities, church groups, detainees support committees, chambers of commerce and industry, the United Nations Special Committee against Apartheid, international trade union federations, the British Labour Party and the Anti-Apartheid Movement.

G. Bizos S.C., representing the family, applied to have eight detainees and ex-detainees give evidence. A Supreme Court judge overruled the state's objections and upheld the application, saying that any appearance of a cover-up would do immeasurable harm.

Witnesses testified that a magistrate took a statement on 19 January from Aggett, who complained of being tortured. His complaint was investigated only three weeks later by a Sergeant Blom who recorded Aggett's renewed statement of being assaulted and given electric shocks. Two magistrates and the Inspector of Detainees made three attempts to see Aggett but were told he was 'unavailable'. The police officer responsible for supervising detainees, who was instructed to visit them every hour, was 'too busy' to see Aggett on the night of 5 February when he died. Maurice Smithers, a fellow detainee, said he saw Aggett through a frosted glass panel doing strenuous physical exercise and being beaten while naked. Aggett was subjected to 'intensive interrogation' for 60 hours between 28 and 31 January by teams led by Colonel Whitehead Major Cromwright and Lieutenant Smith and made to sleep afterwards on a camp bed in the interrogation room. Handwritten and typed versions of statements by Aggett during the interrogation conflicted, and dozens of pages were withheld at the inquest because they contained information 'under investigation'.

When the inquest was resumed on 20 September, nine former detainees gave evidence. Some, who had seen Aggett during his last week, said that his condition had seriously deteriorated. Two days before he died he told Jabu Ngwenya that he had been given electric shocks. Auret van Heerden testified to having been told by Aggett that he was beaten, shocked through his testicles and forced to make a statement linking him to the S.A. Congress of Trade Unions and Communists. Thabo Lerumo saw him being escorted back to his cell only hours before his death. He was in pain, had blood on his forehead and walked with great difficulty.

In his final submission Mr Bizos conceded that Aggett had committed suicide, but said that Cronwright and Whitehead were guilty of culpable homicide.

Mr A. Kotze, the presiding magistrate, ruled in December that Neil had died of 'suicide hanging' because of a feeling of insecurity and guilt resulting from his disclosures of activities of colleagues. Kotze found that the testimony of more than 30 policemen who gave evidence was honest and reliable, whereas the evidence of former detainees was contradictory and inconsistent (SAIRR, 1982: 254–8).

EPILOGUE: DEATH BY EXECUTION

In late 1979 I was asked to visit Morogoro in Tanzania where a school was being planned for ANC recruits on a disused sisal estate. During the next ten years a large comprehensive school was built under the skilled and devoted care of the chief construction engineer Oswald Dennis and his wife Emily, an energetic and competent organiser of the fast-growing section of women, some of whom worked in a garment factory. The buildings included a hospital, assembly hall, pre-school facilities for children of working or absentee mothers, a mechanical workshop and farm stocked with poultry, goats, pigs and cattle. Alfalfa was grown for the livestock and maize for the humans.

The complex was called the Solomon Mahlangu Freedom College (Somafco). The ANC's executive committee decided on the name soon after the execution in Pretoria Central prison of Solomon Kalushi Mahlangu (21) on 6 April 1979. He left South Africa in 1976 after the Soweto revolt, joined Umkhonto, received military training and re-entered South Africa in 1977. In June he and his MK companion Mondy Motloung were cornered by police and white civilians in Goch Street, Johannesburg. Motloung fired a pistol and threw a hand grenade, killing two whites. He was detained and beaten so badly that he was declared unfit because of brain damage to stand trial.

Though Solomon had not used a weapon he was charged with murder by reason of acting in common and with criminal intent for the same purpose as Motloung. The trial judge found him guilty and sentenced him to be hanged. An application to lodge an appeal with the Appellate Division was refused. P.W. Botha, the prime minister, refused to commute the death sentence in spite of many protests from international and domestic groups.

In his last letter to his mother and family in his home town of Mamelodi, overlooking Pretoria, he sent a message which is famous and often quoted. 'My blood will nourish the tree which will bear the fruits of freedom. Tell my people that I love them and that they must continue the struggle.' Francis Meli (1988: 190) wrote that Solomon represented the young generation of liberators who were ready to pay the supreme price for freedom.

On 6 April 1993 his coffin was unearthed at the place where the prison authorities had buried him and taken to the cemetery of Mamelodi. Thousands of mourners, clergy, family and MK guerrillas parading with knees kept stiff stopped at Solomon Mahlangu Square to hear Nelson Mandela pay tribute before escorting the coffin to the grave, where family and comrades-in-arms carried out the last ritual of sprinkling earth on the coffin. 'Dust to dust. Solomon Mahlangu had come home' (*The Weekly Mail*, 6–15 April 1993: 4).

References

CHAPTER 1 EARLY CAPE SOCIETIES

Anderson, A.A., *Twenty-five Years in a Waggon. Sport and Travel in South Africa* (London: 1888).

Armstrong, J.C. and Worden, N., 'The slaves, 1652–1834', in R. Elphick and H. Giliomee (eds), *The Shaping of South African Society, 1652–1840* (Cape Town: Maskew Miller Longman, 1989), pp. 109–62.

Asad, Talal (ed.), *Anthropology and the Colonial Encounter* (London: Ithaca Press, 1975).

Beyers, C.J. (ed.) *Dictionary of South African Biography*, vol. 5 (Pretoria: Human Science Research Council, 1987).

Böeseken, Anna J., *Rapport*, 6 February 1977.

Bosman, D.B. et al., *Tweetalige Woordeboek. Afrikaans–Engels* (Kaapstad: Nasionale Pers, 1936).

Bowles, R.P., *The Indian: Assimilation, Integration or Separation?* (Seaborough, Ontario: Prentice Hall of Canada, 1972).

Branford, Jean, *A Dictionary of South African English* (Cape Town: Oxford University Press, 1980).

Bredekamp, H.C. (ed.), *Afrikaans Historiography and Literature: Past, Present and Future* (Bellvile: University of the Western Cape Institute for Historical Research, 1992).

Bredekamp, H.C., *'Afrikaanse Geskiedskrywing en Letterkunde: Hede, Verlede en Toekoms'* (Bellville: Universiteit van Westkaapland se Institut vir Historiese Navorsing, 1992).

Brown, Richard, 'Anthropology and Colonial Rule. The Case of Godfrey Wilson and the Rhodes-Livingstone Institute, Northern Rhodesia', in Talal Asad (ed.), *Anthropology and the Colonial Encounter* (London: Ithaca Press, 1975), pp. 173–97.

Carstens, W.P., *The Social Structure of a Cape Coloured Reserve. A Study of Racial Integration and Segregation in South Africa* (Cape Town: Oxford University Press, 1966).

Doke, C.M., 'Bushmen of the Southern Kalaha'. Paper reprinted from *Bantu Studies*, Vol. XI, No. 3, together with some additional material (Johannesburg: University of Witwatersrand Press, 1937).

Duggan-Cronin, A.M., *The Bushman Tribes of South Africa. With an Introductory Article on the Bushmen Tribes and Descriptive Notes on the Plates by D.F. Bleek* (Kimberley, The Alexander McGregor Memorial Museum, 1942).

Edwards, Isobel, Towards Emancipation: A Study in Souther African Slavery (Cardiff: University of Wales, 1942).

Eiselen, W.M., 'Christianity and the Religious Life of the Bantu', in I. Schapera (ed.), *Western Civilization and the Native of South Africa. Studies in Culture Contact.* (London: Routledge, 1934), pp. 65–82.

Eiselen, W.M., 'Die Suid-Afrikaanse Inboorlinge' in A.J.H. Van Der Wat et al. (eds), *Geskiedenis van Suid-Afrika*, vol. 2 (Kaapstad, 1951).

Elphick, R. and Malherbe, V.C., *The Khoisan to 1828*, in R. Elphick and H. Giliomee (eds), *The Shaping of South African Society, 1652–1840* (Cape Town: Maskew Miller Longman, 1989).

Elphick, R. and Shell, R., 'Intergroup relations: Khoikhoi, settlers, slaves and free blacks, 1652–1793', in R. Elphick and H. Giliomee (eds), *The Shaping of South African Society, 1652–1840* (Cape Town: Maskew Miller Longman, 1989), pp. 184–230.

Fagan, B.M. (ed.), *A History of Zambia from Earlier Times until* AD 1900 (London: Oxford University Press, 1966).

Fredrickson, G.M., *White Supremacy. A Comparative Study in American and South African History* (New York: Oxford University Press, 1982).

Gie, S.F.N., *Geskidenis von Suid-Afrika, ofs, Ons Verlede* [History of South Africa, or Our Past], 2 vols (Stellenbosch: Pro Ecclesia Drukkery, 1924).

Gluckman, Max, *Politics, Law and Ritual in Tribal Society* (Oxford: Basil Blackwell, 1965).

Guelke, L., 'Freehold Farmers and Frontier Settlers', in R. Elphick and H. Giliomee (eds), *The Shaping of South African Society, 1652–1840* (Cape Town: Maskew Miller Longman, 1989), pp. 66–101.

Hailey, Lord, *An African Survey. Revised 1956. A Study of Problems Arising In Africa South of The Sahara* (London: Oxford University Press, 1957).

Heese, H., *Slawerny in die Afrikaanse Geskiedskrywing* (Institut vir Historiese Navorsing, n.d., c..1991).

Hugo, P. (ed.), *South African Perspective* (Pretoria: Sigma Press, 1989).

Igbozurika, M., *Problem-generating Structures in Nigeria's Rural Development* (Uppsala: The Scandinavian Institute of African Studies, 1976).

International Labour Office, *Indigenous Peoples. Living and Working Conditions of Aboriginal Populations in Independent Countries* (Geneva: ILO, 1953).

Kotzé, C.F., 'A New Regime, 1806–1834', in C.F.J. Muller (ed.), *Five Hundred Years. A History of South Africa* (Pretoria, Academica, 1980), pp. 117–45.

Macmillan, W.M., *The Cape Coloured Question. A Historical Survey* (London: Faber & Gweyer, 1928).

Malherbe, V.C., *These Small People* (Pietermaritzburg: Shuter and Shooter, 1986).

Marais, J.S., *Maynier and the First Boer Republic* (Cape Town: Maskew Miller, 1945).

Marais, J.S., *The Cape Coloured People 1652–1937* (Johannesburg: Witwatersrand University Press, 1957).

Mason, R.J., *Identification of Class in Sotho-Tswana Archaeology. Johannesburg Southern Western Central Transvaal AD 300–1800 Archaeological Research Unit, Multi-graph* (Johannesburg, University of the Witwatersrand, 1987).

Maunier, René, *The Sociology of Colonies. An Introduction to the Study of Race Contact.* vol. 2, ed. and trans. by E.O. Lorimer (London: Routledge & Kegan Paul, 1949).

Müller, A.L., *Ekonomies Geskiedskrywing in Afrikaans.* Referaat gelewer by die Universiteit van die Wes Kaapland, 17 October 1991.

Muller, C.F.J., *500 Years. A History of South Africa* (Cape Town: National Book Printers, 1980; Ist edn 1969).

Nosipho Majeke (pseud. Dora Taylor), *The Role of the Missionaries in Conquest* (Johannesburg: Society of Young Africa, circa 1952).

Oakes, Dougie (ed.), *Illustrated History of South Africa. The Real Story* (Cape Town: The Reader's Digest Association South Africa Ltd, 1988).

Peires, J.B., *The House of Phalo. A history of the Xhosa People in the Days of their Independence* (Johannesburg: Raven Press, 1981).

Roberts, A., *A History of Zambia* (London: Heinemann Educational Books, 1976).

Rogers, B., *Divide and Rule: South Africa Bantustans* (London: International Defence and Aid Fund, 1976).

Saunders, C., *The Making of the South African Past. Major Historians on Race and Class* (Cape Town: David Philip, 1988).

Schuman, C.G.W., *Structural Changes and Business Cycles in South Africa, 1806–1936* (London: King & Son, 1939).

Schapera, I., *The Khoisan Peoples of South Africa. Bushmen and Hottentots* (London: Routledge & Sons. 1930).

Schapera, I. (ed.), *The Early Cape Hottentots described in the writings of Offert Dapper (1688), Willem Ten Rhyne (1686) and Johannes Gulielmus de Gravensbroek (1695).* trans. I. Schapera and B. Farrington (Cape Town: Van Riebeeck Society, 1933).

Schapera, I. (ed.), *Western Civilization and the Natives of South Africa: Studies in Culture Contact* (London: Routledge, 1934).

Schapera, I. (ed.), *The Bantu-Speaking Tribes of South Africa. An Ethnographical Survey* (London: Routledge, 1937).

Schapera, I., *A Handbook of Tswana Law and Custom. International African Institute* (London: Oxford University Press, 1955).

Schapera, I., *Handbook of Tswana Law and Custom* (London: Frank Cass, 1970).

Schapera, I., *Rainmaking Rites of the Tswana Tribes* (Lein: Afrika-Studiecentrum, 1971).

Schapera, I., *Praise Poems of Tswana Chiefs* (n.d.).

Scully, W.C., *Between Sun and Sand. A Tale of an African Desert* (Cape Town: Juta, circa 1898).

South African Institute of Race Relations, *Race Relations*. A Quarterly Journal published by South African Institute of Race Relations. Vol. XV, No. 3 (1948).

Stow, G.W., *The Native Races of South Africa. A History of the Intrusion of the Hottentots and Bantu into the Hunting Grounds of the Bushmen, the Aborigines of the Country* (London, 1905).

Theal, G.M., *Ethnography and Condition of South Africa before A.D. 1505* (London: Allen and Unwin, 1919).

Thompson, L., 'The Forgotten Factor in Southern African History', in Leonard Thompson (ed.), *African Studies in Southern Africa* (London: Heinemann Educational Books, 1969), pp. 1–23.

van der Heever, C.N. and P. de Pienaar (eds.), *Kultuurgeskiedemis van die Afrikaner: Die eerste beskigiwing van die Boere-volksleive in al sy verlakking*, 2 vols (Kaapstad: Nasionale Peis, 1945–50).

van der Walt, AJ., AJ. Wild and A.L. Geyer (eds.), *Geskiedenis van Suid-Afrika*, 2vols (Kaapstad: Nasionale Boekhandel, 1951).

Watson, S., *Return of the Moon. Visions from the /Xam* (Cape Town, The Carrefour Press, 1991).

Wellington, J.H., *South West Africa and its Human Issues* (Oxford: Clarendon Press, 1967).

Wright, H.M., *The Burden of the Present. Liberal–Racial Controversy over Southern African History* (Cape Town: David Philip, 1977).

CHAPTER 2   THE COLONIAL CONQUEST OF ZAMBIA

Barnes, J.A., *Politics in a Changing Society. A Political History of the Fort Jameson Ngoni* (Manchester University Press for The Institute for Social Research. Lusaka, University of Zambia, 1967).

Berger, Elena L., *Labour, Race and Colonial Rule. The Copperbelt from 1924 to Independence* (London: Oxford University Press, 1974).

Brown, Richard, 'Anthropology and Colonial Rule. The Case of Godfrey Wilson and the Rhodes-Livingstone Institute, Northern Rhodesia', in Talal Asad (ed.), *Anthropology and the Colonial Encounter* (London: Ithaca Press, 1975), pp. 173–97.

Burawoy, Michael, *The Colour of Class on the Copper Mines. From African Advancement to Zambianization*, Zambian Papers No. 7 (Manchester University Press for The Institute for African Studies, Lusaka, University of Zambia, 1972).

Colson, E. and M. Gluckman (eds.), *Seven Tribes of Central Africa* (Manchester: Manchester University Press for the Institute of Social Research, University of Zambia, 1959; repr. 1968). (First published by Oxford University Press, 1951, as *Seven Tribes of Central British Africa*.)

Colson, Elizabeth, *The Social Consequences of Resettlement. The Impact of the Kariba Resettlement upon the Gwembe Tonga* (Manchester University Press for The Institute for African Studies. Lusaka, University of Zambia, 1971).

Colson, Elizabeth, 'The Institute under Max Gluckman, 1942–47' and 'From Livingstone to Lusaka, 1948–51, in Mubanga E. Kashoki et al. (eds), *African Social Research, The Journal of The Institute for African Studies* (Manchester University Press for The Institute for African Studies, Lusaka, University of Zambia, 1977), pp. 285–95 and 295–307.

Cunnison, Ian, *The Luapula Peoples of Northern Rhodesia. Custom and History in Tribal Politics* (Manchester University Press for The Institute for Social Research, Lusaka, University of Zambia, 1959).

Davidson, Apollon, *Cecil Rhodes and his Time*, trans. C. English (Moscow: Progress Publishers, 1988).

Davis, J. Merle (ed.), *Modern Industry and the African. An Enquiry into the Effect of the Copper Mines of Central Africa upon Native Society and the Work of Christian Missions made under the auspices of the Department of Social and Industrial Research of the International Missionary Council* (London: Macmillan, 1933).

Epstein, A.L., *Politics in an Urban African Community* (Manchester University Press for the Rhodes-Livingstone Institute, Northern Rhodesia, 1958).

Garth, H.H. and Mills, C.W. (eds), *From Max Weber. Essays in Sociology* (London: Routledge and Kegan Paul, 1948).

Gluckman, Max, 'The Lozi of Barotseland in North-West Rhodesia', in E. Colson and M. Gluckman (eds), *Seven Tribes of Central Africa* (Manchester University Press for Institute for Social Research, Lusaka, University of Zambia, 1961).

Hailey, Lord, *An African Survey Revised 1956. A Study of Problems arising in Africa South of the Sahara* (London: Oxford University Press, 1957).

International Labour Office, *Basic Needs in an Economy under Pressure. Findings and Recommendations of an ILO/JASPA Basic Needs Mission to Zambia* (Job Skills Programme for Africa, Addis Ababa, 1981).

Kashoki, Mubanga E. et al. (eds), *African Social Research* (Formerly The Rhodes-Livingstone Journal), *Human Problems in Central Africa*, Anniversary Issue No. 24 (Manchester University Press for The Institute for African Studies, Lusaka, University of Zambia, 1977).

Long, Norman, *Social Change and the Individual. A Study of the Social and Religious Responses to Innovation in a Zambian Rural Community* (Manchester University Press for The Institute for Social Research, Lusaka, University of Zambia, 1968).

Lungu, G.F., *Administrative Decentralization in the Zambia Bureaucracy. An Analysis of Environmental Constraints*, Zambian Paper No. 18. Institute for African Studies, African Social Research (Lusaka, University of Zambia, 1985).

Meebelo, Henry S., *Reaction to Colonialism. A Prelude to the Politics of Independence in Northern Zambia 1893–1939* (Manchester University Press for The Institute for African Studies, Lusaka, University of Zambia, 1971).

Mulford, David C., *Zambia. The Politics of Independence 1957–1964* (London: Oxford University Press, 1967).

Mushindo, Reverend Paul Bwembya, *The Life of a Zambian Evangelist; the reminiscences*, with an Editorial Foreword by J. van Velsen and a Note by Fergus Macpherson, Communication No. 9 (Institute for African Studies, Lusaka, University of Zambia, 1973).

Mwanakatwe, J.M., *The Growth of Education in Zambia since Independence* (Lusaka: Oxford University Press, 1968).

Oakes, Dougie (ed.), *Reader's Digest Illustrated History of South Africa. The Real Story* (Cape Town: The Reader's Digest Association of South Africa, 1988).

Omer-Cooper, John, *The Zulu Aftermath. A Nineteenth-Century Revolution in Bantu Africa* (London: Longmans, Green, 1966).

Perrings, Charles, 'Consciousness, Conflict and Proletarianization: An Assessent of the 1935 Mineworkers' Strike on the Northern Rhodesian Copperbelt', *Journal of Southern African Studies*, vol. 4, no. 1, 1977, pp. 31–51.

Pim, Sir Alan and Milligan, S., *Report of the Commission Appointed to Enquire into the Financial and Economic Position of Northern Rhodesia*. Colonial No. 145 (London: H.M. Stationery Office, 1938).

Prain, Sir Ronald, 'African Advancement on the Copperbelt', *African Affairs, Journal of the Royal African Society*, vol. liii, 1954.

Richards, Audrey, 'The Rhodes-Livingstone Institute: An Experiment in Research, 1933–38', in *African Social Research*, no. 24 (Manchester University Press for The Institute for African Studies, Lusaka, University of Zambia, 1977).

Roberts, Andrew, *A History of Zambia* (London: Heinemann Educational Books, 1976).

Ross, Rev. Andrew C., 'The African – A Child or a Man. The Quarrel between the Blantyre Mission of the Church of Scotland and the British Central Africa Administration 1890–1905', in E. Stokes and R. Brown (eds), *The Zambian Past. Studies in Central African History* (Manchester University

Press for The Institute for Social Research. Lusaka, University of Zambia, 1966).

Rotberg, Robert I., *Christian Missionaries and the Creation of Northern Rhodesia 1880–1924* (Princeton, New Jersey: Princeton University Press, 1965).

Saffrey, A. Lynn, *A Report on Some Aspects of African Living Conditions on the Copperbelt of Northern Rhodesia* (Lusaka, 1943).

Scudder, Thayer, *Kariba Studies. Volume 11, The Ecology of the Gwembe Tonga* (Manchester University Press for the Rhodes-Livingstone Institute Northern Rhodesia, Manchester: University Press, 1962).

Simons, H. J., 'Customary Unions in a Changing Society', reprinted from *Acta Juridica* (University of Cape Town, Balkema, 1958).

Simons, H. J., 'Prologue' in *African Social Research* (Manchester University Press for the Institute for African Studies, Lusaka, University of Zambia, 1977), pp. 259–73.

Simons, H.J., 'Zambia's Urban Situation', in H. Jack Simons et al., *Slums or Self-Reliance? Urban Growth in Zambia*, Communication No. 12 (The Institute for African Studies, Lusaka, University of Zambia, 1976), pp. 1–32.

Simons, H.J., 'The Institute under Max Gluckman, 1942–47' and 'From Livingstone to Lusaka, 1948–51, in Mubanga E. Kashoki et al. (eds), *African Social Research, The Journal of The Institute for African Studies* (Manchester University Press for The Institute for African Studies. Lusaka, University of Zambia, 1977), pp. 285–95 and 295–307.

Simons, H.J., 'Zambia's Urban Situation', in Ben Turok (ed.), *Development in Zambia: A Reader* (London: ZED Press, 1979), pp. 1–25.

Simons, J. and Simons R.E., *One Hundred Years of Job Reservation on the South African Mines* (International Migration for Employment Working Paper, Geneva, International Labour Office, 1987).

Thompson, Leonard, 'The Forgotten Factor in Southern African History', in Leonard Thompson (ed.), *African Societies in Southern Africa* (London: Heinemann Educational Books, 1969), pp. 1–23.

Tordoff, W. (eds.), *Politics in Zambia* (Manchester: Manchester University Press/Lusaka, distributed by the Institute for African Studies, University of Zambia, 1974).

Turok, B. (ed.), *Development in Zambia: A Reader* (London: Zed Books, 1979).

Turner, V.W., *Schism and Continuity in an African Society. A Study of Ndembu Village Life* (Manchester University Press for The Institute for Social Research, Lusaka, University of Zambia, 1957).

van Binsbergen, Wim M.J., *Religious Change in Zambia Exploratory Studies*, Academisch Proefschrift, Vrye Universiteit te Amsterdam (Harlem: In de Knipscheer, 1979).

Walker, Eric A., *A History of Southern Africa* (London: Longmans Green, 1964).

Watson, William, *Tribal Cohesion in a Money Economy. A Study of the Mambwe People of Northern Rhodesia* (Manchester University Press for The Rhodes-Livingstone Institute, Northern Rhodesia, Manchester: University Press, 1958).

Wilson, Godfrey, *Essay on the Economies of Detribalisation in Northern Rhodesia*, Rhodes-Livingstone Papers, 5 and 6 (Northern Rhodesia, 1941–2).

Wilson, Monica, 'The First Three Years, 1938–41', in *African Social Research*, Anniversary Issue (Manchester University Press for The Institute for African Studies, Manchester: University Press, 1977), pp. 279–83.

CHAPTER 3 PATRIARCHAL RULE

Bennett, T.W. and Peart, N.S., 'The Dualism of Marriage Laws in Africa', in T.W. Bennett et al. (eds), *Family Law in the Last Two Decades of the Twentieth Century* (Cape Town: Juta & Co., 1983), pp. 145–69.

Bodenheimer, E., *Jurisprudence* (New York: McGraw-Hill, 1940).

British Parliamentary Papers (BPP), *c. 1697 Correspondence Relating to the Establishment of the Settlement of Natal* (1853).

Burman, Sandra, 'Roman-Dutch Family Law for African. The Black Divorce Court in Action', in T.W. Bennett et al. (eds), *Family Law in the Last Two Decades of the Twentieth Century* (Cape Town: Juta & Co., 1983), pp. 171–89.

Cachalia, Firoz, *The Future of Muslim Family Law in South Africa* (Centre for Applied Legal Studies, Johannesburg: University of the Witwatersrand, 1991).

Campbell, J., *Myths To Live By* (London: Paladin, 1985).

Cape, G.4., *Government Commission on Native Laws and Customs. Report and Proceedings with Appendices and Minutes of Evidence* (Cape Town: Government Printer, 1883).

Ellis, Havelock, *Studies in the Psychology of Sex*, vol. vi (London: Heinemann, 1928).

Garthorne, E.R., *The Application of Native Law in the Transvaal* (Native Affairs Department, Pretoria, 1924).

Garthorne, E.R., 'Applications of Native Law', *Bantu Studies*, vol. 3, no. 3 (Johannesburg: University of the Witwatersrand, 1929).

Hahlo, H.R., *The South African Law of Husband and Wife* (Cape Town: Juta & Co., 1953, 1963).

Hailey, Lord, *An African Survey. A Study of Problems Arising in Africa South of the Sahara* (London: Oxford University Press, 1957).

Himonga, Chuma, 'Property Disputes in Law and Practice: Dissolution of Marriage in Zambia', in Alice Armstrong (ed.), *Women and Law in Southern Africa* (Harare: Zimbabwe Publishing House, 1987), pp. 56–84.

Krige, E.J. and Krige, J.D., *The Realm of the Rain Queen* (London: Oxford University Press, 1943).

Longwe, Sara Hlupekile, 'Legalised Discrimination against Women in Zambia', Conference on Women's Rights, Mindolo Ecumenical Foundation, 22–24 March 1985 (typescript).

Molokomme, Athalia, 'Marriage – What Every Woman Wants or "Civil Death"? The status of married women in Botswana', in Alice Armstrong (ed.), *Women and Law in Southern Africa* (Harare: Zimbabwe Publishing House, 1987), pp. 181–92.

Mvunga, Mphanza P., *Land Law and Policy in Zambia*, Zambian Papers No. 17, University of Zambia, Lusaka (Gweru, Zimbabwe: Mambo Press, 1982).

Natal, *Commission Appointed to Inquire into the Past and Present State of the Kaffir in the District of Natal. Proc. and Report* (Pietermaritzburg: Government Printers, 1852–3).

Natal, *Despatch with Enclosures from Lt. Governor Scott to his Grace the Duke of Newcastle, No. 34* (1864).

Nathan, Carmen, *You, Your Family and the Law* (Johannesburg: Divaris Stein Publishers, 1983).

Ndulo, Muna, cited in Chuma Himonga, 'Property Disputes in Law and Practice: Dissolution of Marriage in Zambia', in Alice Armstrong (ed.), *Women and Law in Southern Africa* (Harare: Zimbabwe Publishing House, 1987), p. 60.

Nhlapo, Thandabantu, 'Law versus Culture: Ownership of Freehold Land in Swaziland', in Alice Armstrong (ed.), *Women and Law in Southern Africa* (Harare: Zimbabwe Publishing House, 1987), pp. 32–55.

Nube, Welshman, 'The Decision in *Katekwe* v. *Muchambaiwa*: A Critique', *Zimbabwe Law Review*, vols 1 and 2 (Zimbabwe: Legal Projects Centre, 1983–4).

Notulen der Verrigtingen van den Hoog-Edelen Volksraad van den Oranjevristaat in zijne gewone en buitrengewone Jaarlijksche zittingen van 31 Januarij, 1 Mei en 7 December 1876 (Bloemfontein: Die Volksraad, 1876; Bloemfontein: White, Barlow, Drukkers, 1876).

Orpen, J.M., *Reminiscences of Life in South Africa from 1846 etc.*, Vol. 1 (Durban: Davis, 1909).

Schapera, I., *A Handbook of Tswana Law and Custom* (London: Oxford University Press, 1955).

Seymour, S.M., *Native Law in South Africa*, 2nd edn (Cape Town: Juta & Co., 1960).

Simons, H.J., *African Women. Their Legal Status in South Africa* (London: Christopher Hurst, 1968).

Simons, H.J., 'South Africa's Family and Marriage Law Reformed. Towards One System for All South Africans', presented at the Centre for African Studies, University of Cape Town, 26 June 1991.

South African Institute of Race Relations, *A Survey of Race Relations in South Africa, 1976* (Johannesburg: S.A. Institute of Race Relations, 1977).

Stewart, J.'Playing the Game: Women's Inheritance of Property in Zimbabwe', in Alice Armstrong, (ed.), *Women and Law in Southern Africa* (Harare: Zimbabwe Publishing House, 1987), pp. 85–101.

Stewart, Julie and Armstrong, Alice (eds), *Women and Law in Southern Africa* (Harare: Zimbabwe Publishing House, 1990).

Transkei, *Transkeian Territories General Council* (Umtata, 1920).

van der Walt, A.J.H. et al. (eds), *Geskiedenis van Suid-Afrika*, vol. II (Pretoria: Nasionale Boekhandel, 1955).

Transkeian Territories General Council. Proceedings and Reports of Select Committees at the session of *1921*, Annual reports and accounts for *1920* and Estimates of revenue and expenditure for *1921–22*.

Unitata: Territorial New (printers), *1921*.

Walker, Eric A., *A History of Southern Africa* (London: Longmans, Green, 1964).

White, C.M.N., 'Research in Zambian Law', in *African Social Research, June, No. 19*, The Institute for African Studies, University of Zambia, Lusaka (Manchester: Manchester University Press, 1975), pp. 751–6.

Whitfield, G.B.M., *South African Native Law* (Cape Town: Juta, 1929, 1948).

CHAPTER 4   THE STRUGGLE FOR EQUALITY

Basner, Miriam, *Am I An African? The Political Memoirs of H. M. Basner* (Witwatersrand University Press, 1993).

Bazilli, Susan (ed.), *Putting Women on the Agenda* (Braamfontein: Raven Press, 1991).

Benson, Mary, *A Far Cry. The Making of a South African* (London: Penguin Books, 1990).

Berger, Iris, *Threads of Solidarity. Women in South African Industry, 1900–1990* (Bloomington: Indiana University Press, 1992).

Bernstein, Hilda, *For Their Triumphs and for Their Tears. Conditions and Resistance of Women in Apartheid South Africa* (London: International Defence & Aid Fund, 1975).

Bunting, Brian, *South African Communists Speak. Documents from the History of the South African Communist Party 1915–1980*, Editorial Note 1961: 274 (London: Inkululeko Publications, 1981).

Bunting, Sonia, 'The Prisons of Apartheid', in R.M. Segal, (ed.), *Africa in Exile*, vol. 4, no. 4: 42–50 (London: Africa South Publications, 1960).

Desai, Barney and Marney, Cardiff, *The Killing of the Imam* (London: Quartet Books, 1978).

Hailey, Lord, *The Republic of South Africa and the High Commission Territories* (London: Oxford University Press, 1963).

Joseph, Helen, *Side by Side. The Autobiography of Helen Joseph* (London: ZED Books, 1986).

Karis, T and Carter, Gwendolen M. (eds.), *From Protest to Challenge. A Documentary History of African Politics in South Africa 1882–1964*. Vol. 3, *Challenge and Violence 1953–1964*; Vol. 4 (with Gail M. Gerhart), *Political Profiles 1882–1964* (Stanford University: Hoover Institution Press, 1977).

Luckhardt, K. and Wall, B, *Organize or Starve! The History of the South African Congress of Trade Unions* (London: Lawrence and Wishart, 1980).

Mabandla, Brigitte et al. (eds.), *Gender Today and Tomorrow. Towards a Charter of Women's Rights* (University of Western Cape, Centre for Development Studies, 1990).

Matthews, Z.K., *Freedom for my People. The Autobiography of Z.K. Matthews: Southern Africa 1901 to 1968* (Africa South Paperbacks, Cape Town: David Philip, 1983).

Muller, C.F.J (ed.), *Five Hundred Years. A History of South Africa* (Pretoria: Academia, 1969, 1975).

Nkosi, Z., 'The "Fischer" Trial', in *The African Communist*, No. 2, Third Quarter (London: The S.A. Communist Party, 1965), pp. 46–55.

Pampallis, J., *Foundations of the New South Africa* (London: ZED Book, 1991).

Parsons, Neil, *A New History of Southern Africa* (London: Macmillan Education, 1982).

Rake, Alan, 'The Pattern of South Africa's Emergency, in Segal, M. (ed.), *Africa South in Exile*, vol. 5, no. 1 (London: Africa South Publications, 1960), pp. 14–20.

Simons, H.J., 'The Same Boat', in Segal, R.M., *Africa South in Exile*, vol. 5, no. (London: Africa South Publications, 1961), pp. 14–24 (published anonymously).

Simons, H.J., 'Our Freedom Charter', in *Sechaba. Official Organ of the African National Congress South Africa* (London: Sechaba Publications, June 1985), pp. 7–10.

Simons, H.J. and Simons, R.E., 'The Nineteen Days', in Segal, R.M., *Africa South in Exile*, vol. 4, no. 4 (London: Africa South Publications, 1960), pp. 6–21 (published anonymously).

Simons, H.J. and Simons, R.E., *Class and Colour in South Africa 1850–1950* (Harmondsworth: Penguin Books, 1969).

South African Institute of Race Relations, *A Survey of Race Relations in South Africa. Annual Reports from 1930 onwards*, compiled by Muriel Horrell et al. (Johannesburg: SAIR, various years).

Walker, Cheryll, *Women and Resistance in South Africa* (Cape Town: David Philip, 1991).

Walker, Eric, *A History of Southern Africa* (London: Longmans, 1962).

Walshe, Peter, *The Rise of African Nationalism in South Africa. The African National Congress 1912–52* (London: C. Hurst, 1970).

Wells, Julie, *We Have Done with Pleading. The Women's 1913 Anti-pass Campaign* (Johannesburg: Raven Press, 1992).

CHAPTER 5   APARTHEID YEARS

Benson, Mary (ed.), *The Sun Will Rise. Statements from the Dock by Southern African Political Prisoners* (London: International Defence and Aid Fund for Southern Africa, 1981).

Bernstein, Hilda, *No. 46 Steve Biko* (London: International Defence and Aid Fund for Southern Africa, 1978, 1987).

Biko, Steve, *I Write What I Like,* a selection of his writings edited with a personal memoir by Father Alfred Stubbs, C.R. (Anglican Community of the Resurrection) (San Francisco: Harper & Row, 1978).

Black Review, Black Community Programmes, Khoopa, B.A. (ed.) (1972).

Black Review, Black Community Programmes, Mbanjwa, Thoko (ed.) (1974/5).

Black Review, Black Community Programmes, Rambally, Asha (ed.) (1975–6).

Boonzaaier, E. and Sharp, J. (eds), *South African Keywords. The Uses and Abuses of Political Concepts* (Cape Town: David Phillips, 1988).

Branford, Jean, *A Dictionary of South African English* (Cape Town: Oxford University Press, 1980).

Brooks, Alan and Brickhill, Jeremy, *Whirlwind before the Storm. The Origins and Development of the Uprising in Soweto and the Rest of South Africa from June to December 1976* (London: International Defence and Aid fund for Southern Africa, 1980).

Cell, John W., *The Highest Stage of White Supremacy. The Origins of Segregation in South Africa and the American South* (Cambridge: Cambridge University Press, 1982).

Cock, Jacklyn, 'Women in the Struggle for Peace' (Harare: 19–22 April 1989) (duplicated).

Ellis, Stephen and Tsepo, Sechaba, *Comrades against Apartheid. The ANC and the South African Communist Party in Exile* (London: James Currey, 1992).

Hirson, Baruch, *Year of Fire, Year of Ash. The Soweto Revolt: Roots of a Revolution* (London: ZED Press, 1979).

Horrell, Muriel, *Bantu Education to 1968* (Johannesburg: S.A. Institute of Race Relations, 1968).

Inskeep, R.R., *The Peopling of Southern Africa* (Cape Town: David Philip, 1978).

Jenkins, Elwyn, President of the English Academy of Southern Africa, in RRS (1992/3).

Karis, T. and Carter, G.M. (eds), *From Protest to Challenge. A Documentary History of African Politics in South Africa 1882–1964.* Vol. 4, *Political Profiles,* eds Gail M.

Gerhart and Thomas Karis. (Stanford University, Hoover Institute Press, 1977).

Kerr, Alexander, *Fort Hare 1959–48. The Evolution of An African College* (London: C. Hurst and Co., 1968).

Marquard, Leo, *The Peoples and Policies of South Africa* (London: Oxford University Press, 1952).

Matthews, Z.K., *Freedom for my People. The Autobiography of Z.K. Matthews. Southern Africa 1901 to 1968. Memoir by Monica Wilson* (Cape Town: David Philip, 1983).

Meli, Francis, *A History of the ANC. South Africa Belongs to Us* (Harare: Zimbabwe Publishing House, 1988).

Mokoape, Keith, Thengiwe Mtintso and Welile Nhlapo, 'Towards the Armed Struggle', in N. Barney Pityana et al. (eds), *Bounds of Possibility. The Legacy of Steve Biko and Black Consciousness* (Cape Town: David Philip, 1991), pp. 137–42.

No Sizwe, *One Azania, One Nation. The National Question in South Africa* (London: ZED Press, 1979).

Pampallis, John, *Foundations of the New South Africa* (London: ZED Press, 1991).

Phalo, J.B., *The House of Phalo. A History of the Xhosa People in the Days of their Independence* (Johannesburg: Raven Press, 1981).

Pityana, N. Barney, 'Revolution Within the Law?' in N. Barney Pityana et al. (eds), *Bounds of Possibility. The Legacy of Steve Biko and Black Consciousness* (Cape Town: David Philip, 1991), pp. 200–12.

Ramphele, Mamphela, 'The Dynamics of Gender with Black Consciousness Organisations. A Personal View', in N. Barney Pityana et al. (eds), *Bounds of Possibility. The Legacy of Steve Biko and Black Consciousness* (Cape Town: David Philip, 1991), pp. 214–27.

Sharp, John, 'Ethnic Group and Nation. The Apartheid Vision in South Africa', in E. Boonzaaier and J. Sharp, *South African Key Words. The Uses and Abuses of Political Concepts* (Cape Town: David Philip, 1988), pp. 79–99.

Shepherd, R.H.W. and Paver, B.G., *African Contrasts. The Story of a South African People* (Cape Town: Oxford University Press, 1947).

Simons, H.J., *African Women. Their Legal Statue in South Africa* (London: Christopher Hurst & Co., 1968).

Simons, H.J. and Simons, R.E., *Class and Colour in South Africa 1850–1950* (London: Penguin Books, 1969).

Smith, Andrew B. and Pheiffer, Roy H., *The Khoikhoi at the Cape of Good Hope Seventeenth-Century Drawing on the South African Library* (Cape Town: South African Library, 1993).

South African Institute of Race Relations, *A Survey of Race Relations in South Africa* (Johannesburg: SAIRR, various years).

Van der Merwe, Hendrik W. et al. (eds), *African Perspectives on South Africa. A Collection of Speeches, Articles and Documents* (Cape Town: David Philip in association with the Centre for Intergroup Studies, Cape Town, 1978).

Venter, Al J., *Coloured. A Profile of Two Million South Africans* (Cape Town: Human & Rousseau, 1974).

West, M., 'Confusing Categories: Population Groups, National States and Citizenship' in E. Boonzaaier and J. Sharp, *South African Key Words. The Uses and Abuses of Political Concepts* (cape Town: David Philip, 1988), pp. 100–10.

Wilson, Daphne M., *The Struggle of the Cape African Night Schools 1943–1969* (The Centre for African Studies and the Department of Adult Education and Extra-Mural Studies, University of Cape Town, 1991).

Wilson, Lindy, 'Bantu Stephen Biko: A Life', in N. Barney Pityana et al. (eds), *Bounds of Possibility. The Legacy of Steve Biko and Black Consciousness* (Cape Town: David Philip), pp. 15–77.

Publications by H.J. Simons

BOOKS

Simons, H.J. and Ballinger, M.L., *Memorandum on the Need for Penal Reform in South Africa* (prepared for the South African Institute for Race Relations, 1943).
—— and Simons, R.E., *Job Reservation and the Trade Unions* (Enterprise, Cape Town, 1959).
—— *African Women: Their Legal Status in South Africa* (Hurst, London, 1968).
—— and Simons, R.E. *Class and Colour in South Africa 1850–1950* (Penguin, London, 1969; republished International Defence and Aid, London, 1983).
—— et al., *Slums or Self-reliance? Urban Growth in Zambia* (University of Zambia, Lusaka, 1976).

CONTRIBUTIONS TO BOOKS

'Trade Unionism in South Africa', in *Handbook on Race Relations*, ed. E. Hellman (OUP for SAIRR, Cape Town, 1949).
'The Law and its Administration', in *Handbook on Race Relations*, ed. E. Hellman (OUP for SAIRR, Cape Town, 1949).
'Race Relations and Policies in Southern and Eastern Africa', in *Most of the World: The Peoples of Africa, Latin America and the East today*, ed. Ralph Linton (Columbia University Press, New York, 1949).
'What are the National Groups in South Africa?', Paper presented at the Symposium on the National Question, Cape Town: Forum Club.
'Perspectives in Civilization', in *The Western Tradition* (National Union of South African Students (NUSAS), 1958).
'The Status of African Women', in *Africa in Transition*, ed. Prudence Smith (Rheinhardt, London, 1958).
'A Statistical Comment on the Position of Women in Zambia', in *Women's Rights in Zambia: Report of a Consultation* (Kitwe, 1970).
Preface to Watson, G., *Passing for White: A Study of Racial Assimilation in a South African School* (Tavistock, London, 1970).
'The Urban Situation in Zambia', in *Human Settlement in Zambia* (National Housing Authority, Lusaka, 1975).
'Zambia's Urban Situation', in *Development in Zambia: a Reader*, ed. Ben Turok (ZED Press, London, 1979).

227

PERIODICAL ARTICLES

'European Civilization and African Crime', *African Observer* (Bulawayo), 2, 1934.

'The Study of Native Law in South Africa', *Bantu Studies*, 12, 1938.

'Disabilities of the Native in the Union of South Africa', *Race Relations Journal*, 6, 1939.

'Some Aspects of Urban Native Administration', *Race Relations*, 7, 1942.

'The Coloured Worker and Trade Unionism', *Race Relations*, 9, 1942.

'Claims of the African in Municipal Government', *Race Relations*, 13, 1946.

'Passes and Police', *Africa South*, 1, 1956.

'African Women and the Law in South Africa', *Listener*, 55, 1957.

'Tribal Medicine: Diviners and Herbalists', *African Studies*, 16, 1957.

'Tribal Worship', *Africa South*, 1, 1957.

'Mental Disease in Africans: Racial Determinism', *Journal of Mental Science*, 104, 1958.

'Customary Unions in a Changing Society', *Acta Juridica*, 1958.

'No Revolution around the Corner: An Addendum', *Africa South*, 3, 1958.

'What is Apartheid?', *Liberation*, 35, 1959.

'Marriage and Succession among Africans', *Acta Juridica*, 1960.

'The Status of Customary Unions', *Acta Juridica*, 1961.

'Death in South African Mines', *Africa South in Exile*, 5, 1961.

'Prologue', *African Social Research*, 24, 1977 (pp. 259–73).

'Chief, Council and Commissioner', *African Social Research*, 11, 1971.

Index

DATE DUE